Environments in Science Fiction

CRITICAL EXPLORATIONS IN SCIENCE FICTION AND FANTASY
(a series edited by Donald E. Palumbo and C.W. Sullivan III)

1 *Worlds Apart? Dualism and Transgression in Contemporary Female Dystopias* (Dunja M. Mohr, 2005)
2 *Tolkien and Shakespeare: Essays on Shared Themes and Language* (ed. Janet Brennan Croft, 2007)
3 *Culture, Identities and Technology in the* Star Wars *Films: Essays on the Two Trilogies* (ed. Carl Silvio, Tony M. Vinci, 2007)
4 *The Influence of* Star Trek *on Television, Film and Culture* (ed. Lincoln Geraghty, 2008)
5 *Hugo Gernsback and the Century of Science Fiction* (Gary Westfahl, 2007)
6 *One Earth, One People: The Mythopoeic Fantasy Series of Ursula K. Le Guin, Lloyd Alexander, Madeleine L'Engle and Orson Scott Card* (Marek Oziewicz, 2008)
7 *The Evolution of Tolkien's Mythology: A Study of the History of Middle-earth* (Elizabeth A. Whittingham, 2008)
8 *H. Beam Piper: A Biography* (John F. Carr, 2008)
9 *Dreams and Nightmares: Science and Technology in Myth and Fiction* (Mordecai Roshwald, 2008)
10 Lilith *in a New Light: Essays on the George MacDonald Fantasy Novel* (ed. Lucas H. Harriman, 2008)
11 *Feminist Narrative and the Supernatural: The Function of Fantastic Devices in Seven Recent Novels* (Katherine J. Weese, 2008)
12 *The Science of Fiction and the Fiction of Science: Collected Essays on SF Storytelling and the Gnostic Imagination* (Frank McConnell, ed. Gary Westfahl, 2009)
13 *Kim Stanley Robinson Maps the Unimaginable: Critical Essays* (ed. William J. Burling, 2009)
14 *The Inter-Galactic Playground: A Critical Study of Children's and Teens' Science Fiction* (Farah Mendlesohn, 2009)
15 *Science Fiction from Québec: A Postcolonial Study* (Amy J. Ransom, 2009)
16 *Science Fiction and the Two Cultures: Essays on Bridging the Gap Between the Sciences and the Humanities* (ed. Gary Westfahl, George Slusser, 2009)
17 *Stephen R. Donaldson and the Modern Epic Vision: A Critical Study of the "Chronicles of Thomas Covenant" Novels* (Christine Barkley, 2009)
18 *Ursula K. Le Guin's Journey to Post-Feminism* (Amy M. Clarke, 2010)
19 *Portals of Power: Magical Agency and Transformation in Literary Fantasy* (Lori M. Campbell, 2010)
20 *The Animal Fable in Science Fiction and Fantasy* (Bruce Shaw, 2010)
21 *Illuminating* Torchwood: *Essays on Narrative, Character and Sexuality in the BBC Series* (ed. Andrew Ireland, 2010)
22 *Comics as a Nexus of Cultures: Essays on the Interplay of Media, Disciplines and International Perspectives* (ed. Mark Berninger, Jochen Ecke, Gideon Haberkorn, 2010)
23 *The Anatomy of Utopia: Narration, Estrangement and Ambiguity in More, Wells, Huxley and Clarke* (Károly Pintér, 2010)
24 *The Anticipation Novelists of 1950s French Science Fiction: Stepchildren of Voltaire* (Bradford Lyau, 2010)
25 *The Twilight Mystique: Critical Essays on the Novels and Films* (ed. Amy M. Clarke, Marijane Osborn, 2010)
26 *The Mythic Fantasy of Robert Holdstock: Critical Essays on the Fiction* (ed. Donald E. Morse, Kálmán Matolcsy, 2011)

27 *Science Fiction and the Prediction of the Future: Essays on Foresight and Fallacy* (ed. Gary Westfahl, Wong Kin Yuen, Amy Kit-sze Chan, 2011)

28 *Apocalypse in Australian Fiction and Film: A Critical Study* (Roslyn Weaver, 2011)

29 *British Science Fiction Film and Television: Critical Essays* (ed. Tobias Hochscherf, James Leggott, 2011)

30 *Cult Telefantasy Series: A Critical Analysis of* The Prisoner, Twin Peaks, The X-Files, Buffy the Vampire Slayer, Lost, Heroes, Doctor Who *and* Star Trek (Sue Short, 2011)

31 *The Postnational Fantasy: Essays on Postcolonialism, Cosmopolitics and Science Fiction* (ed. Masood Ashraf Raja, Jason W. Ellis and Swaralipi Nandi, 2011)

32 *Heinlein's Juvenile Novels: A Cultural Dictionary* (C.W. Sullivan III, 2011)

33 *Welsh Mythology and Folklore in Popular Culture: Essays on Adaptations in Literature, Film, Television and Digital Media* (ed. Audrey L. Becker and Kristin Noone, 2011)

34 *I See You: The Shifting Paradigms of James Cameron's* Avatar (Ellen Grabiner, 2012)

35 *Of Bread, Blood and* The Hunger Games: *Critical Essays on the Suzanne Collins Trilogy* (ed. Mary F. Pharr and Leisa A. Clark, 2012)

36 *The Sex Is Out of This World: Essays on the Carnal Side of Science Fiction* (ed. Sherry Ginn and Michael G. Cornelius, 2012)

37 *Lois McMaster Bujold: Essays on a Modern Master of Science Fiction and Fantasy* (ed. Janet Brennan Croft, 2013)

38 *Girls Transforming: Invisibility and Age-Shifting in Children's Fantasy Fiction Since the 1970s* (Sanna Lehtonen, 2013)

39 Doctor Who *in Time and Space: Essays on Themes, Characters, History and Fandom, 1963–2012* (ed. Gillian I. Leitch, 2013)

40 *The Worlds of* Farscape: *Essays on the Groundbreaking Television Series* (ed. Sherry Ginn, 2013)

41 *Orbiting Ray Bradbury's Mars: Biographical, Anthropological, Literary, Scientific and Other Perspectives* (ed. Gloria McMillan, 2013)

42 *The Heritage of Heinlein: A Critical Reading of the Fiction Television Series* (Thomas D. Clareson and Joe Sanders, 2014)

43 *The Past That Might Have Been, the Future That May Come: Women Writing Fantastic Fiction, 1960s to the Present* (Lauren J. Lacey, 2014)

44 *Environments in Science Fiction: Essays on Alternative Spaces* (ed. Susan M. Bernardo, 2014)

45 *Discworld and the Disciplines: Critical Approaches to the Terry Pratchett Works* (ed. Anne Hiebert Alton and William C. Spruiell, forthcoming [2014])

46 *Nature and the Numinous in Mythopoeic Fantasy Literature* (Christopher Straw Brawley, ed. Donald E. Palumbo and C.W. Sullivan III, forthcoming [2014])

Environments in Science Fiction
Essays on Alternative Spaces

Edited by SUSAN M. BERNARDO

CRITICAL EXPLORATIONS IN SCIENCE FICTION AND FANTASY, 44
Series Editors Donald E. Palumbo *and* C.W. Sullivan III

McFarland & Company, Inc., Publishers
Jefferson, North Carolina

LIBRARY OF CONGRESS CATALOGUING-IN-PUBLICATION DATA

Environments in Science Fiction : Essays on Alternative Spaces / edited by Susan M. Bernardo.
     p.   cm. — (Critical Explorations in Science Fiction and Fantasy ; 44)
[Donald E. Palumbo and C.W. Sullivan III, series editors]
Includes bibliographical references and index.

ISBN 978-0-7864-7579-7 (softcover : acid free paper) ∞
ISBN 978-1-4766-1503-5 (ebook)

1. Science fiction—History and criticism.   2. Future, The, in literature.   3. Dystopias in literature.   4. Ecocriticism.   I. Bernardo, Susan M., editor of compilation.
PN3433.6.E73 2014
809.3'8762—dc23   2014003861

BRITISH LIBRARY CATALOGUING DATA ARE AVAILABLE

© 2014 Susan M. Bernardo. All rights reserved

No part of this book may be reproduced or transmitted in any form or by any means, electronic or mechanical, including photocopying or recording, or by any information storage and retrieval system, without permission in writing from the publisher.

Cover image: © Photodisc/Thinkstock

Manufactured in the United States of America

*McFarland & Company, Inc., Publishers
   Box 611, Jefferson, North Carolina 28640
     www.mcfarlandpub.com*

Acknowledgments

Without the help of an array of people this book would not have been possible. For their patience and tenacity I thank all the contributors. The support that Wagner College has provided has been key. I would like to thank the Faculty Personnel Committee and the provost for their support and assistance. The staff of Horrmann Library, as always, provided help with locating sources, even on short notice. Special thanks go to Tim Hickey for his work on the text of the book. Thanks to Don Palumbo, who has been easy to work with and encouraging.

Very special thanks to my constant assistant and sounding board, Mark Wagner.

Table of Contents

Acknowledgments vii
Introduction 1

PART ONE
IN THE MARGINS: RECENTERING INDIVIDUALS, SOCIETIES AND ENVIRONMENTS

Heterotopian Possibilities in Science Fictions by Stephen Baxter, Terry Pratchett, Samuel Delany and Ursula K. Le Guin
LAUREN J. LACEY 10

Acceptance of the Marginalized in Marge Piercy's *He, She, It* and Melissa Scott's *Trouble and Her Friends*
MELANIE A. MAROTTA 28

Anathem's Flows of Power: State Space and Nomadology on a Cloistered Planet
JONATHAN P. LEWIS 46

PART TWO
SHIFTING WORLDS THROUGH RE-CREATION

Karel Čapek's *War with the Newts*: Deterritorializing Land and Language
ADAM LAWRENCE 64

Mary Shelley's Literary Laboratory: *Frankenstein* and the Emergence of the Modern Laboratory in Nineteenth-Century Europe
MATTHEW HADLEY 83

Ecotopian London: Morris's Geography of Conservation
MARGARET S. KENNEDY 101

Part Three
Re-Viewing Damaged Worlds Through Quests

Underworlds of Despair and Hope in Cormac McCarthy's *The Road*
    Justin T. Noetzel   120

The Silence of the Subaltern: The Rejection of History and Language in Amitav Ghosh's *The Calcutta Chromosome*
    Shayani Bhattacharya   137

A Case of Terraphilia: Longing for Place and Community in Philip K. Dick's *Do Androids Dream of Electric Sheep?*
    Susan M. Bernardo   154

Discursive Transgressions and Ideological Negotiations: From Orwell's *1984* to Butler's *Parable of the Sower*
    Keith Elphick   171

About the Contributors   191
Index   193

Introduction

Science fiction focused on the environment and the potential future for humans and other animals on the planet well before the more recent interest in green technologies and ecological issues. This concern about the implications of technology and human behavior for the environment makes science fiction a perfect fit for recent ecocritical ideas about space, place and environments as they intersect with literary theory. This collection of essays brings together a focus on environments in post-dystopian moments in science fiction with theoretical ideas to offer readings of science fiction texts from the 19th, 20th, and 21st centuries.

Since its formal establishment in 1992 with the creation of ASLE (Association for the Study of Literature and the Environment), ecocriticism has sometimes contained an uneasy tension between more theoretically oriented approaches and hands on, real world action and political advocacy linked to ecological awareness. Ecocritics, though they take different positions, accept this tension rather than shutting down conversation; so a variety of methods and views have become the norm. All intellectual enterprises involve argument and the response to argument as ways to refine thought, and ecocriticism certainly shares this model. In thinking about how the future of environmental criticism might evolve, Buell points out in *The Future of Environmental Criticism* that the area will develop as a constellation of ideas, rather than be dominated by a particular school of thought (133). In his 2011 *The Cambridge Introduction to Literature and the Environment*, Timothy Clark writes, "The main future challenge for ecocriticism may lie in the way environmental questions will continue to resist inherited structures of thought and are uncontainable within the competence of one intellectual discipline" (203). Of the many possibilities open to ecocritics, literary theory is of special interest. Timothy Morton tackles the mixed response to theory among ecocritics when he says, "Some think that ecocriticism needs what it calls 'theory' like it needs a hole in the head. Others contend that this aeration is exactly what ecocriticism needs" (10). He points out that the act of theorizing is a way "to bring thinking up to date," in the sense that theory helps us question concepts and press ideas forward. Clearly, we have come a long way since Glen Love stated in Glotfelty and Fromm's 1996 *Ecocriticism Reader*, "The decision of those of us who profess has been, by and large, that the relationship between literature and these issues of the degradation of the earth is something that we won't talk about" (227). Recent studies such as Eric Otto's *Green Speculations* and Chris Baratta's edited volume *Environmentalism in the Realm of Science Fiction and Fantasy Literature* (both published in 2012) exhibit the growing interest in ecocritical approaches to science fiction. This book seeks to add to that conversation.

The essays in this book push ecocriticism and the analysis of science fiction forward, and whet our mental appetites by asking some probing questions. How can views of space, place and environment help us understand the visions of the future science fiction offers us? What role do all sentient beings on the planet have in these unfolding futures, and how do all of us help shape and become reshaped by the technological, social and environmental changes we experience, and sometimes even engineer? How do human ideas about place connectedness and the need for context influence choices and outcomes? In bringing an array of theoretical ideas to bear on these questions (from Deleuze and Guattari to Foucault and Yuan), the writers of the essays in this collection address these issues through the texts they discuss and challenge the reader to re-see and re-think. The use of theory, in other words, is not an exercise in intellectual flamboyance, but a way to broaden our understanding of the implications of issues involving space/place/environment.

Space, place and environment are three different, but related, concepts for ecocritics. As Buell explains in Chapter 3 of *The Future of Environmental Criticism*, space is a broad term which "connotes geometrical or topographical abstraction," while we think of place as more personal and associate it with place-attachment (63). Environment is a term we use to refer to the complex surroundings we experience that can include both built and unbuilt nature and usually does not involve the same notion of attachment that place does. Environment is not as broad a notion as space, since we tend to discuss and focus on its specific attributes (everything from toxins to architectural design). Generally, our notion of environment focuses on the physical surroundings we inhabit, rather than any specific emotional link to that setting. On the other hand, "what counts as place," states Buell, "can be as small as a corner of your kitchen or as big as the planet, now that we have the capacity to image earth holistically" (67–8). Buell is also concerned with the potential problems an uncritical notion of place and place-attachment can engender. He cautions against seeing place as something sentimental, or even magical. In the introduction to *Sense of Place and Sense of Planet*, Ursula Heise points out that "the political consequences of encouraging people to develop a sense of place … are far from straightforward and predictable…. There is nothing in the idea of localism itself that guarantees its connection with the grassroots-democratic and egalitarian politics that many environmentalists envision when they advocate place-based communities" (47–48). Heise points out that attempts to influence, change, or create particular places and senses of belonging can have unforeseen outcomes.

Both the unforeseen consequences of place attachment, and our ideas about place itself, can be complex. Humans and some non-human animals have a sense of place, but may also have senses of place that shift over time, since the temporal dimension is also in play (Buell 73). Thus, people may experience a layered or growing/accreting sense of place. A sense of place, then, is not necessarily a static concept, despite our notion that it offers us grounding and stability. Stability can still occur within the changes that our sense of place undergoes, depending on our perception of place. For example, those changes may occur slowly, so we do not see them as disruptive. Even the place, the physical entity, can change, of course. Buell provides the example of the transformation of his boyhood neighborhood into an area of suburban sprawl (73). Memory and our sense of boundaries (ideas of what we include and exclude from our particular place) also help to define and redefine notions of place.

A further complication of the concepts of place and belonging involves the ways the individual human and group fit into that place. As much as people need a sense of place, the place interacts with that need and helps shape the self. Though a sense of place or place-attachment through time comes through people's perceptions, it is also a force that reflects back on us. In other words, the experience of place is a multi-directional dynamic that our perception and desire recognize, rather than a one-way transaction. In science fiction, place is often not the same as setting in the literary sense, since place is not just an envelope for action or even a reflection of character, but has an active part to play in science fiction narratives. In the science fiction texts the writers in this collection address, place is a site of production and often becomes contentious. This collection of essays addresses strategies for working out post-cataclysmic events in science fiction texts through foregrounding the key element of space/place/environment.

Though other books deal with dystopias or environmental issues broadly construed in science fiction, none takes up the intersection between science fiction and the key element of spaces in the forms of both built and unbuilt nature that involve humans, animals and constructed beings. The scholars in this collection offer the reader an array of approaches to this fertile intersection of the science fiction genre and issues and do so as they treat a variety of texts. They all examine the ways these texts depict people, animals and constructed beings and how these beings cope with the realization of their intimate links to space/place, the losses and ruptures that occur with dislocation and the subsequent opening up of possibilities for reconstructing and innovating new structures of self, environments and societies.

In Part One, "In the Margins: Recentering Individuals, Societies and Environments," the essays all focus on what happens to people who are not initially at the centers of their societies and who do not appear to have any control over the array of terrible events that play out in their worlds. Lauren J. Lacey utilizes Foucault's term heterotopias, which he explained as "counter-sites, a kind of effectively enacted utopia which the real sites, all the other real sites that can be found within culture, are simultaneously represented, contested, and inverted." These counter-sites include spaces that host diversity, unity and difference. Her readings of Le Guin's *The Word for World Is Forest* and *The Telling*, along with Samuel R. Delany's *Stars in My Pocket Like Grains of Sand*, focus on these texts' particular ways of creating local, global, and galactic environments. Place in these works engenders both constraint and possibility. Along with the exploration of the encounter between self and other, these texts offer ways to rethink how a heterotopian model might help us re-envision the natural world, technological incursions and globalized power. Melanie A. Marotta's study of Marge Piercy's *He, She, It* and Melissa Scott's *Trouble and Her Friends* comes to the conclusion that the spaces in society that appear most dangerous to the characters actually become more than safe havens for the marginalized—they are utopian and even "communal environments" that "enable them to reject dystopic patriarchal guidelines." Marotta deploys both ecocritical ideas and feminist concepts of the body in her essay. The characters who have suffered in environments that restrict women thus find ways to overcome limitations. In his study of Neal Stephenson's *Anathem*, Jonathan P. Lewis makes the case that forcing the cloistered out of their accustomed, technologically restricted space leads them to reexamine their views of themselves and the world. What appears to be a normal, though rare, event—their "evoking" (being sent out on a mission)—inadvertently engenders possibility because this severing "striates space that the protagonists believed was smooth and sacred."

In Part Two, "Shifting Worlds Through Re-Creation," the essays explore spaces that either undergo radical reinvention or imply various possible reconstructions. By focusing on divergence, Adam Lawrence analyzes Čapek's 1936 work in "Karel Čapek's *War with the Newts*: Deterritorializing Land and Language." He deploys Deleuze and Guattari's notion that supposed minorities have a major impact on the way we see "normal" categories, such as nation, homeland and language. Lawrence also uses Deleuze and Guatarri's idea that the process of deterritorialization-reterritorialization challenges dichotomies. Through the process of disassembling and rearranging, new structures emerge in society. In Čapek's text the Newts engage in this process when they adapt to grasp objects, and especially when they begin to acquire human language. Taking up a classic text, Mary Shelley's *Frankenstein*, Matthew Hadley asks readers to look specifically at a space that is both central to the novel's events and overlooked—the laboratory. As the key space for scientific labor in the text, the literally creative space for Victor Frankenstein, Hadley argues, "the only labor that counts" in the novel takes place in the laboratory. All the other productive spaces that support the creation of narrative become laboratories of a sort themselves—from Walton's ship to the De Lacey's home. Hadley's essay takes up the history of the laboratory and links it to *Frankenstein* as a fundamental way for the novel to frame "its own process of production." Though Victor's creations do not survive, the productive process remains. Margaret S. Kennedy then turns to 19th century Britain for a different view of space and its reconstruction when she investigates William Morris's *News from Nowhere*. This 1890 text describes a revamped, agrarian London and thus posits that a "reversion to a pre-industrial way of living" would be a positive change from the urban setting. In *News from Nowhere* Morris "not only challenges assumptions about the city as unnatural, but reveals Victorian eco-consciousness."

Part Three, "Re-Viewing Damaged Worlds Through Quests," offers essays that focus on the importance of perception and quests as ways of recreating post-cataclysmic environments. Cormac McCarthy's bleak novel *The Road* at first presents a horrendous, ruined world, but then uses underground spaces as areas of possibility and even hope. Human built spaces, such as houses and other structures, represent danger in the novel. By using ideas from such theorists as Bachelard, Fuan, Lane and Giles, Justin T. Noetzel makes the case "that the interior spaces in *The Road* represent the vastness of the unknown," and thus allow the characters to lean toward hope or despair. The journey in *The Road* ultimately leads to a "quest to find the Promised Land." Similarly, Shayani Bhattacharya sees the importance of the quest in Amitav Ghosh's *The Calcutta Chromosome*. As Bhattacharya points out, the novel claims that "to know something is to change it," and this idea means that knowledge is not static, but shifting and mutable. The book presents a quest for an understanding of the very nature of knowledge, rather than a particular piece of information or a medical breakthrough. In trying to retrace Muragan's steps (he had disappeared in Calcutta), Antar discovers a process rather than a particular goal. The subaltern characters, because of their link to an Indian anti-scientific cult, help redefine what discovery means in the text. The "redefined concept of knowledge" the novel offers becomes available only to a few. The city of Calcutta is labyrinth-like and "becomes the epitome of the subversive power of silence." Philip K. Dick's bounty hunter, Deckard, engages in a quest as well, though the world that *Do Androids Dream of Electric Sheep?* describes apparently offers little solace to its characters. In her essay Susan M. Bernardo asks readers to rethink the importance of substitutions and simulacra in the text, and address the issue of terraphilia. The blighted Earth manages to maintain its attraction for both humans and androids not only because the newly colonized Mars is deeply unfamiliar and even more inhospitable than a post World War Terminus Earth, but also because Earth offers freedom to the androids and a lingering sense of place through remnants and replications of art and culture for the humans. That these cultural remnants often take the form of simulacra, as Baudrillard explains them, is far more of a consolation than a problem for the novel's protagonist. Keith Elphick uses the idea of dystopian balance to explain the processes that characters work through in Orwell's *1984* to Butler's *Parable of the Sower*. The characters in these two novels, Elphick argues, learn from and create paths toward change as a result of encounters with their damaged worlds. Characters both adjust to their new environments and renegotiate their pre- and post-disaster notions of identity. These adjustments lead to what he calls "dystopian balance," thus expanding the idea of the critical dystopia offered by Moylan, Baccolini and Sargent.

The essays in this book examine both well-known and less familiar works of science fiction, and help to expand our understanding of the dynamic between environments, people, and others. They engage with the ongoing investigation of notions of space, place and humanity by taking up various theoretical ideas as they read science fiction texts. Though our current world has not completely fallen into a dystopian state, the ideas writers of science fiction present about humanity's responses to a degraded Earth begin to seem less distant and thus more pertinent. Our ability to think beyond our own disasters and imagine ways to manage our shifting selves and environments, then, is not simply an exercise. These readings and analyses of science fiction texts allow us to rethink our views of the world we inhabit, the responsibility and roles we have in shaping that world and how human and world shape each other.

Works Cited

Baratta, Chris. *Environmentalism in the Realm of Science Fiction and Fantasy Literature*. Newcastle upon Tyne: Cambridge Scholars, 2012. Print.

Buell, Lawrence. *The Future of Environmental Criticism: Environmental Crisis and Literary Imagination*. Oxford: Blackwell, 2005. Print.

Clark, Timothy. *The Cambridge Introduction to Literature and the Environment*. Cambridge: Cambridge University Press, 2011. Print.

Heise, Ursula K. *Sense of Place and Sense of Planet: The Environmental Imagination of the Global*. Oxford: Oxford University Press, 2008. Print.

Love, Glen. "Revaluing Nature: Toward an Ecological Criticism." *The Ecocritical Reader: Landmarks in Literary Ecology*. Ed. Cheryll Glotfelty and Harold Fromm. Athens: University of Georgia Press, 1996. 225–240. Print.

Morton, Timothy. *Ecology Without Nature: Rethinking Environmental Aesthetics*. Cambridge: Harvard University Press, 2007. Print.

Otto, Eric C. *Green Speculations: Science Fiction and Transformative Environmentalism*. Columbus: Ohio State University Press, 2012. Print.

Part One
In the Margins
Recentering Individuals, Societies and Environments

Heterotopian Possibilities in Science Fictions by Stephen Baxter, Terry Pratchett, Samuel Delany and Ursula K. Le Guin

Lauren J. Lacey

All readers devoted to the genre know that world building—place, as such—is central to science fiction. Some sub-genres are defined by their settings: utopias and dystopias, for example. This essay focuses on three examples of science fiction narratives that investigate what place is and what it means for what is possible within the bounds of a given narrative: Ursula K. Le Guin's *The Word for World Is Forest* (1976), Samuel R. Delany's *Stars in My Pocket Like Grains of Sand* (1984), and Stephen Baxter's and Terry Pratchett's *The Long Earth* (2012). While each novel is unique in its approach to the concept of place, all three work to demonstrate how the conception of a given place sets the parameters for human subjectivities, for understandings of the nonhuman, and for power dynamics. Beyond focusing on place as a topic of investigation, all three novels pay particular attention to place on a planetary scale. As environmental critic Lawrence Buell puts it, "No genre potentially matches up with a planetary level of thinking 'environment' better than science fiction does" (57). Understanding place on a global scale has never been more important than it is now in relation to impending ecological crises on our world. Indeed, the novels explored here might be defined as "ecoscience fiction," a term Bennett Huffman and others use to describe science fiction that pays particular attention to ecological concerns.

The increasing critical attention to the concepts of place and space, particularly in relation to ecocriticism, has begun to intersect with long-standing discussions of setting and genre in science fiction. After all, genres like dystopia and utopia are about place. For eco-critics, space is an abstract notion, as compared with the "bounded" and "humanly meaningful" notion of place (Buell 145). Keeping that distinction in mind, I have kept to the idea of place for much of this essay. The texts explored in this essay are not dystopias or utopias, however. They are science fictions that imagine a much more complex and interesting third possibility: heterotopia. While we tend to think about utopia and dystopia as genre categories, the terms derive from location, or place. "Heterotopia" is a different kind of category, however, in that it is a functional concept that can help in the process of thinking through the importance of place, particularly within contemporary science fiction. My purpose in working with the idea of heterotopia is not to label specific novels, or even spaces within novels, as heterotopian, but rather to explore a way of thinking about place that is rooted in a philosophy of both/and rather than either/or. From there, it is possible to think about how a heterotopian conception of place reorients the ways we think about subject positions, human/nonhuman relations, and power dynamics—all of which are always tied to place.

Heterotopia is one of those critical terms that garners suspicion because it has been taken up in so many different contexts that it can be difficult to use it in a way that has meaning beyond one particular instance. Its complexity is, however, part of what makes heterotopia so appealing. Michel Foucault is usually cited as the origin of the use of the term in contemporary theory; Joan Gordon calls heterotopia "Foucault's richly generative word" (463). Indeed, the depth of the richness of the term is beyond the scope of this essay, but I do want to take a moment to consider some of the ways the term has been deployed in order to anchor the discussion to follow. One of the most often used definition from Foucault describes heterotopias as "counter-sites, a kind of effectively enacted utopia in which the real sites, all the other real sites that can be found within the culture, are simultaneously represented, contested, and inverted" ("Of Other Spaces"). Here, heterotopias are defined through simultaneity and diversity, unity and difference.

Ralph Pordzik uses this idea of heterotopia as a site of negotiated conflict and testing as a way to think outside of dualistic utopia/dystopia categorizations. After describing how heterotopia gives us a way to understand works that gesture toward something like utopia at the same time as they question the possibility of utopian perfection, Pordzik explains that

> postmodern heterotopia thwarts all efforts on the side of the reader to create a coherent illusion of history, meaning and representation in the text. In the de-totalizing and de-temporalizing space it creates, dissent and discontinuity dictate the course of action, effectively putting into practice in the realm of the literary text the "pluriverse" of concepts, fictions, and discourses that constitutes postmodernism's revisionist agenda [5].

Pordzik's focus on postmodern literature helps to illustrate how the concept of heterotopia can be employed in relation to fictions like those discussed here. My readings of the texts focus on their specific ways of creating environments that link directly to the conditions of possibility for individuals and communities within the narratives. In different ways, all three novels construct spaces of simultaneity that defy simple classification, and, more importantly, that require readers to pay attention to how place creates both constraint and possibility. A "pluriverse" (or, in Pratchett's terms, "multiverse") revises the usual idea of a universe in a way that aligns with a nomadic, fragmented, poststructural conception of subjectivity.

Another literary critic who makes use of the term heterotopia is Kevin Hetherington, who argues that heteropias are sites that can be textual as much as geographical (43). Hetherington provides a detailed discussion of the critical history of the term, and his definition is helpful: "I define heterotopia as spaces of alternate ordering. Heterotopias organize a bit of the social world in a way different to that which surrounds them. That alternate ordering marks them out as Other and allows them to be seen as an example of an alternative way of doing things" (viii). In relation to geographic spaces, such a definition could be applied to any number of "real" locations, from military installations to fetish bars. There are military installations in Le Guin's novel and fetish bars in Delany's, but my interest in the idea of heterotopia here is not about defining spaces within the texts as heterotopian. Instead, I want to take the idea of "alternate ordering" that Hetherington highlights and explore what it means about how place is represented in the fictions discussed below.

In a similar vein, Robert J. Topinka has written about heterotopias as "sites of reordering" rather than as "sites of resistance" (56). He argues, "By juxtaposing and combining many spaces in one site, heterotopias problematize received knowledge by revealing and destabilizing the ground, or operating table, on which knowledge is built" (56). He goes on to affirm that destabilization can lead to resistance, but his focus remains on knowledge production. I am not so sure that it makes sense to separate processes of destabilization—or what I tend to think of as critique or demystification—from resistance, but Topinka's emphasis on knowledge production is essential to an understanding of how science fiction can reorient readers' expectations of environments. Topinka states, "Heterotopias reconstitute knowledge, presenting a view of its structural formation that might not otherwise be visible" (60). Good science fiction is good in part because it is able to intervene in our expectations and create alternative sites. Heterotopia is something more. It is a site that is not a site; it lacks solidity and clearly defined borders. It is a reorganization of the concept of a site.

Given the way heterotopias operate as Other spaces of simultaneity, the instability of the relation between self and other is at their heart. Destabilizing the self/other relation means creating conditions necessary for new and more open subject positions to emerge. Pia Maria Ahlbäck emphasizes how important it is to consider the experience of heterotopia: "What can be absolute about heterotopias, these places of relative otherness, except the individual experiences of them?" (161). Revising Ahlbäck's question a bit, we might consider not just "individual experiences" of heterotopias in the texts discussed here, but the process of subjectivation. How are subjects constructed and maintained within heterotopian places? To what extent do heterotopian ideas of place influence the subject positions within the novels? Foucault's works are infamous for a perceived lack of attention to individual subjectivities, but his concepts of power and knowledge are nevertheless all about the construction of subjects. In an afterword to *Stars in My Pocket* written in 1990, Delany argues against the idea of a coherent, central subject and in favor of a fragmented, poststructuralist one: "I think that any time when there was [...] a notion of a centered subject, especially when related to the white, western, patriarchal nuclear family, not only was it an ideological mirage, it was a mirage that necessarily grew up to mask the psychological, economic, and material oppression of an 'other'" (355). Coherent, centered, unitary subjectivity is, for Delany as for Foucault, a false ideal that supports entrenched power structures. Delany concludes the afterword by saying that "this notion of a fragmented subject as a 'natural' condition" underlies much of his writing, including *Stars in My Pocket*. Heterotopia is a place for fragmented subjectivies to be fragmented, and to stay that way.

The first novel under discussion here, Le Guin's *The Word for World Is Forest*, hints at the possibility of heterotopia as an alternative to colonial power relations and limited modes of subjectivity, as well as environmental devastation. The narrative describes a planetary environment where the indigenous species, which lives in ecological harmony with the forest world, becomes subject to Terran colonizers' genocidal practices. The setting is a planet called New Tahiti, signaling imperial themes, and the plot centers on the conflict between human colonizers and the much more peaceful indigenous Athsheans, who eventually become violent in order to revolt against Terran rule. Overthrowing the colonizers means that some Athsheans have to engage in a kind of violence their people have never engaged in before. The narrative emphasizes how the encounter with humans has permanently changed both the planet and the Athsheans. In the wake of the revolt against the Terrans on New Tahiti, the ambassadors of an emerging interplanetary federation that is more established in Le Guin's later Hainish novels, the League of Worlds, learn important lessons about how to create a galactic federation that is founded on heterotopian rather than colonial enterprise. In what follows, I will focus on how the novel develops the distinction between colonial and heterotopian understandings of place, as well as on the way Athshean subjectivity is described as continuous with, rather than distinct from, the environment.

Carol P. Hovanec writes about "visions of nature" in the novel, exploring how "the collective consciousness of the protagonists and antagonists contains the major American attitudes towards the environment, from the early explorers to the present" (85). The novel shifts perspectives among three main characters, each representing a particular American attitude for Hovanec: Davidson, the Terran captain, Lyubov, a Terran anthropologist, and Selver, a member of the indigenous species. Davidson, the quintessential colonizer and antagonist of the novel, sees nature as something to conquer. For him, women and natives are defined as "other" along with the natural world, all of which are subject to his violent colonizing efforts. Lyubov is a thoughtful scholar who is far more sympathetic than Davidson, but Lyubov is also problematic in his own way because he romanticizes nature and the indigenous species. Finally, Selver represents the native perspective, which is incapable of understanding the human perspective in which the environment is something to be exploited. For Selver and the other Athsheans, nature and consciousness cannot be separated; subjectivity is not distinct from environment, from place.

The novel begins with Davidson's crude, misogynist, racist, colonial perspective, which is almost instantly recognizable as both horribly wrong and familiar. A "new shipload of women has arrived" (Le Guin 9), making him happy and causing him to daydream about "the line of 212 buxom beddable breasty little figures" (9–10). On the other hand, he is concerned about erosion in the newly planted human crop fields: "But he still couldn't see why a soybean farm needed to waste a lot of space on trees if the land was managed really scientifically. It wasn't like that in Ohio; if you wanted corn you grew corn, and no space wasted on trees and stuff. But then Earth was a tamed planet and New Tahiti wasn't. That's what he was here for: to tame it" (10). Davidson sees himself as an agent of civilization, there to make the land produce to satisfy his greed. His use of the word "scientifically" makes the point that a colonial attitude like Davidson's pits science against nature and human against non-human. Such binary logic undergirds all of his thinking; heterotopian simultaneity would never make sense to him. Women's bodies and New Tahiti's lands are there for his use. It is therefore unsurprising that Davidson turns out to have a similarly arrogant attitude toward the Athsheans, whom he derogatorily calls "creechies." His casual mention of genocide exemplifies his attitude toward the Other as he describes to one of his men why he believes the indigenous species is doomed: "They're going to get rubbed out sooner or later, and it might as well be sooner. It's just how things happen to be. Primitive races always have to give way to civilized ones" (21). Davidson's notion of progress requires the domination and even extinction of all things that differ from his own beliefs and desires. His either/or approach means he can see New Tahiti only as a place to conquer, and the way he understands place links directly to his understandings of power, subjectivity, and the nonhuman.

When the narrative shifts perspective in the second chapter, the reader is immediately thrown into an utterly different way of being and thinking. In the first line, the shift is apparent: "All the colors of rust and sunset, brown-reds and pale greens, changed ceaselessly in the long leaves as the wind blew" (35). There is no hint of speaker or context other than the break between chapters, but this is obviously a new and different voice. It goes on, "The roots of the copper willows, thick and ridged, were moss-green down by the running water, which like the wind moved slowly with many soft eddies and seeming pauses, held back by rocks, roots, hanging and fallen leaves" (35). An eco-centric point of view begins to take shape. The wind, leaves, roots, and water are described in a way that suggests their significance, even their agency, while the narrating voice provides no sense of distance—only continuity with the natural world. As the lengthy first paragraph of the chapter continues, the details of the observations begin to take on new meaning:

> The view was never long, unless looking up through the branches you caught sight of the stars. Nothing was pure, dry, arid, plain. Revelation was lacking. There was no seeing everything at once: no certainty. The colors of rust and sunset kept changing in the hanging leaves of the copper willows, and you could not say even whether the leaves of the willows were brownish-red, or reddish-green, or green [36].

The narrative voice laments the loss of what existed before the humans arrived and begins to envision the complexity of a new heterotopian horizon. The language equates experience of the forest with knowledge of events and understanding, which begins to reflect the way in which the native perspective sees nature and consciousness as inseparable.

Soon, the reader learns that the change in narrative tone is because the third person narration has shifted focalization away from Davidson and to an Athshean named Selver. As the chapter unfolds Selver tells members of an Athsheans tribe he does not know about his experiences with "yumens," one of whom (Davidson, it turns out) raped and killed Selver's wife. The Terrans treat Selver and other Athsheans as sub-human slaves to be used for labor and Terran pleasure. Lyubov intervenes when Selver goes after Davidson in a very un–Athshean manner. Utlimately, Selver helps to lead a revolt in which he and other Athsheans kill their human captors. It is the first time any of his people have committed murder, and everyone who hears Selver's story is concerned with this new thing—this new act that is so against their culture yet seems to have become necessary since the Terrans' arrival. The behavior of the humans is incomprehensible to them. They do not distinguish between place and self, between forest and people, so the destruction of the forest is particularly impossible for them to understand.

Interestingly, the Athsheans have a kind of reversed gender structure in which the females are the rulers and decision makers, and some of the males—only the gifted and learned—are "dreamers," who are able to "see" in their dreams and to offer their insights to the female rulers. As I will discuss below, Delany's novel also plays with gender categories, emphasizing how provisional subject positions really are—even those that we commonly assume to be inherent or essential. In Le Guin's novel, the gender reversal among the Athsheans is a subtle but important way to signal the relationships among culture, place, and subjectivity. It also becomes clear that even before the Terrans invaded and enslaved his people, the Athshean world view was already somewhat heterotopian. Selver's thoughts illustrate that point: "They were not all one people on the Forty Lands of the world. There were more languages than lands, and each with a different dialect for every town that spoke it; there were infinite ramifications of manners, morals, customs, crafts; physical types differed on each of the five Great Lands" (47). The desire for conquest and the need for homogeneity that marks nearly every word and deed Davidson offers is absent from the indigenous culture. Difference did not mean danger to them in the way that it does to Davidson.

Lyubov, the human anthropologist who befriends Selver and fights Davidson's model of colonial dominance, takes over in chapter three. The reader learns that Lyubov and other scholars consider the Athsheans to be members of the human species. There is an ancestral link to Terrans (humans from Earth) as well as to humans on other planets. Therefore, for Lyubov the Athsheans are not a lower life form; their otherness does not make them less than, just different from Terrans. Lyubov wants to learn from and about the Athsheans, but it soon becomes clear that the other colonizing Terrans do not respect him or his work. He is, however, able to help to convince visiting non-humans who represent the brand new League of Worlds of some of the threat the Terrans pose, saying, "'We have killed, raped, dispersed, and enslaved the native humans, destroyed their communities, and cut down their forests. It wouldn't be surprising if they'd decided that we are not human'" (75). The colonists wind up being told by the authorities back on Terra that they must cease contact with the native humans. Lyubov complicates things since he is open to new possibilities, to new ways of thinking and being. He does not believe in a single model of civilization, nor does he believe in the hierarchical model of power that Davidson and the other Terrans adhere to. Still, Hovanec's point, discussed above, that Lyubov romanticizes, is accurate. He assumes Athsheans to be incapable of murderous violence, when it turns out that they are capable once they face Terran colonizers.

In this novel, colonial domination seeks to destroy difference and create homogeneity, while the heterotopian possibility of simultaneity and difference is always just beyond reach for those who wish to embrace it. As the novel continues, Davidson's thinking deteriorates from hateful to paranoid as he becomes increasingly frustrated by his colleagues' willingness to cooperate with orders from Earth. He winds up defying orders and attacking a native village. His actions lead to a major revolt in which Selver and others of his people kill or capture all of the humans in the main settlement. Lyubov, too, is killed, although Selver tries to warn him to leave the camp. After a few years pass, the humans are picked up by the group that had once heard Lyubov's concerns, and Selver meets with the representatives of the League of Worlds who explain that the world will be protected and that no more aliens will arrive for generations. The new model of the League of Worlds is one of gradual integration; Selver's planet will eventually be given an opportunity to join, but only if it wants to do so. However, for Selver and the other native humans on his planet, the Terran colonizers have brought changes that cannot be undone. They are postcolonial subjects now who have learned to objectify other humans to the point of being able to kill them. Heterotopia is not utopia. The conflict between Terrans and Athsheans will change the Athsheans, even if no other alien arrives for generations. Nevertheless, the events on Selver's planet teach the new League to approach new worlds differently and to avoid colonial situations in favor of heterotopian ideals.

The Word for World Is Forest demonstrates how a heterotopian model differs from a colonial one, and emphasizes how important the relationship between subject and environment really is. Davidson's essentializing rants are peppered throughout the text, but they grow increasingly violent in tone and intent up to the point where he simply does not trust anyone but himself. His view of the world as a place to own, subdue, and use is mirrored by his inability to see humanity in the natives he refers to as "creechies," in the Terran women he sees as being provided for his convenience, and in his treatment of other Terrans whose views and race differ from his own. He cannot, in fact, grant subject status to anyone or anything outside of himself. Selver's understanding, in complete contrast to Davidson's, is that the world is part of him and he is part of the world. The Athshean model of subjectivity aligns with a heterotopian conception of place, and with embracing the other, the nonhuman in a nonhierarchical way.

Stars in My Pocket Like Grains of Sand is another example of science fiction set on a faraway planet populated by both an intelligent native species and humans. Delany's novel takes place during a different time in the relationship between species, after humans have lived on the planet Velm and coexisted with the native evelm for generations. Nothing is simple in this text; it is a complicated, frequently disorienting, narrative in which the experience of heterotopian simultaneity is shared by the characters and the reader. Marq Dyeth, the (human) main character and narrator of most of the text, is an "Industrial Diplomat" whose work has to do with the transfer of technology across worlds. Figuring out what a hand gesture or a particular pronoun means on a planet he has never visited before is a frequent problem for Marq. His efforts to make sense of the people and places around him are mirrored and multiplied in the reader's experience of the text.

Narrative complexity is certainly one way to evoke heterotopian possibilities. Like Le Guin's *The Word for World Is Forest*, *Stars in My Pocket Like Grains of Sand* offers more than one narrative perspective. Here, the Prologue, "A World Apart," written in the third person (as opposed to Marq's first person narration of most of the novel), describes Rat Korga's experience on his home world where he is socially marginalized in part due to some "prenatal brain damage," and in part for his homosexuality. Much later in the novel the reader learns that Rat's preference for sexual partners who are much shorter than he is further marks him out as deviant on a world where height is supposed to determine sexual attraction. Delany begins his novel with a figure whose entire existence has been on the margins of his society which judges him according to rules that, to the reader, can only seem arbitrary and unjust. At the beginning of the novel Rat has essentially given up; he undergoes "Radical Anxiety Termination," which hinders his ability to think for himself but is supposed to allow him to be happy. After the treatment, Rat is sold by the company that administers it as a worker who will follow orders and winds up being treated as a slave. Rat (the name comes from the treatment he undergoes and is used pejoratively on his world for all "rats") is caged, whipped, sexually assaulted, and generally treated as an object without any subject status. There is no place for someone like Rat to be anything more on his world.

At one point Rat gains access to "General Information," or "GI," a kind of intergalactic internet to which one can link one's mind. As he grows accustomed to GI, and able to think through and with it, Rat comes to a sense of what it means for him: "The new condition was not so much an alternate voice loud enough to drown the voices of childhood as it was a web, a text weaving endlessly about him, erupting into and falling from consciousness, prompting memory and obliterating it" (Delany 34). Access to GI changes everything for Rat. The drowning of "voices of childhood" means a shift away from the constant reminders of his defects, while the "text weaving endlessly about him" offers a different mode of subjectivity. When Rat resurfaces later in the novel, he has permanent access to GI. The heterotopian cyberspace of GI creates the possibility of a new kind of subjectivity for Rat that is not contingent upon the rules of his home world. Rat's story is merely the prologue to the rest of the novel, but it sets the tone for the story to come and establishes a number of important themes—including power relations, subject positions, and access to knowledge.

The main portion of the novel is subtitled "Monologues: Visible and Invisible Persons Distributed in Space," emphasizing the relationship between subjectivity and place yet establishing a sense of complexity. It is written in the first person from Marq Dyeth's human perspective. One example of the complexities in Marq's narrative is the way the novel treats gender and sexuality. Phrases like "But after all, I'm a woman" (68) pop up in Marq's narration, but his name and other signals suggest he is actually a man. To make matters more confusing, even Marq does not understand the meaning of the use of the pronoun "he" on the planet he visits at the beginning of his section. Eventually, we learn that on Marq's world, and on the world he had been visiting:

> "She" is the pronoun for all sentient individuals of whatever species who have achieved the legal status of "woman." The ancient, dimorphic form "he," once used exclusively for the genderal indication of males […] for more than a hundred-twenty years now, has been reserved for the general sexual object of "she," during the period of excitation, regardless of the gender of the woman speaking of the gender of the woman referred to [73].

"He" and "she" are used, but they have to do with the speaker's sexual interest in the object, not gender. Such a narrative move certainly destabilizes the ground upon which the reader's understanding usually stands. Throughout the reader's experience of the novel, gendered pronouns hold simultaneous, conflicting meanings; in order to make sense of Marq's narration the reader has to adjust to the way pronouns work for "her."

Marq's narration of his experiences on his home planet of Velm further the sense of heterotopian place. He has grown up with human and evelmi friends and family, and to him the large size, long claws, multiple tongues, and hard scales of the evelmi are perfectly normal, as are the three evelmi sexes: male, female, and neuter. His narration of a meeting with one of his sisters illustrates how the narrative links subjectivity and a heterotopian concept of place:

> Bu lolloped across the stones, the wet tufts on her legs dripping about her claws, the scales on her back a glister of purples and browns. She leaped against me, bronze claws hooked over my shoulders (yes, the gold-clawed apprentice in the butcher shop hails from a different continent than Bu), small tongues playing over my mouth. I opened wide so she could be sure to taste me properly. Her eyelids signaled madly the sign we had both agreed on, when we were fifteen years younger—me sixteen and just emerging from human adolescence, she fifteen and just emerging from evelm infanthood—would be my name to her [174].

Here, there is no interpretive distance between Marq and the experience because this is normal for him. He tells us about greeting his sister in a manner that is consistent with how he understands his own body and his own subjectivity. Marq understands Bu's desire to taste and finds it to be completely normal. Possibilities multiply in passages like this. Heterotopias contain the potential for all things. The parenthetical reference to a different evelm and her greeting earlier in the text furthers the heterotopian sense of multiplicity and possibility. As strange as this scene between Marq and Bu is, it is only one way of greeting on his world which, like ours, contains infinite variations simultaneously.

One of the important points about heterotopian concepts of place is that they inevitably undermine utopian ideals. Like Le Guin's novel where the utopian possibility of Selver's people is disrupted by a Terran attempt to create a different kind of utopia, Delany's novel takes care to remind the reader that utopia is both dangerous and impossible. One of the central plot points of the novel has to do with a conflict between two different groups who seek to have political dominance on each world: the Family and the Sygn. As Marq puts it, "with the Family trying to establish the dream of a classic past as pictured on a world that may never even have existed in order to achieve cultural stability, and with the Sygn committed to the living interaction and difference between each woman and each world from which the right stability and play may flower" (80), there is always a sense of conflict between achieving a kind of idealized "family" and embracing all possibilities. Clearly, the Sygn is the more heterotopian option.

Marq and his family see themselves as aligned with the Sygn. Marq and his siblings were adopted into his "stream"—the word they use instead of family. There is no need for genetic links or the kind of restrictive notion of purity that seems to be associated with the Family. Nevertheless, there are hints about human violence against the evelm in the northern part of the planet so that it is impossible to describe Velm as a place of peaceful coexistence. Marq describes the "most common form of government on Velm" as "an efficient bureaucratic anarchy" (105). Such a structure aligns beautifully with a heterotopian notion of place. Neil Easterbrook, who looks at heterotopia in other novels by Le Guin and Delany, argues, "A 'humanist' liberal utopia is an isotopia; a postmodern liberal utopia is an authentic anarchy, a heterotopia. The schema of a heterotopia is the rhizome: a model of rhetorical, semiotic, intertextual, heterotropic space—convoluted, oxymoronic, folded back on itself, distinctly poststructural" (70). Velm and the Sygn are excellent examples of Easterbrook's point. There is no promise of a single utopian vision, but there is the possibility for multiplicity, conflict, and proliferation.

It turns out that Rat's world, Rhyonon, was deciding between membership in the Sygn or the Family, but succumbed to "Cultural Fugue," which is a constant danger in the universe of the novel. Both groups, Sygn and Family, are efforts to stabilize worlds so that they do not experience Cultural Fugue. Again, it makes sense to think of the Sygn as embracing a heterotopian model of place and governance, while the Family represents an attempt to create an idealized utopia. Choosing one model or the other has great importance in the novel, since Cultural Fugue means the destruction of an entire planet. Rat is the only survivor on his planet; he is rescued by people associated with GI who discover that he and Marq Dyeth are each others' "perfect erotic objects." Someone from GI who knows Marq brings Rat to him in an effort to give Rat a new life on Velm, however Rat and Marq's relationship brings the threat of Cultural Fugue to Velm. They cannot be together, and the sense of heterotopian complexity takes over completely by the end of the novel. In the Epilogue, Marq talks about what it is like to arrive on a world at dawn, explaining that "you become intensely aware how arbitrary a concept dawn is" (Delany 335). Arbitrary, yet significant. Finding meaning, connection, purpose in heterotopia is daunting for Marq, and losing Rat after only a brief but intense time together makes it that much harder. Delany's novel simultaneously describes heterotopian place, fragmented subjectivity, and the complexities of such a model of existence.

The complicated nature of heterotopia is also explored in *The Long Earth*, by Stephen Baxter and Terry Pratchett. It is the first book in a series that rests on a premise that changes the way space and place operate. In the year 2015, humankind discovers that our Earth is only one among a possibly infinite number of other Earths, and—more importantly—that most humans can access those other Earths through a process called "Stepping." The story is told through a third person narrator focalizing different characters in different chapters. A large portion of Baxter and Pratchett's novel tells the story of one particular boy/young man: Joshua Valienté. Joshua is a "natural stepper" who can move from world to world with ease and without the aid of a device. The main plot focuses on Joshua, who is recruited by an artificial intelligence entity called Lobsang who claims to be a reincarnated Tibetan motorcycle repairman. Lobsang wants to explore, to find out what is out there, and he and Joshua head as far west into the Long Earth as they can go. Along the way they determine that there is a threat to the Long Earth; a single-minded life form that is driving all other life forms eastward, toward our Earth. It is worth pausing to emphasize that the particular danger the novel describes is one that wishes to homogenize, to devour difference—a distinctly un-heterotopian way of approaching place.

One of the most interesting elements of *The Long Earth,* for the discussion here, is the way the discovery of all of those other Earths—none of which, by the way, include human life—alters the conditions of life on our Earth, or "Datum Earth" as it is called in the novel. Jack Green, who worked in software before the discovery of the Long Earth, offers an example of how things have changed. He is a middle-class pioneer who leaves Datum Earth with total strangers to settle in a new place, "a hundred thousand worlds away" (Baxter and Pratchett 92). As he travels over Datum Earth to arrive at the proper place to begin Stepping, he observes,

> And so you never knew who you might meet at the next rail station. Pioneer types, come back to buy a new set of bronze tools and to have their teeth fixed. High-tech hippies, trading goat cheese for mastitis cream.

> Once, a woman dressed like Pocahantas blissfully clutching a white wedding dress in a cellophane cover, and there was a whole short story just in her smile. People with new ways of living all jumbled up together in the Datum, at least for the duration of their journeys [90–1].

Jack Green's description is the epitome of a heterotopian conception of place and an accompanying fragmented sense of subjectivity. With all of the Long Earth available to them, people have begun to create new possibilities for themselves. The sense of multiplicity and simultaneity pervades the novel, and links to the subject positions people occupy. In fact, one way this novel helps to further an understanding of heterotopia is through the ways it connects the new knowledge of space with new subject positions. In this passage, the woman whose smile is a story is just one example of how the vastness of the Long Earth (as the entirety of the new range of worlds is called) has created a heterotopian sense of possibility.

Another important aspect of the Long Earth is the degree to which natural landscapes become significant. All of those other worlds, with a variety of animal life and even other sentient beings but without humans, are wildernesses for humans used to Datum Earth. Over and over again, Steppers find themselves grappling with what it means to be vulnerable to nature and to know that there is so very much of it out there. Helen Green, Jack's daughter, explains, "You do feel like you're out in the wild. Back home on the Datum I was living on top of centuries of other people's efforts to *tame* everything. Here the forest has never been cleared, the swamps never drained, the river never dammed or leveed. It's strange. And dangerous" (156). In part, the discovery of the Long Earth means a return to earlier modes of living in relation to the natural world. Like *The Word for World is Forest*, *The Long Earth* recognizes that a different conception of place must take into account the nonhuman. The "tameness" of Datum Earth is an anomaly in the vastness of the Long Earth, and should bring to mind Davidson's desire to tame New Tahiti in Le Guin's novel. Just as *The Long Earth* emphasizes the link between heterotopian space and subjectivity, it also highlights how incredibly anthropocentric our usual models of space are. In other words, heterotopian space, with its convolutions and contradictions, has the advantage of not needing to focus on human needs, wants, desires, etc. Indeed, the "human" seems far too close to a singular reality in the context of heterotopia, where the sheer magnitude of all that is nonhuman makes its presence known.

Nevertheless, human beings do not easily relinquish the desire to control, conquer, and contain. At one point in Joshua's travels with Lobsang, they reach West 33156, the number designating how many steps away from Datum Earth it is. Joshua describes it as "a typical Ice Belt world" full of snow belts and almost no actual water, and he observes,

> On the outcrop to which they were anchored, black rock protruding through the snow, stood a natural monument: a lonesome pine, big, elderly and isolated. But the tree had been neatly cut down close to the root, the tangled branches and the upper trunk lying discarded on the ground, and a pale disc of core wood exposed to the air. An axe had evidently been used [117].

Joshua is fittingly stunned by the careless killing of a single tree. It turns out to have been human scientists looking for climate records from tree rings. This is just one of the signals that humanity is in danger of making the same thoughtless mistakes it has made on Datum Earth on all of the new worlds. Obviously, scientific curiosity taking precedence over the life of the tree is deemed a problem here, much like Terran colonialism or the Family's attempts at homogenization are critiqued in the other novels. Indeed, the scientists who cut down the tree in the passage above engage in the exact same act as the humans who clear cut Selver's home in Le Guin's novel.

As people begin to move around the Long Earth, a distinction between two groups begins to form. Some steppers become nomads, while others work to settle the new Earths. In many ways, it seems that the settlers are looking for a kind of utopia, while the nomads embrace the idea of a "multiverse," or a heterotopia. Jack Green and his daughter are part of those seeking a utopian model. Joshua is a nomad. Twice during his travels with Lobsang he stops at a settlement that is clearly an attempt at utopia—Happy Landings. Joshua is skeptical: "And Joshua felt oddly uncomfortable, once more. A slight feeling you get when everything is so *right* that it might have gone all the way around the universe and come back metamorphosed into *wrong*" (319). As in *The Word for World Is Forest* and *Stars in My Pocket Like Grains of Sand*, utopia is problematic here. There is room in the vastness of the Long Earth for just about everything, but there is something troubling about efforts to make one, perfect place.

Predictably, the poor and the disenfranchised on Datum Earth are eager to find new places and new possibilities, while the landed and privileged are just as eager to extend their holdings on as many worlds as possible. Police Sergeant Monica Jansson is another key character. She considers how the "Long Earth Trading Company," with its colonial name and goals, operates on a world three steps removed from Datum Earth, describing workers who realize the vastness available to them: "As soon as they realized that they could be using their strength to build something for themselves, they tended to start agitating to join one of the new Companies and go trekking off into the deep crosswise to colonize—or else [...] they simply walked away, into the endless spaces" (80). Power dynamics have to change with the freedom of the Long Earth.

The discovery of the Long Earth does not mean total freedom for everyone, however. It turns out that a substantial portion of the population simply cannot move between worlds. Joshua quickly recognizes the danger of the situation: "Suddenly humanity was fundamentally divided—even if it didn't know it yet" (154). Rod Green, Jack's son, is one of the people who cannot step; his family leaves him behind on Datum Earth, and at the end of the novel, acting as part of a fringe political group that is against stepping, he plants a nuclear bomb in Madison's capital. Most, if not all, of the people manage to step away; those who cannot step are carried by those who can. As the novel ends, the sequel titled *The Long War* looms with wars on at least two fronts: the entity in the Long Earth devouring difference and the humans on Earth who want to close down the possibility of the Long Earth. Both the entity and the radicals on Datum are dangers to the heterotopian nature of the Long Earth.

The texts discussed here offer ways to rethink how a heterotopian understanding of place can help us to reevaluate the importance of place in relation to subjectivity, power, and the nonhuman. Thinking beyond our usual conceptions of utopia can allow for a different model that these science fiction novels have begun to explore. All three novels juxtapose heterotopias with dangerous colonial/imperial/utopian models of place/subjectivity. If the goal is to "tame" the nonhuman, the Other, the difficult, in order to create a place of safety and security for the few who are granted subject status and positions of power, we are already doomed. Perhaps there can be a different kind of goal, one that allows for difference and simultaneity, and that understands subjectivity to be nomadic, contingent, and fragmented—and open. Certainly the nonhuman, and many of the human, inhabitants of our world would benefit from a more heterotopian approach to place.

Works Cited

Ahlbäck, Pia Maria. *Energy, Heterotopia, Dystopia: George Orwell, Michel Foucault and the Twentieth Century Environmental Imagination*. Åbo: Åbo Akademi University Press, 2001. Print.

Baxter, Stephen, and Terry Pratchett. *The Long Earth*. New York: Harper, 2012. Print.

Buell, Lawrence. *The Future of Environmental Criticism: Environmental Crisis and Literary Imagination*. Malden, MA: Blackwell, 2005. Print.

Delany, Samuel R. *Stars in My Pocket Like Grains of Sand*. Middletown, CT: Wesleyan University Press, 1984. Print.

Easterbrook, Neil. "State, Heterotopia: The Political Imagination in Heinlein, Le Guin, and Delany." *Political Science Fiction*. Ed. Donald M. Hassler and Clyde Wilcox. 1997. Columbia: University of South Carolina Press, 2011. 43–75. Print.

Foucault, Michel. "Of Other Spaces." 1967. *Foucault Info*. Trans. Jay Miskowiec. Web. 14 February 2004.

Gordon, Joan. "Hybridity, Heterotopia, and Mateship in China Mieville's *Perdito Street Station*." *Science Fiction Studies* 30 (2003): 456–476. *MLA International Bibliography*. 3 October 2012.

Hetherington, Kevin. *The Badlands of Modernity: Heterotopia and Social Ordering*. New York: Routledge, 1997. Print.

Hovanec, Carol P. "Visions of Nature in *The Word for World is Forest*: A Mirror of the American Consciousness." *Extrapolation* 30.1 (1989): 84–92. *MLA International Bibliography*. Web. 14 September 2012.

Huffman, Bennett. "Postmodern Ecocriticism in the Science Fiction Novel: J.G. Ballard and Ken Kesey." *The Environmental Tradition in English Literature*. Ed. John Parham. Burlington, VT: Ashgate: 2002. 64–74. Print.

Le Guin, Ursula K. *The Word for World Is Forest*. New York: Tor, 1972. Print.

Pordzik, Ralph. *The Quest for Postcolonial Utopia: A Comparative Introduction to the Utopian Novel in the New English Literatures*. New York: Peter Lang, 2001. Print.

Topinka, Robert J. "Foucault, Borges, Heterotopia: Producing Knowledge in Other Spaces." *Foucault Studies* 9 (2010): 54–70. Web. 10 May 2012.

Acceptance of the Marginalized in Marge Piercy's *He, She, It* and Melissa Scott's *Trouble and Her Friends*

MELANIE A. MAROTTA

In Marge Piercy's *He, She, It* (1991) and Melissa Scott's *Trouble and Her Friends* (1994), the female protagonists, Shira Shipman, Cerise, and Trouble/India Carless, leave patriarchal dystopias in favor of utopias that accept the marginalized. While the patriarchal areas appear to emphasize community, the communities have been constructed in accordance with the needs of the leaders (in most cases the leaders are corporations) kept in mind and not those of its populace. Piercy's Shira resides in a patriarchal enclave, the Yakamura-Stichen dome, while Scott's Cerise and Trouble appear in an unnamed city and on the nets, their world's virtual landscape. Each aforementioned residence aims to restrict the movements of the female protagonists and force them to conform to the communal ideal. The patriarchal enclaves, Y-S dome, and the unnamed city, appear on the surface to be ideal utopic environments, the proverbial Garden of Eden; however, it becomes clear that these areas oppress the protagonists.

Shira, Cerise, and Trouble escape these so-called utopias, preferring instead the physically dangerous frontier. For Shira this area is the Glop, the environmentally-damaged expanse where the poverty-stricken reside, and Tikva, the freetown where she spent her childhood. Cerise and Trouble choose the nets and Seahaven, a city which appears both on the nets and in reality. Although these areas are dangerous to the physical well-being of these characters, the protagonists have no other option but to flee from the patriarchal enclaves and reside here if they wish to be free to form their own identities. Throughout science fiction, there is the appearance of the dystopic area that the unconforming masses live in, preferring instead freewill and the constant threat of physical harm to the appearance of safety and mental and physical domination. While these areas may appear to be dystopias they are, in fact, utopias for the marginalized. This study investigates the assertion that Shira, Cerise, and Trouble must go to the utopias for the marginalized because the social constructs in place in these areas, these communal environments, enable them to reject the dystopic patriarchal guidelines and reclaim their true identities. As Piercy's text opens, Shira's experiences inside the Y-S dome reveal the elitism of the patriarchal utopia.

In reference to the construction of the utopia, theorist Ruth Levitas observes that the U.S. has a long-standing tradition of attempting to fabricate the utopia (180). Significantly, as revealed through Levitas' analysis of the various forms that utopias take as seen in J. C. Davis' *Utopia and the Ideal City*, the concept of the utopia appears in multiple incarnations, but each form is problematic (185–189). In essence, the inhabitants of the utopia repeatedly face an imperfect utopia rather than experiencing their utopian ideal (185–189). According to Mircea Eliade, humanity has immersed within its collective psyche primordial symbolic images (16). The theorist continues to note that the "symbols never disappear from the *reality* of the psyche" (16). In other words, humanity creates what it believes it misses, what it longs for, thereby having "'nostalgia for Paradise'" (16). As depicted in Piercy's novel, the issue is that as humanity formulates a utopia it tends to manufacture a dystopia which includes a hierarchal system favoring exclusion rather than inclusion. Piercy's narrator notes that "there were twenty-three great multis that divided the world among them, enclaves on every continent and on space platforms. Among them they wielded power and enforced the corporate peace: raids, assassinations, skirmishes, but no wars since the Two Week War in 2017" (3). Here, the multi appears as the protector figure, but of itself rather than humanity. The multi construct is shown as controlling not only in Norika (the former U.S. and Canada), but the planet at large. Notably, space has entered the equation and the multis are in the midst of conquering this area as well. Istvan Csicsery-Ronay, Jr., in "Cyberpunk and Neuromanticism" observes that one of the traits of the cyberpunk text is the presence of the "evil (megacorporations/police states/criminal underworlds)"—they appear in the form of the antagonist that threatens the way of life and, in some cases, the existence of the protagonist (184).

In Piercy's text, the multi that receives considerable attention and appears as the greatest risk to Shira is Y-S. This patriarchal corporation, which is located in the former U.S. and in space, demands conformity in its employees. For instance, Shira is Jewish and while in the corporate enclave she must hide her religious beliefs, so much that she is referred to as a marrano, "a term borrowed from the Spanish Jews under the Inquisition who had pretended to be Christian to survive" (Piercy 2). Immediately, it becomes clear that Shira's multi is a faux-utopia, a space that ensures life through the oppression of personal freedoms. Y-S has its own ideology, a feature Shira notes as common to all multis. First, in order to be admitted to a multi, one must work for the corporation. In Shira's society, if a student does exceedingly well in the Grand Exam, that student is placed in an auction and bid on by universities. When Shira receives her auction results, rather than appearing as a moment of privilege, the process is reminiscent of a slave on the auction block headed into an environment that restricts personal freedoms. After her education has been completed, Shira is once again purchased, only this time it is by Y-S. In reference to Shira's education and position at Y-S, the narrator notes that "she had gone to school in the affluent quadrant of Europa—so she had had no choice but to come here" (2). Immediately upon introduction in Piercy's novel, Shira's inability to conform to Y-S's ideology and social hierarchy becomes apparent. As previously stated, Shira hides her true religion and worships in secret. Piercy's narrator reveals that "all multis had their official religion as part of the corporate culture" (2). As do others, including her ex-husband, Shira appears to follow the "born-again Shintoism of Y-S" so to placate the corporate entity (2). By worshipping Judaism, Tikva's religion, Shira breaks one of Y-S's rules while simultaneously ensuring that the religion of Tikva's people continues to exist. Shira is essentially caught between worlds—she resides in Y-S and follows enough of Y-S's rules in order to ensure survival, but just barely.

While residing in the Y-S enclave, Shira reveals that her corporate progress has been stunted and that she is incapable of becoming a true representative of the Y-S ideal. The narrator observes, "Here she was desperately lonely and constantly in minor trouble" (3). In this multi as with the other corporate bodies, many of the populace are so eager to please the corporate entity, thereby protecting themselves from what lies outside the dome, that they are willing to undergo appearance-altering surgery, which ensures that they conform to the Y-S ideal. In fact, when pregnant Shira carries her son to term, an event practically unheard of in Y-S, Shira does so because she fears the corporation's "conditioning" of the child (192). Due to her uncommon behavior, Shira is willing to risk stretch marks in order to have a full-term pregnancy, she appears as an oddity to others in the enclave (192). By taking control of her body, Shira rebels against Y-S's constant domination of her physical form. The effects of a character's environment on the creation of his or her self connect SF to reality in Piercy's novel. The Glop looms threateningly throughout Piercy's plot, as do other remnants of the apocalyptic environmental disaster. For instance, Shira and Yod are attacked by organ pirates while swimming, surviving only because of Yod's physical presence. Piercy creates the body not only as a signifier of hierarchal position and as a commodity, but also as a site of resistance. When they go swimming they choose to do so even though death looms on the horizon. As part of a freetown, Shira has the ability to behave as she pleases, to physically look as she desires. For instance, once she arrives in Tikva, Shira's grandmother cuts her hair short, removing the long tresses favored by Y-S. She does, however, keep her Y-S ocular implant. By retaining the implant, Shira always has a reminder that Y-S has influenced the manner in which she has viewed the world and herself. As Bruce Sterling highlights in his ground-breaking preface to *Mirrorshades*, "Certain central themes spring up repeatedly in cyberpunk. The theme of body invasion: prosthetic limbs, implanted circuitry, cosmetic surgery, genetic alteration" (346). In *He, She, It*, it is commonplace for a character residing in a multi to alter his or her appearance: for example, while in Y-S, Shira plugs in and speaks to Gadi Stein, her childhood friend. Gadi works as a stimmie producer, a creator of artificial environments for escapists. Shira examines his appearance and notes that he has dyed his hair gray and his face brown, so that he may appear to conform to the image of both the stimmie producer and as a member of Uni-Par, Gadi's multi, which prizes fame and artificiality above all else.

As Shira observes when she is passing a group of schoolchildren who have been surgically altered in accordance with the Y-S image, appearance discloses position in the Y-S hierarchy. In other words, the levels of plastic surgery increase to denote superiority in the hierarchy.

While employed by Y-S, Shira does not alter herself surgically, but she does wear the backless suit, which reveals to others her position as a techie. Csicsery-Ronay, Jr., states, "Cybernetics provides the pretext for the mechanized control of social life, of the body itself ..." (185). The multis are positioned in Piercy's text as the stereotypical cyberpunk corporations, the organizations that regulate the lives of those in their proximity. Even though Csicsery-Ronay, Jr.'s assertion was made regarding the concept of the cyborg, it nonetheless can be applied to Shira's society (185). Since many work to supplement the multis' need for technological components, the corporations do, in fact, have "control of [the] social life, of the body itself ..." of many of Piercy's characters (185). The oppression of the characters by the multis is not always successful and creates a desire for resistance rather than compliance. Csicsery-Ronay, Jr., notes that in the cyberpunk world, "in a universe where the forces of innovation are constantly tinkering with human beings' own information processing systems through telematics, drugs, and surgical intervention, the regulator of experience (ego? self? spirit?) can no longer accept any experience as worth more than any other. The only standard is thrill ..." (191). When applied to Piercy's text, a later cyberpunk novel, Csicsery-Ronay, Jr.'s statement is found to be partially true—it is accurate to state that some of Piercy's characters, Gadi for instance, are "thrill"-seekers who employ technology to do just that while others use it as a tool to achieve survival and even autonomy from the multis (191).

While owned by Y-S, Shira desperately attempts to comply with Y-S's guidelines, but the power of her family's ideology over Shira's self is compelling. In reference to Shira and her identity, the narrator states, "She always felt too physical here, too loud, to female, too Jewish, too dark, too exuberant, too emotional" (Piercy 5). Shira is self-conscious about her appearance and her behavior when immersed in Y-S society; subsequently, she brings the ill effects of this learned behavior to Tikva upon her return. For example, when Shira goes swimming with Yod, she is hesitant to remove her clothing in front of him, thereby revealing her naked body and subsequently becoming vulnerable. Shira feels exposed, an emotional reaction foreign to a resident of Tikva. According to Shira, residing in a multi meant strict control over the body: "She had since lived in cultures, like Y-S, that had fierce injunctions concerning what parts of the human body should be displayed in what circumstances" (100). Through Shira's character, Piercy examines "sex roles" in her text, frequently implying that with this new post-apocalyptic society comes change in what was previously considered the norm for humanity (100). Once Shira begins to reintegrate herself into Tikva society, she becomes more comfortable with her body, thus regaining control over her identity. Over time spent in Tikva with Yod, Shira begins to develop an emotional attachment to the cyborg and starts a sexual relationship with him. It is only once she returns to Tikva that Shira feels a sense of self-worth. It is in this community that she is appreciated for her contributions to science—she works with Avram on his project—and for whom she is as an adult. It should be noted that Shira separates herself from Tikva during her adolescence when she discovers that Gadi has cheated on her with a classmate of hers. Upon advice from Avram, Shira goes to Europa to attend university; she then joins Y-S as one of its most promising commodities. *He, She, It* is essentially a bildungsroman: throughout the text Shira's progression from childhood to adulthood is portrayed alongside Yod's. When Shira joins Y-S, it appears odd since Y-S is a patriarchal entity and Shira is from a matrilineal family. Once Shira rejoins Tikva, the meaning of Shira's previous behavior becomes clear—she has been looking for an escape from her former life, which is one that includes Gadi. Shira is unable to make the transition from childhood to adulthood thereby releasing her childhood insecurities until she rejoins Tikva society. It is only then that she recovers from the false direction that she has taken and steers herself towards true self-acceptance. When the novel begins, however, Shira is searching for stability in her life, so she attempts to integrate the patriarchal guidelines of Y-S into her identity.

Shira is torn between worlds and clings to her only security, her son Ari. She has refused the societal guidelines taught to her by her grandmother, Malkah, in an effort to socially conform to her new society. First, Malkah has directed her not to marry, but Shira has gone against her wishes and entered into a marriage contract with Josh Rogovin. In order to forget her past, specifically the love that she has for Gadi, Shira attempts to please both Josh and Y-S, thereby accepting the patriarchal hierarchal guidelines set in place by Y-S. Second, Malkah has falsely led Shira to believe that in her family a woman's mother is to raise the woman's child. Malkah has Shira's best interests in mind when she gives misinformation to Shira: Riva, Shira's mother, is an information pirate and is wanted by the multis so, as a result of her status, Malkah must raise Shira. What Shira does not understand in this phase of her life is that while the societal rules of Tikva are there to protect its inhabitants, those of Y-S are created to ensure the survival and superiority of the corporation. The individual's needs are insignificant to the multi. For example, after Y-S has sent assassins to attack Malkah and other Tikva citizens, a meeting is arranged in order to discover the reason for the attack. According to Eliade, once introduced to the utopia humanity develops a "nostalgia for paradise" (17). Significantly, Eliade warns against having this desire to seek paradise for the image may be to an unknown degree "desecrated, degraded and artificialised" (18). At the meeting Shira learns that if she reenters the Y-S community, she is to be rewarded; Shira is to join Ari on Pacifica Platform, a Y-S owned platform in space, or the three are to move to Y-S in Nebraska. Eliade's warning is validated at this point in the plot (18). Shira momentarily is tempted by Y-S; however, she comes to the realization that by accepting Y-S she would betray Tikva and its citizens, even causing their deaths. Once she rejoins Tikva's community, Shira learns that she must place the needs of others above her own. At the meeting, unfortunately, the allure of Y-S is still strong, so she does not immediately refuse its offer. As a result of Shira's hesitation to reject Y-S (her desire to reenter what she believes is paradise, blinds her to the truth behind the meeting with Y-S) many are killed, including Riva. It should be noted that Riva fakes her death in order to hide from the corporations' assassins. Before they attack, the representatives of Y-S reveal that the only choice that they truly intended to offer Shira was whether or not she was going to return with Y-S willingly, or be taken by force. Up until this meeting, Shira still believes in Y-S as the paradise, a part of her is convinced that the meeting is to be about her custody case rather than Y-S's relation with Tikva. Once the meeting ends in violence, with Shira, Yod, and Nili fleeing from the scene and reaching Tikva with the news that Riva has been killed, then Shira understands her mistake, that she has been misled by the false promise of paradise. While in the lab repairing Yod, Shira realizes that "she had engaged in fatal wishing. Fantasizing about recovering Ari, she had gone eagerly to the meeting, ignoring the danger" (Piercy 223). In the beginning Shira accepts the beliefs of the people in the Y-S dome instead of following the belief system in place from her original community (her grandmother and that of Tikva). Consequently, she loses custody of her child and her decisions drastically affect her family as a whole.

While still a part of Y-S, Shira becomes unhappy in her marriage to Josh, so she proceeds with a divorce. Unfortunately for Shira, as Csicsery-Ronay, Jr., has observed, both the corporation and its material need, cybernetics, dominate the human existence in Piercy's cyberpunk text (184–185). During the custody trial, one of the interchangeable Y-S representatives informs Shira that she has only been awarded visitation with her son, and that her husband has full custody. This information is significant not only because it shows the patriarchal ideological behavior present in Y-S, but also because it reveals Y-S's true nature, that the corporation values wealth over people. Carlen Lavigne observes that while cyperpunk was a ground-breaking genre when it emerged in the 1980s, it "was also criticized for being misogynist and classist; its virtual realities and digital escapism represented a white, middle-class, heterosexual and very male perspective" (preface). As the verdict in Shira's custody case is announced, she immediately notices that Y-S has altered her son's surname; instead of stating hers, Y-S has given Ari's surname as Rogovin, which is Josh's. Due to the corporate ideology of Y-S, when women enter into marriage contracts, they do not change their surnames to their husbands.' By giving Ari her surname, Shira reveals that she still follows the ways of her former community, and by altering it Y-S communicates its desires for its citizens and itself, while simultaneously rejecting Shira. When the news is related to Shira, Josh immediately gloats after which Shira's lawyer informs her that this verdict has occurred because "'your ex-husband has a higher tech rating than you do'" (Piercy 4). Once Shira loses custody, she panics. Piercy's protagonist has been struggling with her identity; however, she was secure in the knowledge of her role as mother. Once her son is taken from her, she is uncertain of her future.

In her discussion of what constitutes feminist cyberpunk and the issues that appear in this literature during the 1990s, Lavigne observes that various writers including Piercy and Scott focus on "'feminine' issues such as gender, motherhood, ecology, religion and community" (introduction). Significantly, the issues that Shira faces in her post-modern 2059 society are quite similar to those in the 1990s—many women still faced workforce discrimination, they struggled with leaving their children and returning to employment, while simultaneously men were more often triumphant in custody cases (introduction). Notably, while highlighting authentic concerns for women in *He, She, It*, Piercy also features the displacement some women felt which came with their changing identities (introduction). Not only does Shira lose custody because she resides in a patriarchal society, but also because of Y-S's economic drive to sustain and protect itself. In reference to the cyberpunk novel, Lavigne states that cyberpunk "produced an exploration of capitalism, technology and the human condition" (introduction), and Csicsery-Ronay, Jr. reveals that the "dominant telechtronic cultural powers ... are insatiable in their appetite for new commodities and commodity fashions" (183). The decision in the custody trial is made on the basis of Shira's position in the corporation, Josh's transfer to Pacifica, and Riva's threat to Y-S.

Once Shira hears the verdict she starts to unravel and is no longer as conscious of minding Y-S's societal protocol. For example, Shira runs frantically out of the courtroom to pick-up Ari from daycare. Even though Y-S's behavioral guidelines dictate that employees must appropriately greet peers of a superior rank and must not randomly roam on moving sidewalks, Shira pays no attention to Y-S decorum as her world comes apart around her. The verdict causes Shira to be less conscious and less caring about whether or not her behavior complies with Y-S directives; however, this response is only temporary. She reverts to her former self-conscious self almost immediately as she thinks about the trouble her rebellion has caused her in the past. Subsequently, Shira attempts to successfully reinsert herself into Y-S society—she has a relationship with another man—but then she discovers that Josh has taken Ari to Pacifica. It is then that Shira learns part of the truth about the custody decision, that Y-S desperately wants humans to go into space. Shira alludes to the fact that because there might be radiation on Pacifica, and because no Y-S citizen may be moved to space without his or her permission, Y-S has ruled in favor of Josh because Josh has chosen to go. The cyberpunk corporation fulfills its own needs and gives little thought to human desires unless they correspond with that of the corporation. Lavigne discusses the characters in the 1980s cyberpunk novel, thereby revealing how the novel reflected North America's economy and workforce (ch. 1). In particular, Lavigne observes that the characters are "devalued as interchangeable and easily replaceable assets within corporate society ..." (ch. 1). On multiple occasions, Shira denotes her worth to the corporation, stating that "she had been sacrificed for the needs of the multi" (Piercy 16). Y-S is an economically-driven conglomerate and, in order to ensure that its needs are met, custody is decided in favor of Josh. Y-S utilizes its staff, Shira's supervisor and the caregivers at Ari's daycare, to isolate Shira and make her feel unwanted. Significantly, it is the loss of her son that drives Shira to return to Tikva where she discovers the other reason for her loss of Ari.

Once her house computer tells Shira that Josh has left for Pacifica, she chooses to accept Avram's offer for work for him in Tikva. Avram, Gadi's father, works with cybernetics, and when she arrives home she discovers that he has, once again, created a cyborg, a golem named Yod. While there, Shira delves into her past and discovers pertinent information about her mother, namely that she steals information from the multis. Interestingly, Riva was also owned by one of the multis, Alhadarek, until she became an information pirate. The purpose of the information pirate is twofold: to take power away from the multis through the removal of information, thereby making the multis vulnerable, and to free information from the control of the multis and give it to the public. It is a mark of the post-cyberpunk writer, the new wave of female authors in this field, that Piercy does not have her console cowboy the hero of her text. According to Sterling, the image of the "mirrored sunglasses" became the representative icon of the 1980s cyberpunk "movement" (344). Sterling continues, "They are the symbol of the sunstaring visionary, the biker, the rocker, the policeman, and similar outlaws" (344). Once again, the physical form is highlighted as a key element of the cyberpunk text. The character of Riva, however, fits into this mold while Shira does not. Both characters have escaped the clutches of the all-encompassing corporation, but only one emerges as the hero of the community, the space that still offers individuality for its inhabitants. Riva takes on the stereotypical cyberpunk protagonist image as the lone wolf, the figure who hides behind a surgically-constructed exterior and works to preserve his or her individuality. When Riva arrives at Tikva, she has been surgically altered to appear as the elderly sister of Malkah; this disguise is meant to conceal her from the assassins sent by the multis to kill her for her repeated thefts of information. It is significant that when the meeting between Shira and Y-S concludes in excessive violence, the only remnants of Riva to be found are a few mechanized parts and a foot. The former cyberpunk protagonist has all but been obliterated and replaced with the new model, Shira. Lavigne observes that Piercy in both *He, She, It* and *Woman on the Edge of Time* highlights the changing role of woman during the second wave of feminism (ch. 8). In her text, Lavigne calls attention to the mother figure in *He, She, It* showing the differing roles that Malkah, Riva, Shira, and Nili take: "Shira in *He, She and It* balances her work as a programmer with her role as a single mother" (ch. 8). No longer is the cyberpunk protagonist alone in the quest for liberation. As Piercy shows in *He, She and It*, the new cyberpunk hero, Shira, has a family and a community to protect, therefore driving her to ensure their safety. The old protagonist, Riva, has to be destroyed, to be almost obliterated, in order to make way for one that would not separate herself from her community, would not disappear to search for the "thrill" (Csicsery-Ronay, Jr., 191). At the conclusion of Piercy's text, Shira remains in Tikva becoming a Base Overseer, a position vacated by Malkah. Instead of riding off into the proverbial sunset like the standard console cowboy after Y-S is no longer a threat, Shira stays in Tikva to preserve the freedom that the freetown offers.

In Scott's *Trouble and Her Friends*, once again a new wave of cyberpunk author alters the construction of the standard protagonist. Cerise and Trouble are lesbian netwalkers, those who traverse the nets; consequently, they live in two different worlds, each with its hierarchy and social guidelines. As in Piercy's novel, the primary industry in Scott's text is the creation and ownership of technology. While some characters work with information legally, others like Cerise and Trouble are shadowwalkers—they deal in information illegally obtained from corporations on the nets. They also choose to be implanted with the "full-sense" brainworm rather than walk the net using the dolly-slot, "which gave a text-speech-and-symbol interface" only (Scott 14). The brainworm permits netwalkers to have a bodily experience, an inclusive experience, rather than not being emotionally connected to the nets. Conflicts arise when the brainworm and the shadowwalker position are outlawed; since Scott's protagonists have chosen to become shadowwalkers and to be implanted, they face societal displacement. Consequently, these two protagonists, much like Piercy's Shira, must conceal their true identities, thereby separating their true selves from the self that they display in the city. Through the implant, the protagonists show that they control the technology rather than allowing the technology to control them (Leary 256): they have elected to appear as individuals instead of accepting the dolly-slot used by the masses. In his essay, "The Individual as Reality Pilot," Timothy Leary examines what he terms the "cyberpunk," noting specific traits and instances in which this person exists in pop culture. Significant to this study is Leary's analysis of Matthew Broderick's character in *WarGames*, one which Leary calls "an Electron Jock. A Quantum Wizard"; in other words, this character, while appearing in a different medium than the novel, is a standard cyberpunk protagonist (256). After Leary captures a moment of rebellion for Broderick's protagonist he notes, "Okay, we get it. Matthew is ungovernable. He's a cyberkid" (256). As Leary notes, this trait signifies the epitome of the cyperpunk protagonist—hero, if you will, for standing up to the controlling corporations (256). Whether it be in the first or second wave of cyberpunkists, this fact remains unchanged: a corporate entity seeks to dominate the individual, and the individual rebels preferring instead his or her identity over conformity. When Scott's novel begins, one of the protagonists, Cerise, is now alone; she has arrived home to discover that Trouble has moved out. According to Csicsery-Ronay, Jr., when he relates a list of traits commonly found in the early cyberpunk novels, the main character "hooks up with rebellious and tough-talking (youth/artificial intelligence/rock cults) who offer the alternative, not of (community/socialism/traditional values/transcendental vision), but of supreme, life-affirming *hipness* ..." (184). In Scott's text, Cerise has a partner in net-walking; however, she is much more than someone with whom Cerise may rebel against the corporate entity (Csicsery-Ronay, Jr. ,184). Csicsery-Ronay, Jr., reveals that one of the tasks that the cyberpunk duo complete is a defiance of the corporation's control (184). Cerise and Trouble are not only business partners, but also romantic partners. When Cerise is first introduced, she is in her apartment discovering that half of the netwalking equipment, Trouble's half, has been removed, signifying that Trouble has dissolved both their personal and business relationships. Due to a federal bill called the Evans-Tindale, which is put into effect regarding the nets, Cerise and Trouble's relationship has been placed in jeopardy as has their community.

Instead of being faced with the standard corporate entity—a business per se—Cerise and Trouble's lifestyle is being threatened (successfully for the time being) by the U.S. federal government and the bill. While Cerise is in her apartment attempting to discover whether Trouble left her a note, a reporter defines the bill, "Evans-Tindale, like the Nunberg Act before it, redefines so-called cyberspace as a particular legal jurisdiction, and establishes a code of law governing these electronic transactions" (Scott 15). Cerise continues to observe that "Evans-Tindale also meant that there was no longer any possibility of legalizing the brainworm" (16). When Trouble is receiving the surgery to upgrade her brainworm, the narrator captures her thoughts, in particular how dangerous having a brainworm is for a person. According to Scott's intrusive narrator, the installation process and traversing the net both have the ability to render a person catatonic or can even cause death. The narrator then observes the hierarchy of the net, noting, "Maybe that was why it was almost always the underclasses, the women, the people of color, the gay people, the ones who were already stigmatized as being vulnerable, available, trapped by the body, who took the risk of the wire" (128–129). When the novel opens, it becomes clear to the reader that through the passing of this bill, Cerise has lost more than her relationship with Trouble, she has also lost her position in the social hierarchy and her community.

As Cerise searches for a note from Trouble she uses her brainworm to enter the nets. While she is searching for information about Trouble's whereabouts, she enters Miss Kitty's saloon, a space that the duo have frequented in the past. Immediately upon entrance, Cerise notices the difference in the atmosphere in the saloon, specifically that the IC(E), the "Intrusion Countermeasures (Electronic)," has become more dangerous and that her progress is being followed (18). It is almost too late when Cerise learns that her entrance to the saloon is unwanted; after she asks Miss Kitty's icon about Trouble the IC(E) attacks and she faces near-death. After the passing of Evans-Tindale, the nets have changed and they are no longer the utopian space of Cerise's past. For the netwalkers, particularly those with the brainworm, the nets, as Csicsery-Ronay, Jr., has observed, provide a "thrill" for those who are permitted to enter (191). It is telling that Miss Kitty's space is configured as a saloon from the construct of the U.S. West since "Miss Kitty deals in ... data, stolen, borrowed, invented, even imagined, and in the commerce of messages passed unread" (Scott 18). It is logical that this space, the nets and the U.S. net in particular, contain images of the U.S. West; later, Cerise and Trouble enter the nets where their icon images have now been changed to take on the form of the cowboy. It is a space that offers, as the U.S. West did, danger for thrill-seekers, an unlimited amount of material goods, and power to those who wish to reign supreme.

According to Levitas, "earthly paradise myths," stories about utopic places, contain many common traits, including "abundant food and water, clement weather, absence of conflict, fountains of youth and difficulty of access" (186). While the nets do not offer an "absence of conflict" (186) and, in fact, Cerise and Trouble thrive on encounters with corporations from which they steal information, the nets do offer a space in which to earn an income and, more importantly, they exist as a utopia for the marginalized. Lavigne states, "While still often concentrating on themes of alienation, works such as *Arachne* and *Trouble and Her Friends* also explore small, fringe communities and relationships that exist along societal margins. While the protagonists may be alienated from society, they are not alienated from each other" (ch. 3). Cerise portrays the nets before Evans-Tindale as idyllic, as a place of unlimited freedom for netwalkers. Levitas reveals that "the essence of utopia seems to be desire—the desire for a different, better way of being" (209). It is on the nets that Cerise and other netwalkers have formed a community, one that can fulfill their needs and desires, but the bill places this community in jeopardy. As a result, this community fragments until a new community, one that operates under the confinement of the nets laws, can be formed.

As Cerise enters the bar, Marco Polo, and attempts to find her friends, she examines others in the bar and makes the following significant statement: "netwalkers didn't as a rule congregate in the real world. It took something like this to bring them together" (Scott 28). Throughout the text Cerise simultaneously describes her friends in affectionate terms while observing their differences from others in their society. Cerise labels them the "oddball group" citing the brainworm and their sexual orientation as the only reasons why she believes they are friends outside of the nets (21). Once Evans-Tindale passes, Cerise relates her feelings of displacement, her sense of being alone once more. After a confrontation between her group and those that dislike brainworm users, Cerise observes that "whatever else Evans-Tindale had done, it had broken the old community of the net, divided the old-style crackers, the ones who relied on the dollie-boxes, from the ones who used the brainworm—and was that the intention?" (36). Once Evans-Tindale becomes reality, the utopic nets, the individual, and the community in the nets no longer exist. The disappearance of Trouble signifies the start of the disintegration of Cerise's community of friends. The group of friends in the bar fragments because they are no longer crackers—no workspace commonality—and because they fear going to prison. It should be noted that the first result of the Evans-Tindale is the conviction of a cracker, David Terrel, for armed robbery, a conviction which carried with it time in prison. Once their communities are dissolved (the nets' community first and then the group of friends), both Cerise and Trouble relinquish the individuality that the netwalker identity provides and conform to the standards set by their new society. Fortunately, this condition, which is established to ensure survival, is only temporary.

While walking to the bar, Cerise remembers her life before becoming a netwalker, thereby revealing the displacement within society that those without access to the nets face. As she passes the dollie-girls, young females so desperate for technology that they have "indentured themselves" to a local secretarial school, she notes that not only are they criminals willing to attack passers-by, but also that she used to be a dollie-girl (24). As she nears the group, she is attacked and they attempt to rip her brainworm from her body. Cerise defends herself, revealing as she does the lengths she will go to defend her position as a netwalker. To many in Cerise's society, power is associated with becoming a netwalker, as is a societal position either as a cracker, or as an employee for a corporation. Once Evans-Tindale is passed, the form of the U.S. net is altered and Cerise conforms to meet the new standards as does Trouble. According to Lavigne, "Three years later, Cerise is working for a megacorporation and Trouble is a systems operator at a small artists' co-op; both have been assimilated into society, and 'legitimate' jobs'" (ch. 4). Due to the fear of the consequences connected to breaking the laws associated with the Evans-Tindale bill, both characters attempt to leave their past lives behind, but their true selves and also a netwalker using Trouble's name, refuse to allow them to do so. The community has now been fragmented, its inhabitants separated from each other by force.

When Scott returns to Cerise and Trouble three years have passed and the protagonists have obtained legal employment positions. Even though the characters have attempted to conform to accepted societal standards, they refuse to entirely obey the guidelines. For example, both characters continue to work on the nets; however, their actions are now primarily legal (they both still use the brainworm although in secret). Trouble has moved into an artists' co-op in an attempt to locate a new, accepting community. While there she has taken a position as a syscop, an employment position through which she regulates the use of the nets by the inhabitants of the co-op. This new grouping is not an authentic community for Trouble as she is concealing her past from them. When agents from Treasury, those that patrol the nets, arrive at the co-op Trouble reveals that she fears that her past will be exposed to them as well as the members of the co-op. Like Trouble, if one does not have true acceptance from a societal group, then this entity cannot be considered a community.

Cerise is now an employee working IC(E) security for the corporation, Multiplane. Cerise not-so subtly rebels against the conventions of her position; for example, she has chosen garish make-up that "was subtly wrong for her job, like the rest of her look …" (Scott 68). Ceylan

Ertung discusses the appearance of both the first and second-wave of cyberpunk in her essay, focusing specifically on those deemed feminist and that deal with the body. Ertung observes that with feminist cyberpunk female writers moved away from the masculine ideologies found in first-wave texts, thereby highlighting instead equality between the sexes (77–82). In her analysis of the masculine, Ertung examines William Gibson's character Molly Millions, who is "a technologically enhanced female assassin. With her surgically implanted mirror shades in her eyesockets and 'double-edged, four-centimeter blades' hidden beneath her 'burgundy nails' Molly, according to Laurie Leblanc reverses the stereotypical gender definitions" (82). Gibson's character, while remaining female, assumes traits considered masculine; she also lays claim to those that are usually seen as derogatory to women making them just a body rather than a person (Ertung 82). Scott, however, with Cerise's character uses the body as a tool to signal rebellion: "the skirt a little too short, the jacket too mannish, with none of the affectations or compromises of corporate femininity. The heels of her shoes were painted the same stark fuchsia as her nails" (68). While she will willingly work for the corporation, Cerise refuses to accept this entity as her new community. While Ertung cites Leblanc as seeing that "Molly is a 'cyborg woman in a masculine role'" (82), Cerise refuses to be confined to either gender type, preferring instead to appear as the individual; however, her individuality cannot be completed while she still works for the corporation. It is only when Cerise and Trouble create a new community that they can individuality be considered authentic.

Once Trouble reappears on the nets—this is an imposter who has taken control of the name and reputation—Cerise and Trouble attempt to form a new community. Clearly their old communities cannot be reformed because Evans-Tindale restricts the behavior of the friends and of the former nets community. As a result, the duo must attempt to create new societal groupings, ones that are able to function in a world that is regulated by the bill and the Amsterdam Network Conventions. In order to save Trouble from prison, Cerise and Trouble make contact with their former group of companions—those from the bar and from the nets. Cerise and Trouble are once again involved in illegal activity and, by doing so, they have once again become members of the nonconformist population. The issue is that this behavior cannot continue to occur under Evans-Tindale; in order to form a community that can exist successfully on the nets and in person, virtual Seahaven must be reformed under the jurisdiction of the Conventions. Once this act occurs, both Cerise and Trouble, who act as virtual Seahaven's governing body, not only can continue to work on the nets, legally of course, but they also can proceed with their goal of abolishing the bill and having the U.S. sign the Conventions. When Mabry, a Eurocop, offers the position of mayor of virtual Seahaven to Trouble, he tells her, "'You could do it. Times are changing; the wire doesn't matter so much anymore—too many people have them now'" (Scott 370). In this statement Mabry reveals that no longer are Cerise, Trouble, and the others marginalized, rather they have been accepted because it is they who can enact change for the future. In both Piercy and Scott's texts, the protagonists must alter the make-up of their respective societies in order to ensure survival of themselves and their way of life.

Through an examination of Shira, Cerise, and Trouble's final communities, it becomes clear that the primary function of these communities is to be inclusive. While providing a network of support for those within them, these communities ensure that the individuality of the protagonists and other inhabitants is prized rather than existing as a cumbersome burden needing to be obliterated. In *He, She, It*, Piercy creates contrasting societies, specifically those of Tikva and Y-S. As a second-wave cyberpunk writer, Piercy creates a text in which not only does the underdog dominate the larger oppressive entity, but also the female protagonist appears as the victor while coming to the realization that the key to her survival is both her individuality and her inclusion in an accepting community. In Scott's novel, again a second-wave cyberpunk writer alters the form of the text, and has two female protagonists create two communities in which one is free to exist as an individual. Scott cites adaptation as the key to survival in her text, as her protagonists must create new communities in response to an oppressive societal alteration, the Evans-Tindale bill. Interestingly, both writers have employed the use of adaptation, thereby modifying the standard cyberpunk text in order to give voices to the marginalized.

Works Cited

Csicsery-Ronay, Jr., Istvan. "Cyberpunk and Neuromanticism." *Mississippi Review* 47/48 (1988): 266–278. Rpt. in *Storming the Reality Studio: A Casebook of Cyberpunk and Postmodern Science Fiction*. Ed. Larry McCaffery. Durham: Duke University Press, 2007. 182–193. Print.

Eliade, Mircea. *Images and Symbols: Studies in Religious Symbolism*. 1952. Trans. Philip Mairet. Princeton: Princeton University Press, 1991. Print.

Ertung, Ceylan. "Bodies That [Don't] Matter: Feminist Cyberpunk and Transgressions of Bodily Boundaries." *Edebiyat Fakültesi Dergisi/Journal of Faculty of Letters* 28.2 (2011): 77–93. *MLA International Bibliography*. Web. 5 July 2013.
Lavigne, Carlen. *Cyberpunk Women, Feminism and Science Fiction: A Critical Study*. Jefferson, NC: McFarland, 2013. Kindle.
Leary, Timothy. "The Individual as Reality Pilot." *Mississippi Review* 47/48 (1988): 252–265. Rpt. in *Storming the Reality Studio: A Casebook of Cyberpunk and Postmodern Science Fiction*. Ed. Larry McCaffery. Durham: Duke University Press, 2007. 245–258. Print.
Levitas, Ruth. *The Concept of Utopia*. Oxford: Peter Lang, 2010. Print.
Piercy, Marge. *He, She, It*. 1991. New York: Ballantine, 1993. Print.
Scott, Melissa. *Trouble and Her Friends*. New York: Tor, 1994. Print.
Sterling, Bruce. "Preface from *Mirrorshades*." *Mirrorshades: The Cyberpunk Anthology*. Rpt. in *Storming the Reality Studio: A Casebook of Cyberpunk and Postmodern Science Fiction*. Ed. Larry McCaffery. Durham: Duke University Press, 2007. 343–348. Print.

Anathem's Flows of Power
State Space and Nomadology on a Cloistered Planet

JONATHAN P. LEWIS

After completing the historical science fiction epic *The Baroque Cycle* (2003–2004), Neal Stephenson engaged some of the tropes of more traditional speculative science fiction in his follow-up, *Anathem* (2008). Set on an Earth-like planet called Arbe, *Anathem* projects a world with sixty centuries of recorded history including three apocalypses, called "Sacks" in the novel, that each nearly wiped out society. The driving plot device is the discovery of a massive alien spacecraft in orbit above Arbe's poles. Stephenson further picks up plot points from his novels *Snow Crash* (1992) and *The Diamond Age* (1995) to explore the chaos and reformation of societies after complete social, economic, and political breakdowns, and he follows Walter A. Miller's *A Canticle for Leibowitz* (1960) by positing a cloistered culture that has survived an apocalypse.[1] Finally, the novel engages the contentious dynamic between a society's political and intellectual powers in a thorough criticism of recent real world attacks on rationalism and intellectualism by the American far right that is more indebted to Plato than to Asimov.

Anathem explores many subjects, including the multi-world theory of quantum mechanics, but the strength of the novel is its examination of the natures of intelligence and learning and how societies rebuild in the wake of social, economic, political, and environmental apocalypses. Stephenson engages familiar science fiction tropes such as depictions of dystopic, post-apocalyptic societies reforming, and discoveries that the aliens orbiting the planet are actually earthlings, and *Anathem* explores some of the more recent developments in AI, the psychology of human intelligences, and quantum computing inside and outside the physical spaces of the Concents, cloistered spaces that are similar to our universities where the brightest, and in many cases the strangest, most inquisitive minds are found. The Concents annually take and isolate young Arbans who exhibit gifts for math, science, language, and other talents. Each new Avout is given a new name and three, and only three, possessions, and they are reborn as future philosopher-kings.

Overall, Stephenson's depictions of power are often far more fluidic than the dystopic visions of such predecessors as George Orwell or Aldus Huxley, but like Orwell and Huxley, Stephenson often engages contemporary politics in his novels, and *Anathem* is no exception. In particular, the novel interrogates the myriad ways that politicians seek to control academics through the power relations between the "Sæcular Powers," the novel's collective term for the ruling political powers on Arbe, who control the planet's political landscapes outside the academic worlds of the Concents. Inside the Concent walls, Stephenson's monk-like "Avout" made up of male "fraas" and female "suurs" believe themselves to be free from the intervention of changing political winds outside their gates, unlike contemporary America academics who often depend on industry and governmental grants as their life-blood. The novel thus enters a Platonic debate about what happens when metaphysicians are yanked out of the safety of their caves and forced to work on such practical questions as "What shall we do about the gigantic spaceship that is orbiting our planet and dropping huge metallic rods into our volcanoes and wiping out our cities?"

At the same time, because this text is a serious work of literary fiction, Stephenson asks his readers to consider the real world results of recent governmental interventions into the workings of the American university system through *Anathem*'s setting within and without Arban Concents. In 2011, for example, Tom Coburn, a medical doctor and Republican senator from Oklahoma, released a report entitled "The National Science Foundation: Under the Microscope." In his introduction, Coburn argued that

> very few of the proposals submitted for NSF financial support represented transformative scientific research according to most grant reviewers surveyed. Taxpayers may also question the value of many of the projects NSF actually chose to fund, such as: How to ride a bike; When did dogs became

man's best friend; If political views are genetically pre-determined; How to improve the quality of wine; Do boys like to play with trucks and girls like to play with dolls; How rumors get started; If parents choose trendy baby names; How much housework does a husband create for a wife; and When is the best time to buy a ticket to a sold out sporting event [4].

These examples might appear frivolous to some—but even a small wine producing state like North Carolina generates $1.28 billion annually and supports 7,600 jobs (NC Wine Fast Facts). I would hardly call research into quality control for such an industry useless, nor would I imagine that Coburn would label "frivolous" the research project grants from the National Science Foundation given to, say, the University of Tulsa's Graduate School for such projects as Drilling Research and Petroleum Reservoir Exploitation. But the point is two-fold: (1) the Senator should know how often pure research into seemingly scientific dead ends like the networking of remote computer terminals (DARPA was funded by the NSF in the 1970s) impacts society in undreamed of manners; and (2) as a medical doctor, Coburn should know that NSF research into genetics and the interaction of humans and animal species has led to many unforeseen insights into virology and epidemiology. I do not believe that Senator Coburn opposes all federal funding—far from it as he has recently asked for grants to rebuild Moore after the recent terrible tornadoes. But what is important here for *Anathem* is that since the conjoining of the universities to the military industrial complex to defeat National Socialism and the Empire of Japan in the 1940s, American academics, like all of Stephenson's protagonists, have had to fight against domination by the government in order to secure their freedom. This situation creates a Deleuzian rhizome of state space and nomad space that fluctuates between domination by the State and lines of flight that take academics in unexpected directions.

Gilles Deleuze and Félix Guattari's "schizoanalysis" grounds my discussion of *Anathem* here because of this tension between the political and education powers in the novel as seen in the semi-permeable walls of the Concents and the flows of power from the Concents and the Sæcular world surrounding them. In *A Thousand Plateaus*, Deleuze and Guattari use the terms "rhizome" and "rhizomatic" to describe the condition of modern Western civilization, though one of their chief models for the rhizome comes from the Mongol Empire's "war machine" from the thirteenth century.[2] The fluidic, adaptive, and rapacious Mongol empire created what Deleuze and Guattari call "nomad" or "smooth space," which may be unknown, unmapped, or unfamiliar, or in the case of the Empire, held by a moving, flexible army. The Mongol smooth space of seemingly countless warriors on horseback pouring out of the steppes was opposed by the structured and mapped State, or "striated," spaces of Western Europe with their far-less flexible foot soldiers who were largely no match for the speed of the Mongols. And so it is in *Anathem* where the striated State space outside the academic Concents has used the Concents' walls to lock the unpredictable dangerous Avout inside smooth space. But because of the presence of the spaceship, smooth space erupts out of the Concents and into State space.

As I have argued elsewhere, most of the conflicts in Stephenson's works can be profitably viewed through the larger lens of the Ares/Athena rhizome fully articulated in *Cryptonomicon* and *The Baroque Cycle*.[3] In this view, the tension between the kinds of human behaviors the Greeks separately identified as the mindless rage and bloodlust of Ares are opposed by the intellect and guile of Athena—in *Snow Crash* the force of hackers like Hiro Protagonist within the smooth space of the virtual world of the Metaverse is opposed by the power of televangelist cum military leader L. Bob Rife, and in *The Diamond Age*, the structured Neo-Victorian State must find innovation within through the destabilizing efforts of nanotechnology engineers like John Hackworth and his work with the anarchistic Drummers, a collective intelligence seemingly outside the controls and laws of any State. In *Cryptonomicon* and *The Baroque Cycle*, there are a series of rhizomes that form through and because of the actions of the various generations of the Waterhouse and Shaftoe families around issues of war, freedom, slavery, gold and the global economy, and networks of information. In *Anathem*, the Avout are clearly Athenian and the State powers, who would use the Avout as delivery devices for neutron bombs to destroy the spaceship and its aliens, are just as clearly Aresian.

In postulating such rhizomes, Stephenson's novels nearly always depict struggles that drive scientific innovation, war, and commerce in his long views of history—he reaches back to the dawn of the Enlightenment with Isaac Newton's childhood in *The Baroque Cycle* and looks forward hundreds of years after the death of Kurt Gödel in *Anathem*. In this text, we see this dynamic as the State drafts the Avout to striate space that the Avout believed was smooth and sacred. So the question that emerges is what happens when the State Powers bring the Avout

out of the darkness of their Platonic seclusion and force them to act in the light of the dystopic Sæcular world?

Against the Sæcular powers, the Avout form the other force on the planet, and the Powers that Be are terrified of them. The Avout's power of pure thinking—most of the main characters in Anathem were deposited by families too bewildered by their offspring to know what else to do with them—is beyond the Sæculars' grasp and control. To employ Deleuze and Guattari's useful metaphor from *A Thousand Plateaus*, the two forces create a rhizome, and lines of rupture form both in and outside the Concent walls. The Sæcular world functions as Deleuzian State, or striated space, and the mathic world of the Concents functions as smooth space: "Where there is no State and no surplus labor, there is no Work-model either. Instead, there is the continuous variation of free action, passing from speech to action, from speech to enterprise, all in a strange chromaticism with intense but rare peak moments or moments of effort that the outside observer can only 'translate' in terms of work" (491). Inside the Concents, there is a great deal of continuous action and hard work: the Avout keep bees; make paper, wine, and beer; raise and educate the children given to them; take astronomical observations; hone martial arts; record their history, and complete any variety of mental and physical activities. There is no surplus labor—every action is taken to learn a lesson, work a proof or experiment, or otherwise keep the Concent functioning without State support in the form of grants as in contemporary American universities. However, while the Avout would like to believe otherwise, they are not free from interference from the State.

As Louis Althusser argues in "Ideology and Ideological State Apparatuses (Notes towards an Investigation)": "The ultimate condition of production is therefore the reproduction of the condition of production. This may be 'simple' (producing exactly the previous conditions of production) or 'on an extended scale' (expanding them)" (127). And so it is on Arbe; the State controls the Avout in several ways by granting the Avout existence so long as the Avout don't cause too much trouble and go on existing as they have for nearly a millennia since the last Sack. First, the State imposed diet renders the male Avout sterile, and second, the fraas and their female counterparts, the suurs, can own no property and have no role in secular society *except* when the State needs them. The key here is that the Concents are jails, albeit very productive, safe, and voluntary jails—but they are carceral nonetheless because once

Avout enter the Concent system, they are loathe to leave, and those who are Anathemized are shamed and shunned. The Avout go to the Concents because these spaces *appear* to allow them to live and work free from governmental control—but they submit to the rules of the Concents and can be thrown back into the Sæcular world if they refuse to follow the basic guidelines. But this freedom is illusory, as the Sæcular powers can pull any and all Avout they want and/or need from the Concents. Stephenson here again follows Althusser:

> The reproduction of labour power requires not only a reproduction of its skills, but also, at the same time, a reproduction of its submission to the rules of the established order, i.e., a reproduction of submission to the ruling ideology for the workers [here, the Avout], and a reproduction of the ability to manipulate the ruling ideology correctly for the agents of exploitation and repression, so that they, too, will provide for the domination of the ruling class "in words" [132–33].

Because they submit to the ruling ideology, the Avout raise their own food and are left largely to their own devices. They are devoted to purity in thought and reason, and use their physical and mental isolation to prevent contemporary trends in political favor to influence their work. In this way, Stephenson sets up the Concents as perhaps ideal forms of contemporary Terran universities where courting political favor—especially in the form of grants—may be part and parcel of being in the academy. The novel's most close-minded and dangerous characters make up part of the novel's critiques of today's notorious political attacks on climatology, biology, and history from the far right.[4]

While the Avout work hard to be largely autonomous inside their consecrated spaces, any true agency and autonomy are illusory. The maths must communicate with the Sæcular Powers who retain the ability to shape policy within the Concents, and critically, remove needed Avout from Concents to accomplish specific goals. Thus the Avout only *appear* to be free—they are protected from without by the Sæcular Powers' security forces (and the Concents' thick walls and strong gates), and the Avout have had their research tools and results shaped and limited by the Sæcular Powers in three historical Sacks. The Avout are not permitted to own anything but three possessions: a "New Matter" cloth "bolt," a belt-like "cord," and a "sphere" that can be expanded, contracted, and illuminated. The reason for this austerity is not a vow of poverty, but rather limiting laws set by the Second Convox of Concents following the First Sack of the Mathic world, two centuries after the "Terrible

Events"—events on Arbe likened to such Earth events as World War Two, the Holocaust, and the nuclear attacks on Japan. 190 years after the Terrible Events, the Avout discovered how to manipulate nucleosynthesis to create New Matter—essentially designing matter from the nucleus up. Like his exploration of the nanotechnology rhizome in *The Diamond Age*, Stephenson's New Matter clearly had many unintended and deleterious effects on Arbe, as the First Sack occurs only 21 years after its creation. The sacks each nearly destroy the Concent system, but as Deleuze and Guattari suggest with any rhizomatic structure of power and knowledge, the Concents reorganized after each Sack along new lines of flight, or as Deleuze and Guattari write, "the abstract line, the line of flight or deterritorialization according to which they change in nature and connect with other multiplicities.... A rhizome may be broken, shattered at a given spot, but it will start up again on one of its old lines, or on new lines" (9). The Avout give up, or have taken away depending on one's point of view, the creation of new matter after the First Sack, the use of "syndactic devices"/digital computers after the Second, and "Dowments"/financial support systems after the Third. Their libraries survived, however, and the most isolated maths remained unviolated, sealed from within and without, with skeleton crews of Avout locked behind the gates, and, after a time, the Concents reopened for Apert, a ten day carnivalesque period held every year, decade, century, and millennium for each of the four divisions or "Maths" within the world of Avout. In each Sack, only the "inviolate" Thousand Year sections of only three Concents were not destroyed—it turns out that these three Thousander Maths store the nuclear waste created before the First Sack.

In this cycle of Sacks, Stephenson suggests the critiques by the political right in America to undermine research into global warming, evolution, and the like. While such attacks on the left and the academy have been commonplace since at least the 1950s, recently, the right has ratcheted up its rhetoric, calling the contemporary American university nothing more than a left-wing ideological brainwashing machine, and trying to cast doubt on established science. United States Representative Paul Broun of Georgia, a medical doctor with a degree in chemistry from the University of Georgia, who sits on the House Science, Space and Technology Committee, recently said on September 27, 2012, that

> All that stuff I was taught about evolution, embryology, Big Bang theory, all that is lies straight from the pit of hell. It's lies to try to keep me and all the folks who are taught that from understanding that they need a savior.

There's a lot of scientific data that I found out as a scientist that actually show that this is really a young Earth. I believe that the Earth is about 9,000 years old. I believe that it was created in six days as we know them. That's what the Bible says [Pearce n.p.].

Such statements are, of course, complete nonsense. But Broun and his allies among the Fundamentalist Christian Right in America are dangerous; such views are antithetical to science and research into the very real problems presented by anti-biotic resistance and global warming to name just two facts Broun et al. dispute. He many be entitled to his opinion, but Broun's position on the House Committee for Science, Space and Technology puts him in a place where he can do great harm to the universities that depend on government and industry for research grants to solve such problems as drug-resistant tuberculosis, rising sea levels and alternative energy sources. Other dangerous fundamentalist anti-scientists on powerful Committees in the Legislature include Senators James Inhofe from Oklahoma, Marco Rubio of Florida, and Lindsey Graham of South Carolina, and Representative Michelle Bachmann from Minnesota. Inhofe's influence is especially pernicious as he is a Young Earther and Biblical Literalist, and one of largest recipients of lobbyist money from the Oil Industry and the author of the anti-science, anti-intellectual *The Greatest Hoax: How the Global Warming Conspiracy Threatens Your Future* (2012).

Many on the right—perhaps most vociferously David Horowitz in print and Rick Santorum in public statements—call American universities "liberal indoctrination machines"; Santorum decried President Obama's attempts to increase access to college, famously telling ABC's George Stephanopolos that "the indoctrination that occurs in American universities is one of the keys to the left holding and maintaining power in America" (Montopoli n.p.). Horowitz's claims have been both celebrated and condemned, but what matters here regarding Santorum, Broun, and Todd Akin is that the American university is under attack for a lack of objectivity—but the right does not want objectivity, and it certainly does not want to deal with truths like evolution throwing into grave doubt any claims about all life being created in its present form only a few centuries ago. What matters here is that such "leaders" as Broun and Akin have attacked all academic freedom in order to placate their campaign contributors from the hydrocarbon industries and have actively sought to starve research into global warming and green energy. In short, the right seeks control over the universities' research agendas, something that the universities must attempt to thwart. More importantly, such efforts to corral research give novelists like Stephenson ample space to show the rhizome of fear and need between the Sæcular Power and the Concents, and he draws his sharpest critiques of contemporary politics and the academy with the closing of spaces within the Concents.

Anathem shows that the Avout have no real power until afforded it by the State—the main characters in the novel end up blasted into space to destroy the alien ship's capacity to attack Arbe—much like most academics often have little real power at their universities. While the State gives the Avout the agency to destroy the aliens' ability to make war on the planet Arbe, the Sæcular Power also surreptitiously turns the Avout into living bombs by introducing what Stephenson calls "Everything Killers"—likely neutron bombs—into their bodies as alleged health monitors to destroy the alien craft as a last ditch effort to save Arbe. Again, what the State appears to deterritorialize it quickly reterritorializes.

It is Stephenson's suggestion of a more austere university, not constrained by the need for government funding, that truly marks this novel as an important critique of contemporary politics. Not unlike today's graduate students and even faculty alike, the Avout are poor—they own nearly nothing individually except their bolt, chord, and sphere—while the Concents themselves are powerful. Stephenson's philosophers are more like peasants than kings—some, like the main characters in *Anathem*, are rather poor and lead hard lives because their Concent is in a region more northerly and colder than others. The Avout form a collective; rather than lose the collected wisdom of the Concents altogether, the Avout reorganized after each Sack to ensure the Concents' survival—every time, in short, the State striates the Mathic world, the Avout launch a line of flight into smooth space. The Sæcular Power keeps tabs on the kinds of research being published by the Avout, and so the Avout are caught by the push and pull of nomad and State space. On the surface, the Avout's lines of flight appear to open up smooth spaces completely separate from the Sæcular world. Empires, regimes, city-states, et cetera rise and fall outside the Maths' walls, but the Avout are largely unaffected. When needed by the State, however, the Avout are quickly controlled and striated by the Sæcular Powers in moments of crisis like the discovery of an asteroid on a collision course with Arbe, or a massive alien spacecraft settling into orbit above the planet's poles.

In the novel, this push and pull first affects a savant named Paphlagon among the 100 year Avout; he, like his "fid" (or graduate student), Orolo among the Tenners, discovers the spacecraft above Arbe and is evoked, removed from the Concent, because of his expertise in astrophysics and his theory of multiple cosmos. Deleuze and Guattari state that the engineer is "caught between a rock and a hard place, between the war machine that nourishes and inspires [such savants] and the State that imposes upon them an order of reason" (362). Paphlagon's "Voco," or rite of evocation from the Math, sends shock through the Concent and occurs at the same moment as the astronomical laboratories and observatories at all the Concents are locked to the Avout. The State needs him, so they take him; the idea of the Concents' autonomy is shattered.

Further, the key questions facing the Avout in the novel is whether a destructive paradigm shift can be prevented from occurring. In the face of new information, like the discoveries that there are intelligent beings from other worlds orbiting their planet, and that these beings are from not just from different planets, but different cosmoses from Arbe and each other, can Arbe not devolve into the destructive chaos of a Fourth Sack? In the 902 years since the Third Sack, the Avout have existed more or less unchallenged by the Sæcular Power—until *Anathem* opens. Further, this rhizome of power is part of a repressive Ideological State Apparatus: "the State is explicitly conceived as a repressive apparatus. The State is a 'machine' of repression, which enable the ruling classes ... to ensure their domination over the working [or in *Anathem*, the Mathic] class, thus enabling the former to subject the latter to the process of surplus-value extortion" (137).

To put it another way, the Sæcular Power imprisons the brilliant in the Concents. In other words, the Concents are able to exist because they allow the Sæcular Power to control the population of brilliant, hence dangerous, minds. As Brian Massumi argues in his *User's Guide to Capitalism and Schizophrenia*: "Ask any politician what a school is for, and the answer will be: To build good citizens. The essence, therefore, is 'to-make-young-body-docile'" (25). In other words, the Avout patrol and corral their own to educate the young fraas and suurs to keep these inquisitive minds from rising up against the repressive State and to provide space for the best minds to remain hidden from state control as they advance from ten year "commitments" to hundred and then to thousand year maths. Indeed, such "difficult" minds either find their way to the maths because the schools and religious organizations fail them, or they are given to the maths by exasperated parents. Each generation replicates the Avout who will keep the Concents from running into ruin, or as Althusser says:

> Children at school ... learn the "rules" of good behaviour, i.e., the attitude that should be observed by every agent in the division of labour, according to the job he is "destined" for: rules of morality, civic and professional conscience, which normally means rules of respect for the socio-technical division of labour and ultimately the rules established by class domination [132].

While the Avout believe they are free from interference from the non-mathic world, the Concents are only allowed to exist because the Sæcular Powers allow them to; the Avout gave up areas in their pure pursuit of knowledge—a form of repression—and they perform a delicate balancing act between freely exploring the world of ideas and the worlds of new discovery. Those of us who see contemporary conservative attempts to discredit the academy's work as frivolous or a waste of taxpayer dollars surely recognize this conflict.

Caught in this tension is a Ten Year fraa named Erasmus or "Raz," the main character in, and narrator of, *Anathem*. Raz is in his late teens and looking forward to his first Apert—the carnivalesque period of ten days every year, ten years, 100 years, or 1000 years when Avout from different maths can freely travel outside the Concents' walls while the Concents welcome visitors—since being "Collected" into a math called Saunt Edhar as a boy during the previous Apert for the Tenners. When his first Apert comes, Raz excitedly leaves Saunt Edhar to seek out members of his biological family, but he finds the world outside the Concent's walls dirty, ugly, loud, and he quickly hopes for the end of Apert. Some of the new Avout come willingly and ask to join the Concents, while some parents too poor or too frazzled by difficult children surrender them at the gates, and the State dumps other children into the Concents. Stephenson uses a character named Barb, who appears to have an Arban form of Asperger's, as an example of a character whose parents are desperate for the Concents to adopt their son. The Concent of Saunt Edhar, and Raz in particular, takes Barb in and gives him a space where his startling intelligence is allowed to explore dynamics, physics, calculus, and engineering largely unfettered while Raz learns to become a more patient teacher—a graduate student learning first hand how to deal with a difficult freshman. Another character named Yul grew up too isolated from the maths to be Collected, but rejects the orthodoxy proposed by the different "Arks" or churches on Arbe because he figures out that the planet is much, much older than the Arks' holy texts allow.

Raz was collected as a poor but intelligent boy; he narrates the novel, and brings us into the novel as both observer of the action and confused participant. A huge clock controls the gates—every year it opens the Year gate, every ten years the Decade Gate goes up as well, every hundred years the Century Gate joins them, and every thousand years the Millennial Gate goes up too.[5] Raz narrates the novel and brings us into the novel as both observer of the action and confused participant. During Apert's approach, Raz carefully delineates marked boundaries that are both permeable and symbolic, and between the mathic and non-mathic worlds that are made of stone and water features. The imagery is clearly meant to invoke images of ancient Rome and the system of aqueducts that ran water into the heart of the Empire:

> The praxics had [powered the gates separating the maths] with water power.... The water in that pipe, pressurized by gravity, erupted in a pair of fountains from the pond that lay just outside the Day Gate.... Drains were plumbed into its bottom and throttled by monumental ball-valves of polished granite. One of them fed a series ponds, canals, and fountains that beautified the Primate's compound, and farther downstream, formed part of the barrier between the Unanrian and the Decenarian maths. Three other drains connected to systems of pipes, siphons, and aqueducts that ran out toward the Year, Decade, and Century Gates. Those systems were dry except at Apert. Now the clock's descending weights had opened two valves and allowed water to rush from the pond to flood the Year and Decade systems [60–61].

Stephenson amplifies the connection between Rome and the Concent here in the use of decorative and functional fountains as well as the complex water engineering. As the Avout voluntarily follow most bans on genetic and atomic engineering inside the Concents, these divides would be easily traversed but for their symbolic values. But more important for my purposes is the use of water here—as Deleuze and Guattari say, "the sea is smooth space par excellence, and yet was the first to encounter the demands of increasingly strict striation" (479). And the control of water through aqueducts and decorative water features striates the smooth spaces into the separate maths within the larger Concent. The release of this water powering of the gates and fountains open the mathic world to the accumulation of ideas since the last Apert. In the Apert that opens *Anathem*, the Day, Year, and Decade spaces open, and the

Avout to roam about the Sæcular world for ten days. So the rhizome of the water, stone, and gates form a semi-permeable boundary that allow the Avout and the non–Avout to mix together, albeit briefly, which is Deleuze and Guattari's point—rhizomes are permanently in motion and only briefly—if ever—resolved, just as we see with today's attacks on academic freedom and so-called liberal bias in the academy by the right wing of American politics.

As stated, the walls of the Concents are semi-permeable. Each year, decade, century and millennium, the different gates open and the maths adopt new Avout. Further, each Apert brings an influx and outflow of new books and monographs (at least those deemed appropriate for the Avout) to and from the Maths' respective libraries. But the gates that separate the maths within the Concents are constructed as screens so that sounds but not sights move easily between the maths. For example, Raz and the other Tenners can hear but not see the Hundreders and vice versa. And those who wish to make a more serious commitment to the Avout life can also decide to "graduate" from their math and join the next higher math by making their way through a labyrinth—Paphlagon was waiting for Orolo to make his way from the Tenners to the Hundreders before Paphlagon was Evoked.

In *Anathem*, the rhizome of power and force is shown before Apert begins when the Sæcular Power forces the head of the Concents, "First Among Equals" the Warders Regulant, to close the astrological observatories called the starhenges at the top of each Concent. They do this in an attempt to prevent the Avout from discovering that an alien ship is in orbit above Arbe. This show of state power opens a line of flight of force for one particularly ingenious and persistent stargazer. This fraa is Orolo; he was Paphlagon's best student before Paphlagon advanced to the Hundreder Math, and he is Raz's tutor and the most brilliant astronomer in the ten-year math at the Concent of Saunt Edhar. Like the Sæcular Power, Paphlagon and presumably many other fraas and suurs at other Concents, Orolo detects the alien ship, and, prior to the closing of the starhenge, learns that "speelycaptors," the novel's term for digital video cameras, are able to see into space. So, breaking many of the rules of the Concent and risking being "Anathemized," or thrown back to the Sæcular world; during Apert, Orolo steals mead from the Concent and trades it for a speelycaptor and continues to try to observe the spacecraft orbiting over Arbe. When his actions are discovered, Orolo is indeed exiled from the mathic world. But Raz and his friends decipher his actions and discover the spacecraft without aid of telescopes or other tools locked in the starhenge, and continue Orolo's work inside the math.

By calling attention to Paphlagon and then Orolo, the Sæcular Powers arouse curiosity about the work they do. Because Paphlagon and Orolo are the leading astronomers in their respective maths, their fids naturally focus their investigations on the heavens—just the opposite of what the Sæcular Powers want them to do. Thus each use of force against the Avout creates a line of flight away from the Powers That Be, and we see that the desire to control the Avout only increases the Avouts' desire to resist this restriction of the field information. Three Sacks resulted from such previous flows of power and nearly all the Avout died. Here again, we see how the rhizome operates at the Concents—smooth space erupts in the form of the discovery of the extra–Arban spacecraft, and the powers that be immediately attempt to reterritorialize the means of its discovery. But because the Concents are full of the most brilliant and inquisitive minds on the planet, flight lines of curiosity keep erupting within the Concents and those inside the Concents keep churning and pushing against the attempts to limit their fields of knowledge.

While this flow of force and power goes on in the Mathic world, it turns out that a similar struggle is going on above Arbe. One group, called the Fulcrum and made up especially of Terrans or Earthlings aboard the ship, wants to reach out in peace to the Arbans, but the Pillar, a different faction among the aliens and in control of the ship's weapons systems, wants to strip Arbe of the resources the ship needs to continue its voyage without connecting with the Arbans. Again we see the rhizome of power and force as the Pillar seeks only to striate Arbe as they dominate and take what they want, while the Fulcrum seeks to open communications. The Pillar makes its presence clear through two gestures: first, they light up the three Concents, including Saunt Edhar, that are repositories of nuclear waste. Second, after one of the Terrans escapes the alien ship in a small craft and comes to the surface of Arbe, the Pillar drops a large metallic rod into a dormant volcano in an attempt to destroy the craft and those Arbans who attempted to investigate the craft and its pilot, who, it turns out, had been mortally wounded by the Pillar before she had escaped.

Before these events, like Plato's philosopher-kings in training, the Avout begin to be called out of their Cave—following Paphlagon's Voco, the Sæcular Power calls Erasmus and dozens of other Avout to a vast conference to deal with the discovery of the craft. They are, quite literally, dragged from the safety of the Concents where they dwell in the dark protection of the walls and gates doing their work, largely free from interference from the Sæcular Power. Stephenson mirrors Plato's Cave here through the nested worlds of a multiverse that "speak" to each other. The Avout must confront the light of their ignorance. At the same time, the Sæcular Power is defined by their simultaneous terror of the Avout and need to control their existence against such emergencies as planet killing asteroids and aliens, who of course turn out to be Earthlings as well as three other humanoid species from differing cosmoses.

Therefore, *Anathem* opens significant debates about the natural order of the educated classes in our own time and place. The novel asks whether our universities can do enough to ensure intellectual freedom for the average citizen in a country where the current right wing political leadership is more and more hostile to learning. Further, our entire country is more dependent on science and engineering, especially with regard to computers and digital information networks, biological engineering, and the keeping of history. So why are our "Sæcular Powers" trying to striate further and further what little smooth space remains in our Concents of higher learning? And so the novel forces those of us in the academy to consider whether we will be sacked by the radical right or find our lines of flight, and in that respect, *Anathem* is a call to arms.

Notes

1. See also Mordecai Roshwald's *Level 7* (1959) and Paul Cook's *Duende Meadow* (1985) among other texts. Thanks to my colleague Josh Stein for these suggestions and his help shaping the overall essay.

2. See "1227: Treatise on Nomadology:—The War Machine" in *A Thousand Plateaus*, pages 351–423.

3. See for example "House of War, House of Peace" in *Tomorrow Through the Past: Neal Stephenson and the Project of Global Modernization* (Newcastle: Cambridge Scholars, 2006), 114–32).

4. It may be of interest to note that Stephenson grew up at Iowa State University where his father was a professor of electrical engineering and his mother was a researcher in the biology department. Both his grandfathers and his mother's brother were also university professors.

5. Stephenson drew the idea of the Clock from the Long Now Project's proposed 10,000-Year clock.

Works Cited

Althusser, Louis. "Ideology and Ideological State Apparatuses." 1970. Reprinted in *Lenin and Philosophy*. Trans. Ben Brewster. New York: Monthly Review Press, 1971. 127–88. Print.

Coburn, Tom A. "The National Science Foundation: Under the Microscope." United States. Cong. Senate. April 2011. Web. 13 April 2013.
Deleuze, Gilles, and Félix Guattari. *A Thousand Plateaus: Capitalism and Schizophrenia Vol. 2*. 1980. Trans. Brian Massumi. Minneapolis: Minnesota University Press, 1987. Print.
Inhofe, James. *The Greatest Hoax: How the Global Warming Conspiracy Threatens Your Future*. Los Angeles: WND Books, 2012. Print.
Massumi, Brian. *A User's Guide to Capitalism and Schizophrenia: Deviations from Deleuze and Guattari*. 1992. Cambridge: MIT Press, 1999. Print.
Montopli, Brian. "Rick Santorum: Left Uses College for 'Indoctrination.'" CBS News. January 25, 2012. Web. 5 April 2013.
"North Carolina Wine Fast Facts." North Carolina Department of Commerce. 2013. Web. 13 April 2013.
Pearce, Matt. "U.S. Rep. Paul Broun: Evolution a Lie 'From the Pit of Hell.'" *Los Angeles Times*. October 7, 2012. Web. 5 April 2013.
Stephenson, Neal. *Anathem*. New York: William Morrow, 2008. Print.
―――. *The Baroque Cycle*. 3 vols. New York: William Morrow, 2003–04. Print.
―――. *Cryptonomicon*. New York: Avon, 1999. Print.
―――. *The Diamond Age, or a Young Girl's Illustrated Primer*. 1995. New York: Bantam, 2000. Print.
―――. *Snow Crash*. 1992. New York: Bantam, 2000. Print.

Part Two
Shifting Worlds Through Re-Creation

Karel Čapek's *War with the Newts*
Deterritorializing Land and Language

Adam Lawrence

Czech author Karel Čapek, who was acutely aware of the power of both the printed word and broadcasted political speech in 1930s European culture, viewed language as the key component in exploitation. His satirical masterpiece *War with the Newts* (1936) explores the power of language to dupe, transform, and control segments of society, and the monumental consequence of transforming both language and land into an interlocking ideology.

Čapek's strange and disturbing novel concerns the discovery and eventual exploitation of a species of salamander that possesses the ability to grasp objects such as knives, walk upright, and learn human languages. Initially co-opted for cheap labor and then conditioned to support the war effort, the Newts ultimately revolt and use underwater drills to break up the major continents and submerge the planet in water. Because it was written during the Nazi rise to power, *War with the Newts* has been viewed as a satire of militant expansionism and the ideological perversion of a mass population. My impression is that Čapek understood his Newts not simply as a "representation" of human territorial behavior, but *also* as an accurate depiction of Darwinian natural selection, which propels organisms to create, invent, and multiply in order to ensure survival of the species. Moreover, the Newts' adaptability—at least initially—enables them to evolve along a path very similar to *Homo sapiens*, interacting with a diverse number of other species, developing communication skills, and creating habitations for survival and comfort. Human populations, on the other hand, cannot resist the temptation to study, dissect, assimilate, and co-opt these creatures who possess the enviable characteristic of seemingly endless *environmental adaptation*. The consequence of this exploitation is that after the Newts evolve into a pseudo-human society, they begin to imitate the worst of human behaviors.

Specifically, it is through *enunciation*—and not just bodily movements—that these salamanders absorb and propagate the damaging expansionist ideologies disseminated by the human species. But the Newts' repetition of such ideas functions as parody, which is the consequence of forcing a marginalized group to think and speak in a new language. According to Gilles Deleuze and Félix Guattari, figures of so-called "minority," whether they be part of a marginalized ethnic, social, or sexual group (and the Newts surely fit this description), have a fundamental impact on the way we normally understand "major" categories of being: nation, homeland, and language (*A Thousand Plateaus: Capitalism and Schizophrenia* 102). Deleuze and Guattari replace the rigid dichotomies of "minor" and "major" with the dual concept of deterritorialization-reterritorialization—an interrelated process, partly inspired by Darwinian theory, in which an act or expression either rearranges the parts of a structure, carries those parts away and modifies them, or sets aright that disassembled structure and stabilizes it (87–88). As it will be discussed in the first section of the essay, this process is generally apparent in the way that the novel is plotted: the "story" of the Newts appears to be linear, but we discover that the orderliness of the narrative is engineered by the politicians and businessmen who wish to present a history of progress, from savagery to "civilization." Deliberately and unwittingly, a segment of the scientific community contributes to this artificial "history" when it attempts to taxonomize the Newts. In both cases, the seemingly stabilized identity of the Newts is undermined by the discovery that they have multiple "origins" and that they possess biologically divergent characteristics. From a Darwinian point of view, Newt evolution has "branches" of development, or variations,[1] which most humans are not aware of.

The second section of the essay considers how these scientific anomalies, which are a sign of that species' unique evolutionary path, are finally recapitulated by humans as an inferiority complex; the Newts are encouraged by politicians and businessmen alike to embrace the ideological abstractions of patriarchal nationhood as a way of compensating for their apparent shortcomings. However, when the Newts are dispersed across the planet, the attempt to impose uniformity fails. Employing Deleuze and Guattari's terminology, we could argue that these ideological notions are themselves dispersed and carried away through the concrete acts of flight and enunciation: the Newts leave their original "home," and while they are subsequently co-opted by nations, they nevertheless multiply into many racial variations; although the Newts do literally dismantle geographical space by splitting it into pieces and causing the major continents of the world to bifurcate, this is a *natural* response to their exploitation and enforced proliferation (they are "grown" in farms and incubators); ultimately, the Newt "tongue" loses its monolingual status once these racial and geographical boundaries are dismantled. Moreover, Čapek conceives of "space" as both a malevolent phantasm and a potentially liberating concrete set of coordinates—as an ideological notion of unity and purity, and a material circumstance of bodies intermingling and proliferating.

Plotting the War with the Newts: Reterritorializing History and Taxonomizing Difference

In most instances, summarizing plot is a tedious although necessary task; in the case of Čapek's novel, tracking the plot structure enables us to see the arbitrary nature of the Newts' "story," and to grasp the insidiousness of the narrative of their so-called progress towards "civilization." For example, the first few chapters of Book One appear to explain the origin of the Newts' evolutionary path: Captain J. van Toch "discovers" the Newts in Devil Bay, off the island of Tanah Masa, west of Sumatra, Indonesia while hunting for pearls. It is only much later (in the chapter titled "Andrias Scheuchzeri" and in the Appendix, "The Sex Life of the Newts") that we find out about this creature's physical characteristics and mating rituals: neither van Toch nor his eventual business partner, G. H. Bondy, have the foggiest notion about the Newts' biology or linguistic capacity. Romantically intrigued by van Toch's "fairy tale" about teaching the Newts to hunt pearls (Čapek 42), Bondy agrees to finance a global pearl-hunting enterprise. Bondy's "Salamander Syndicate" (Book One, Chapter 12) ensures that the Newts will continue to function as a "story" of *humanity*'s progress: as the chairman of the Pacific Export Association, Bondy proposes to transform van Toch's romantic but "slightly foolish" enterprise (101) by exploiting the untapped potential of this now gargantuan Newt population (amounting to around six million). Books Two and Three dramatize the consequences of these plots (both the events of the novel and the strategies of its principle characters). For example, the larger "history" of the Newts (Book Two, Chapter 2) is a multi-authored compendium detailing—not always in the correct order—momentous events, such as the colonization of new islands (in the wake of the Syndicate of Book One) and the setting up of Newt incubators (122); the gradual development of the "Newt problem" (142) related to the ambiguity surrounding their education, political affiliations, and linguistic capability; and the development of Newt labor and Newt-built machines for the construction of dams. Suffice it to say, humans are responsible for reterritorializing an uneven, mysterious, and divergent "history," and, as a consequence, for propelling the Newts forward in their destruction of the world. The novel is brilliant for its satire of traditional plotting, which imitates the conventional wish to impose artificial linearity, order, and causality, but also to conveniently ignore actual logic.[2]

This satire is aided by the fact that *War with the Newts* is a *roman feuilleton*, which is a "pastiche of the most diverse kinds of writing: newspaper articles, memoirs, scholarly works, manifestoes, etc." (Harkins 95). Chapter 8 of the first book, and the entire second book, contain excerpts of scientific reports; an eighteenth-century manuscript with the original typeface (Čapek 93-94); footnotes that contain news dispatches (121-24, 141-42, 150-51); fragments from the censored Newt manifesto (158); and other sundry minutes and extracts of meetings and conferences.[3] All of this—the catalogue of typeface and tongues—contributes to the babbling confusion of the book's middle section and its catastrophic final book. While the novel itself brims with knowledge (facts, speculations, neat articulations of theories), the characters that populate it grasp only small portions of the text—and now the Newt-infested environment—in which they live.

The great irony of the second book, "Up the Ladder of Civilization," is that while the enterprise first initiated by Bondy's Syndicate has moved forward, much of the more significant research on Newt biology has been forgotten, if not completely ignored. "Up the Ladder of Civilization" really means *along the steps to war* (Suvin 278), and this war is the consequence of the failure to consider fully the possible "future" of the Newt. This crucial middle section, which, as the narrator indicates in its first chapter, consists largely of the "history of the newts" (Čapek 120), is a summary of countless view points and is characterized by an almost haphazard fragmentation of logic and sense.[4] The unidentified narrator apparently gives no thought to the matter that this history is incomplete, but confidently asserts that "the making of history [is] now taking place wholesale" (121). In support of Bondy's belief that "Utopia" is possible through economic enterprise, the narrator adds that "we simply cannot wait a few hundred years for something good or bad to happen in the world" (121–22). The reterritorializing mechanism required to contain this mass of documents known as "history" is turned towards the Newts themselves who remain scattered about the globe. Through the machinery of incubators, the Salamander Trade (125f.), and universal Newt education (142–45), the Newts are organized into a "story" about *human* progress. The rational and optimistic narrator of the "history" boasts that "nature is not, and never has been, as enterprising and purposeful as human production and commerce" (123). However, while the Newts give the impression that they have just begun their career—as pearl hunter (Chapter 1, Book One), film monster (Chapters 6–7, Book One), circus performer (Chapters 5 and 10, Book One), or dam builder (Books Two and Three)—it turns out that they have been employed by Nature for centuries in any number of operations. After the war of words in the first book, *Andrias Scheuchzeri* (the supposed genus of these salamanders) still exists in a shroud of mystery.

Even though the "history" is basically non-linear in structure, as the omniscient narrator describes in a lengthy disclaimer (119–20), the voice of this work would have us believe that, as Bondy had proclaimed in the famed Salamander Syndicate, "the future of the Newts is now beyond any doubt" (105). However, because organic development frequently leads to unexpected results (called "mutations"), a doctrinal faith in official History is not only limited but dangerous. Unlike the writers of the "history," then, we must return to the moments in which the Newts' evolution already shows signs of diverging from the norm, and the moments in which this divergence begins to graft itself onto the history (and evolution) of *Homo sapiens*.

While it is true, as Suvin argues, that the Newts enter "the life of mankind [...] under a cloud of delusions and misperceptions" (276), there is no shortage of scientific studies and learned scholarly articles on Newt biology and their evolutionary past. Two chapters in Book One (Chapters 8 and 11) as well as the Appendix include carefully documented analyses of fossil remains and salamander genera, as well as studies of the Newts' evolution and their social and sexual life. While one intellectual claims that the Newts are an "unscientific hoax and pure fantasy" (73), two others speculate that *Andrias Scheuchzeri* may be "antediluvian man" (75) or "Miocene man" (95). In these opposing views lie two kinds of warnings: on the one hand, an academic scolds his peers for engaging in sensational mythologizing; on the other hand, two academics strive earnestly to write about the facts as they appear, to enlighten, and to engage in a "learned" discussion (92) that may prevent future "delusions and misperceptions." However, one issue that contributes to the Newt "problem" of the second book is the dispute over the identity of this unusual salamander species. As we learn in the first scientific chapter of the first book ("Andrias Scheuchzeri"), scientists from all across the world "discover" their own genus of Newts and begin to wage "a furious scientific war against the giant salamanders of other nations" (78). The word choice here is meant to indicate not only the "war of words" that erupts in the scientific community, but also the ways in which the Babylonian confusion of tongues can undermine the goal of sharing knowledge. But Čapek is not so prejudiced as to suggest a universal translation: the proliferation of Newt genera deriving from eighteenth- and nineteenth-century explorations of the South and Central Pacific—the "Megatriton moluccanus" from the Dutch Sunda islands Dgillo, Morotai, and Ceram; the "Cryptobranchus salamandroides" from the French islands Takaroa, Rangiroa and Raroire; and the "Pelagotriton Spencei" from the English Gilbert islands (77)—indicates how such a translation has already been at work in the desire to taxonomize everything for the glory of king and empire and in the language of science. In this initial instance at least, the Newt is important insofar as it has distinct and verifiable affiliations; the subject of the Salamander genera is important insofar as it is a *legitimate* field of study, and this status is reached when scientists become the "fathers" of their discoveries: Johannes Jakub Scheuchzer gives birth to *Andrias Scheuchzeri*, H. W. Spencer (perhaps a parodic nod to the noted Social Darwinist, Herbert Spencer) gives birth to *Pelagotriton Spencei*, and so forth. The "war" that is waged, then, is one between potential patriarchs, and it indicates the ways in which chauvinistic politics instigate cultural wars between nations. As a result of these disputes, our narrator concludes, "that whole important business of the salamanders was never sufficiently resolved on the scientific side" (78).

Čapek's point is that there is no simple resolution and that intellectual cooperation and convergence rather than competition and censorship might assist in understanding the Newts better. Moreover, as we follow the plot of the novel we simultaneously discover all the ways that humans plot the "war" with the Newts, and yet no character ever really sees how obvious the causal relation is between human arrogance/shortsightedness and the destruction of the planet. While the stories and plots about the Newts (where they came from, what tasks they were capable of performing, and how they might fit into human history) continually change, the narrative maintains the consistent goal of stabilizing—ordering, reassembling—a Newt population that is more diverse than humans realize.

This diversity is made apparent in the second scientific chapter of Book One ("Men-Lizards"), which may be a parodic reminder of Čapek's earlier "vitalist" or "relativist" works,[5] sparkling as it does with the Bergsonian intonations about "a major mutation *in actu* [in progress]" (91), or the endlessness of Nature's "creative operation" (92). However, it is perhaps too hasty to conclude that vitalism was a mere stage in Čapek's writing, especially since much of the satire in this work points to the inability to *foresee* the workings of "creative evolution" or the "life force" that operates despite our belief in the eternal laws of science. "[T]here is no universal biological law," Henri Bergson writes, "which applies precisely and automatically to every living thing. There are only *directions* in which life throws out species in general" (16).

Professor Vladimír Uher, whose findings are summarized in this scholarly chapter titled "Men-Lizards," writes in a similar spirit when he speculates on the possibility that some "powerful vital *élan* [...] had so suddenly and extensively revived the arrested existence of an evolutionarily backward and indeed near-extinct creature" (Čapek 92). His theory begins to blossom: If the Newt had evolved in what appears to be an almost spontaneous mutation, perhaps as a way of making up for "the hundreds of thousands and millions of years of evolution that it had missed!" (95), what was it still capable of? Was it still capable of catching up to *Homo sapiens* or, given its unpredictable "vital *élan*," even surpassing it? These are speculations, of course, exuberant ruminations resulting from an undated (but likely early eighteenth-century) newspaper report Professor Uher was given describing a crew's discovery of strange salamanders fitting the description of *Andrias Scheuchzeri*. Provocatively, the report tells of how, after the men hunt down most of the salamanders and slay them, two live ones are brought aboard, but, as the ship is crossing near Sumatra, they ultimately escape from the casks in which they have been imprisoned, climb out the windows of the "steerage," and throw themselves into the water (94).

This fragment, while certainly apocryphal, exists alongside other similarly speculative theories about the Newts' history, and offers both a confirmation that *some* Newts may very well have derived from the South Pacific as well as a counter to the belief that Captain van Toch was their original "liberator" (Test 3). In this alternate "history," the Newts display early signs that they can "revolt" when provoked by either nature or humans. But, Uher discovers, his fellow creatures are not interested in a story that has ceased to be fashionable, a sentiment that displays the first signs of his own dwindling "life force" as a writer. Convinced that his readers have become "sick and tired of those newts" and opting instead for something "different" (Čapek 95–96), the editor of the *Lidové Noviny* rejects Professor Uher's scholarly studies and, as a result, "the article on the evolution and future of the newts was never published" (96).

Up until the middle of the Book Two, the Newts remain stabilized, although clearly underestimated. For this reason they are appropriate exemplars of how animals and hominids are both ordered by language (taxonomy of type: *Andrias Scheuchzeri, Homo Sapiens*, and so forth), and yet create *dis*order as soon as they speak (acquiring new languages and mispronouncing them). As Deleuze and Guattari write, "Language is made not to be believed but to be obeyed, and to compel obedience [...]. Language is not life; it gives life orders. Life does not speak; it listens and waits" (*A Thousand Plateaus* 76). For the time being at least, the Newts listen while they are ordered, and they wait...

The Attraction of Affiliation: Reterritorializing/Deterritorializing Land and Language

While readers discover that the Newts are scientifically anomalous because of their unique evolutionary path, the majority of the humans within Čapek's fictional world sees only an undifferentiated mass of exploitable workers. However, because they do differ physiologically from the population into which they incorporated, the Newts are ultimately reterritorialized as a nation with an inferiority complex. The whole second half of the "history" of Book Two is taken up with report after report detailing the inferior and maligned status of the Newt, and yet, right to the end (to the last days of the so-called "Golden Newt Age," Čapek 169), the Newts are congratulated for their slave-like work ethic and their willingness to demean themselves. In one particular sequence, a Czech couple comes across a Newt that speaks their language and begins a conversation about Czech history. To their surprise, the Newt knows nothing about contemporary history but can recite by rote the old woeful and wretched details of the country's past. He speaks excitedly of the Thirty Years' War when "the Czech land was then turned into a desert drenched with blood and tears," and speaks proudly of the "three hundred years of servitude" that followed (149). In this situation where hardship is glorified, Čapek "not only mocks his fellow-countrymen for wallowing in past sufferings but shrewdly shows how this kind of pride in humiliation can be fostered in others" (Maslen 84). On the one hand, the Newts are indeed an inferior race, exploited by business and science for ambivalent purposes: greed, the enlightenment of society, and the creation of a pseudo-human labor force to replace the already massive human one. On the other hand, the Newts are transformed into a vengeful fraternity bent on the total exploitation of the entire globe. The Salamanders multiply at an astronomical rate, aided and abetted as they are by both the artificial incubators and the natural evolutionary "vital élan" described in the first book by Professor Uher. In this work, Suvin rightly notes, "a limit was found beyond which the pseudo-human became clearly evil," particularly when the Newts "grow into an analogy to the Nazi aggressors" (276). This analogy is confirmed in the third book when German nationalists begin praising the superiority of the "Baltic Newt" (Čapek 192–96).

It is reasonable to find the answer to the Newts' aggression and terrible reterritorializations in their biology: the studies show that, in everything—in sexual courting, in community organization, and in industry—their society is organized by a male collective, "We, the Male Principle" (113). But it is also fair to suggest that their behavior has been influenced by "secondary impulses," which correspond to the ideological abstraction of male "honor" and dominance; these impulses do not, in other words, derive from any biological necessity (Reich vii–ix, xii, 130,

140, 253, 295). The Newt behavior is, of course, comparable to the male portion of *Homo sapiens* that also tries to marginalize the female population, form into collectives, and court aggressively as it consumes and builds. No Newt is ever really a slave to his courtly aggression, just as no man is; but each organism finds that the result (the fertilization of eggs) will raise his own status in his particular community and contribute to his own feeling of self-worth. Van Toch sees something of this male pride in his "tapa-boys," even if he is unfamiliar with their sexual life or social organization; he flatters their male ego and the result is that—at least for a time—they bind themselves to him and to the more successful "Male Principle" of the capitalist world. More so than even his Robots, Čapek's Newts apparently "evolve" according to the demands of capitalism, which can proclaim with all confidence "the spectacular spread and progress" (122) and the "strong and steady ascent" of the Newts (164). Here we have a vulgarized version of Darwinism, leading to the greatest ideological perversion of all: *fascism*. After the Newts allow themselves to be employed in the new hyper-industrialist milieu, when the exploitation reaches its peak, they then turn on their masters and carry out the destruction of the human world. So we can say with accuracy, "no, the masses were not innocent dupes; at a certain point, under a certain set of conditions, they *wanted* fascism, and it is this perversion of the desire of the masses that needs to be accounted for" (Deleuze and Guattari, *Anti-Oedipus: Capitalism and Schizophrenia* 29). This "perversion" can be distinguished from its previous form—mutation, deviation, divergence—since, in the form it takes here, fascist desire, these characteristics are co-opted for the purposes of irrational hatred.

The "open-ended" nature of the novel's conclusion—in which the "author" is unsure "how it [the story, the world] goes on" (Čapek 241)—reflects Čapek's Darwinian faith in an "undirected" evolution, leaving us with more than one possible future for *Homo sapiens* and *Andrias Scheuchzeri*. Indeed, the final conversation between the author and his "inner voice" (235–41) invites us to invent our own ending. On the one hand, the Newt *mass* becomes a State apparatus comparable to a military dictatorship, destroying whole fleets of ships and splitting apart continents in order to construct as many new coasts as possible, with the intention of creating a monolithic Newt kingdom. On the other hand, the Newts operate as a molecular aggregate linked already to the multiple continents of the world, and to the scattering and diffusion of State authority. This is why the mechanism of "co-option" is so important: the typically large quantity of the oppressed group supplies the State with multiple organs of power which are fuelled by a *ressentiment* reappropriated by the "enemy" (*you are an inferior bastard tribe!*) and redeployed in paternal affection (*you are OUR superior legitimate sons!*). From the State's point of view, the pathway from inferiority to superiority is a linear one, "striated" or punctuated in a series of steps like the most rigid model of evolutionary descent or ascent: such a model encourages the "little man" to see in his new affiliation the "natural" progression towards higher and enlightened things. In this way, the Newts reterritorialize on the basis of a phantasmal notion of place and space: they become affiliated with a "nation," which is, of course, an ideological abstraction.

However, from the point of view of the molecular aggregate, or the diffused and divergent "masses" that are "constantly flowing or leaking from classes" (Deleuze and Guattari, *A Thousand Plateaus* 213), the pathway is "smooth" and "the points are subordinated to the trajectory" (478): such a model encourages the co-opted Newt to see legitimacy as one more stoppage, as one more damned affiliation, not to mention one more way to be "fucked over" (*Anti-Oedipus* 23). After all, the supposed leader of the organized Newts, who calls himself "Chief Salamander," is really a human, "Andreas Schultze" (Čapek 239), perhaps a sly reference to "Adolf Hitler," and therefore just one more anthropoid con artist. In other words, in a certain sense, the Newt must understand that he is not really a human, that he need not *be* a human, but that he can take flight from this fascist horde, this State-driven production frenzy. In this way, the Newt (having broken off from the pack, from the horde) deterritorializes on the basis of a more concrete sense of space: he is allied to a place insofar as it contributes to survival.

This survival instinct is apparent as early as Chapters 6 and 7 of Book One, when we first see and hear the Newts: while B-movie actress "Miss Lily Valley" is cavorting in the waves on set for one of her cheesy films, she is approached by several Newts who make demands for a "Nyfe" (59). Readers will recall that they were originally supplied with knives to defend themselves from sharks, so the suggestion is that the Newts are searching for more weapons of survival. However much we might view this episode as an example of the Newts' capacity for violence, we should not forget that it is meant to mirror *Homo sapiens*' acquisition of similar survival tools during its evolution. For both Newt and human, evolution means not so much steady advancement as a continual process of advancement and retreat. Deleuze and Guattari describe the process in the following way:

> We already know the importance in animals of those activities that consist in forming *territories*, in abandoning or leaving them, and even re-creating territory on something of a different nature [...]. All the more for the hominid: from its act of birth, it deterritorializes its front paw, wrests it from the earth to turn it into a hand, and reterritorializes it on branches and tools. A stick is, in turn, a deterritorialized branch. We need to see how everyone, at every age, in the smallest things as in the greatest challenges, seeks a territory, tolerates or carries out deterritorializations, and is reterritorialized on almost anything—memory, fetish, or dream [*What Is Philosophy?* 67–68; original emphasis].

This type of "becoming" occurs in the novel when the Newts use knives to pry open oysters and to kill predatory sharks, and when they manufacture drills to build dams. In both cases, the acquisition of tools represents a reterritorialization, where a "challenge" (hunger, predatory threats, or overpopulation) is resolved when the organism falls back on an implement, relies on something other than its body to perform tasks. At the same time, however, the operation of these tools enables a deterritorialization as both food and enemies are carried away—for sustenance, for survival—and single pieces of land (coastlines, underwater bedrock) are broken up and carried away.

This process of deterritorialization-reterritorialization occurs most dramatically when the Newts begin to acquire human languages. Consider the following lengthy passage, which describes the onset of the so-called "Newt problem":

> With the nationalisation of Newt education the whole business was simplified: Newts in each country were simply taught in the national language. Although the salamanders *picked up* foreign languages rather quickly, and with enthusiasm, their linguistic skill exhibited some peculiar shortcomings, due, on the one hand, to the configuration of their vocal organs and, on the other, to what one might call psychological reasons. They had difficulties, for instance, with the pronunciation of long polysyllabic words and tried to shorten them to one syllable which they then uttered in a brief and rather croaky manner. They said "l" instead of "r" and tended to lisp their sibilants. They *dispensed* with grammatical endings, never learned to differentiate between "I" and "we," and they could not care less whether a word was of feminine or masculine gender [...]. In short, every language was *characteristically transformed in their mouths* and somehow economically reduced to its simplest and most rudimentary form. It is worth noting that their neologisms, their pronunciation and their primitive grammar

were *rapidly being adopted by* the dregs of dockside humanity, on the one hand, and what is known as society, on the other. From there this *manner of expression spread* to the newspapers and soon became general. Even among humans *grammatical gender often disappeared, endings were dropped, inflexion became extinct* [Čapek 146; emphasis added].

Here language acquisition is characterized in terms of grasping, dispensing, transforming, imbibing, proliferating, and disappearing—all the gerund participles that relate to the Newts' physical development as they find and use tools, consume food, and spread themselves across various territories. In terms of Deleuze and Guattari's conceptual framework, there are certainly instances of reterritorialization, where the Newts are simply *given* languages, reflecting how language exists "to compel obedience" (*A Thousand Plateaus* 76). But there are also numerous occurrences of deterritorialization, where, for example, the Newts mispronounce or lisp certain words, eliminate letters, and completely modify the grammatical structure of a language. While we know that the reduction of language to the lowest common denominator is a tendency here, we cannot at the same time miss the deterritorializing process in which parts of the whole are carried away. These are wrestings and wrenchings propelled by circumstance. As reterritorialization, this indifference to grammar and linguistic inflection and gender may reflect the Nazis' imperialist and racist policy of purifying the Newt language of its foreign elements, thereby stabilizing it; but as deterritorialization, this failure to differentiate between individuality and collectivity may exemplify the natural diffusion of centralizing languages through the habitual utterances of the people, of the masses (including both Newts and humans): it is certainly notable that the working classes—denigrated by the pompous narrator as "dregs of dockside humanity"—have adopted the newly transformed *Newtese*. The repetition of the various world languages leads to a mongrelization of the unitary language.

For all of the above reasons, we might disagree with the apparent voice of reason, the fictional philosopher Wolf Meynert, who, in his great work on the whole Newt "problem" (Book Three, Chapter 5), characterizes the Newt as a "homogeneous, uniform and, as it were, consistent mass," and as "biologically equally primitive in all its parts" (Čapek 199). In his more recent analysis of the novel, M. Keith Booker takes Meynert at his word: "The newt society values not quality, but quantity, and Čapek reinforces the suggestion that he is really talking about modern human society rather than newt society" (Booker 111).[6] However, there is still so much evidence that individual Newts can and do acquire languages and make them their own. The instances of this seem so minor in the face of the faceless Newt horde that destroys the planet at the end of the novel; however, if, as Booker argues, Čapek is reinforcing the connection between the Newts and humans, he is nevertheless lamenting the positive creativity that is lost when both Newt and human give in to the compulsion to embody a purely patriarchal society, when studies show (again, about both Newts and humans) that there are alternatives available. Moreover, we are not meant to accept Meynart's view at face value: he is analyzing the Newts from the typically human point of view; he is anthropomorphizing them and, in effect, ensuring that their "homogeneous" and "uniform" identity will be accepted as fact.

The Chief Salamander specifically makes use of this reterritorialization, coordinating the Newts of the world in order to instigate a massive series of earthquakes. Yet, the chief's expansionist ideology—disguised as a plea for the Newts' necessary survival—is exposed in his very manner of speech, which is Newt-like and yet suspiciously *human*. Here is how his first European-wide transmission is described: "From [a] protracted unending hum [of the radio wavelength] suddenly came a terrible croaking voice [...] described [by listeners] in similar terms: *hollow, quacking, as if artificial, and simultaneously enormously magnified by a loudspeaker* [...]" (Čapek 215; emphasis added). The characteristic "croak" is mentioned (see also 149), but there is something fake about it, as though a human has deliberately distorted his voice and projected it. Such is the world as Čapek knew it—one in which the latest technologies (mainly radio and print media) could be used to dupe the masses; however, now it seems reasonable to argue that this aggregate is much more complex than the businessmen, politicians, scientists, and philosophers in the novel would have us believe.

Conclusion: "transitional [...] zones of indiscernibility"

Čapek composed *War with the Newts* during a period in which fascism was seeking to "mobilize the middle strata" (Hobsbawm 143), including the "little men," of society. It is clear that this mobilization is largely successful, and yet this ideological victory does not prevent Čapek from demonstrating smaller biological and linguistic rebellions. Again, the open-ended conclusion seems the best evidence of this remaining Darwinian faith in the unpredictable ways of nature, rather than in some "natural order." Darwinian theory provides a useful way of undermining ideologies of homogeneity, or the belief that nature can be categorized rigidly into types and taxonomies, methods of reducing bodies to a limited set of behaviors. By Čapek's day, it was abundantly apparent that Darwinian theory had altered the entire social order of the Victorians: it was no longer valid to accept the biblical account of creation, and the theory of separate and specialized variations; it seemed more likely that all humans were the product of the slow and sometimes unforeseen modification of formerly nonhuman species (see Darwin 636–49). As Darwin writes early in *The Origin of Species*, "Indefinite variability is a much more common result of changed conditions than definite variability, and has probably played a more important part in the formation of our domestic races" (26). The arbitrary acceptance of only certain kinds of variation (i.e., Anglo-Saxon, Caucasian, and Christian) was therefore a clear sign of racial and moral prejudice. This hypocrisy has already been noted above. Darwin himself characterized the conflict between indigenous groups and their oppressors with some sympathy: "And as foreigners have thus in every country beaten some of the natives, we may safely conclude that the natives might have been modified with advantage, so as to have better resisted the intruders" (111). In such a scenario, the human attempt to impose its will on the environment is undermined by nature's "preservation" of valuable characteristics and survival skills; as Darwin adds, nature "cares nothing for appearances, except in so far as they are useful to any being." Such a theory, which helped to "relate man to the 'under-world of life,'" was useful to the underclasses in Britain (Desmond and Moore 508) and must surely have appealed to the "little people" of Čapek's society.

All the way through *War with the Newts*, and especially in Book Two, Čapek is similarly satirizing "progressivist" views of evolutionary development. Specifically, "up the ladder of civilization" mockingly references the classic misunderstanding of Darwin's description of how organisms change and evolve. Darwin—as Gould, Deleuze and Guattari, and others have demonstrated—placed emphasis on variation and change as the central trend of evolution, and not on progressive development upward; it was only by chance, by accident, that certain species vary in such a way as to achieve notable specialization: e.g., apes with a consciousness and the ability to make war with the objects they can grasp. Deleuze and Guattari in particular reinforce that the "hominid"'s evolution comprises a series of advances and retreats, grasping and releasing space as the situation demands.

There is, moreover, a subtle Darwinian lesson implied in Čapek's novel: that the beautiful complexity of one society becomes savage, destructive, and ultimately sterile when it attempts to impose its creativity and inventiveness on other societies; in other words, where it prefers automatism over individuality. Brilliantly, Čapek's novel illustrates how the rise and fall of empires and of totalitarian regimes derives in part from the very biological impulses that drive the individual organism along its evolutionary path: the sexual milieu is not simply the analogy to another society (that of *Homo sapiens*), but is an earlier stage of evolution in general. The exception here, "in part," indicates that, for Čapek (as for Darwin, as for Deleuze and Guattari), it is not "natural" for a man to want to dominate and exploit his neighbors because it is not part of the human's "biological core" (Reich vii-viii), even though he may employ his strength and cunning towards this very goal when certain conditions spur him on. As Elana Gomel elaborates for us, "When violent power is misread as a law of nature, it elevates itself beyond ethical judgment" (406). The violators—van Toch, Bondy, and especially the ubiquitous Chief Salamander who organizes the bifurcation of the planet—see themselves and especially the Newts as "agent[s] of natural order": more so than in Wells's day, vulgarized versions of Darwinism have become fully entrenched in political ideology as the justification for war-mongering and genocide. What produces a creative tension, however, is the fact that the Newts are both the oppressed and the oppressor. This tension is perfectly illustrated when we consider that the Newts' uneven and unpredictable development is deliberately misread as a journey "up the ladder of civilization" and as a justification of nature's cruel progress towards perfection. As a result of this misreading, the "post-Darwinian inversion of benevolent natural theology into a gospel of cruelty paves the way for the sacred science of massacre" (Gomel 411).

The Newts' anomalous adaptation to human society and their ability to operate for a time as equal partners to their human counterparts suggests the sort of symbiotic relation that might have developed had the salamanders not been exploited for profit. Their unpredictable changeability and their capacity to infiltrate human society suggest that Čapek's pseudo-humans still function in a socially critical way. We might put the matter thus: In *War with the Newts*, the novelty (the Newt) grafts itself onto certain aspects of the mundane or empirical world, slowly and gradually transforming it, almost imperceptibly, in the same way that a virus can alter the structure of any organism over a period of time. This deterritorialization provides a way of gauging how deviations enter into society and affect (or infect) that society, and how "monsters" become a part of how *Homo sapiens* understands its own evolution as a species. For the Newt embodies humankind's potential to evolve into open communities, to diverge from the normal set of relations, to embrace what conservative ideologies call the "perverse" and the "monstrous," to reject the doctrine of *ressentiment* and part company with the "little man," and to diverge from—or deterritorialize—the laws that would seek to restrict mobility and change. This strategy is available precisely because the Newts are a "minority"—however large, however similar they appear. As Deleuze and Guattari write in *A Thousand Plateaus*, "the more a language has or acquires the characteristics of a major language, the more it is affected by continuous variations that transpose it into a 'minor' language" (102). However much they are exploited, and however much they become absorbed into the human population, the Newts deterritorialize the unitary notions of "nation," "homeland," and "mother(father) tongue." Because of their "peculiar shortcomings" (Čapek 149), the Newts simply cannot offer a perfect imitation of human speech and habits, mispronouncing, lisping or lopping off parts of language until it is incomprehensible. But this is Čapek's satirical ploy. Compared to the all-too-human language of the "Chief" Newt, the real Newt languages (which are many) convert these ideological abstractions of land and language into a series of "transitional [...] zones of indiscernibility" (Deleuze and Guattari, *A Thousand Plateaus* 101).

Notes

1. In *Full House: The Spread of Excellence of from Plato to Darwin*, Stephen Jay Gould refers to the competition in contemporary evolutionary thought between "ladders" of progression and "branches" of deviation, or "individual pathways chosen with prejudice versus entire systems (full houses) and their complete variation" (62).

2. Gould also speaks to this human instinct to embrace the ideology of progressive development: "We are story-telling creatures, products of history ourselves. We are fascinated by trends, in part because they tell stories by the basic device of imparting directionality in time, in part because they so often supply a moral dimension to a sequence of events: a cause to bewail as something goes to pot, or to highlight as a rare beacon of hope" (30).

3. In his book *The Animal Fable in Science Fiction and Fantasy*, Bruce Shaw notes

that the novel's form was due in part to its serialization: "Čapek had not only to fill spaces and make a tale flow from one issue to the next, [but] he had also to hold his readers' interest." I think it quite appropriate, given Čapek's Darwinian slant, that the novel "*grew* over two years, published in installments from 1935 to 1936" (138; emphasis added).

4. As John Clark and Anna Lydia Motto put the matter, "the reader is never allowed to settle for consistency and complacency" when it comes to the "oscillating" significance of the Newts: indeed, the reader can track the accumulation of errors, misinformation, and plain negligence which contribute to the Newts' "ubiquity and multifariousness" (11).

5. Harkins argues that Čapek's writings of the 1910s and early 1920s exemplify an "ethical relativism," or the "discovery of the freedom, richness, and variety of a relativist world" (72), hinted at in the conclusion of *R.U.R.*

6. Booker seems more on the mark when he notes that there is a Bakhtinian strategy at work in the novel: "the book is constructed from a complex patchwork of texts imported from a variety of genres and discourses, endowing the work with an overt Bakhtinian heteroglossia that acts to combat the single-mindedness of the authoritarian tendencies Čapek wishes to oppose" (108). Bruce Shaw also notes the presence of Bakhtinian "carnivalesque" in the novel (136–37).

Works Cited

Bergson, Henri. *Creative Evolution*. Trans. Arthur Mitchell. New York: Henry Holt, 1911. Print.

Booker, M. Keith. *Dystopian Literature: A Theory and Research Guide*. Westport: Greenwood Press, 1994. Print.

Čapek, Karel. *War with the Newts*. Trans. Edwald Osers. North Haven: Catbird Press/UNESCO, 1999. Print.

Clark, John R., and Anna Lydia Motto. "At War with Our Roots: Karel Čapek Revisited." *Studies in Contemporary Satire: A Creative and Critical Journal* 14 (1987): 1–15. Print.

Darwin, Charles. *The Origin of Species by Means of Natural Selection, or The Preservation of Favored Races In the Struggle for Life*. New York: Modern Library, 1998. Print.

Deleuze, Gilles, and Félix Guattari. *Anti-Oedipus: Capitalism and Schizophrenia*. Trans. Robert Hurley, Mark Seem, and Helen R. Lane. Preface Michel Foucault. Minneapolis: University of Minnesota Press, 1983. Print.

———, and ———. *A Thousand Plateaus: Capitalism and Schizophrenia*. Trans. Brian Massumi. Minneapolis: University of Minnesota Press, 1987. Print.

———, and ———. *What Is Philosophy?* Trans. Hugh Tomlinson and Graham Burchell. New York: Columbia University Press, 1994. Print.

Desmond, Adrian, and James Moore. *Darwin: The Life of a Tormented Evolutionist*. New York: W. W. Norton, 1991. Print.

Gomel, Elana. "From Dr. Moreau to Dr. Mengele: The Biological Sublime." *Poetics Today* 21.2 (Summer 2000): 393–421. Print.

Gould, Stephen Jay. *Full House: The Spread of Excellence from Plato to Darwin*. Cambridge: Belknap Press, 2011. Print.

Harkins, William. *Karel Čapek*. New York: Columbia University Press, 1962. Print.

Hobsbawm, E. J. *Nations and Nationalism Since 1780: Programme, Myth, Reality*, 2d ed. New York: Cambridge University Press, 1994. Print.

Maslen, Elizabeth. "Proper Words in Proper Places: The Challenge of Čapek's *War with the Newts*." *Science-Fiction Studies* 14 (March 1987): 82–92. Print.

Reich, Wilhelm. *The Mass Psychology of Fascism*. Trans. Theodore P. Wolfe. New York: Orgone Institute Press, 1946. Print.
Shaw, Bruce. *The Animal Fable in Science Fiction and Fantasy*. Jefferson: McFarland, 2010. Print.
Suvin, Darko. *Metamorphoses of Science Fiction: On the Poetics and History of a Literary Genre*. New Haven: Yale University Press, 1979. Print.
Test, George A. "Karel Čapek's *War with the Newts*: A Neglected Modern Satire." *Studies in Contemporary Satire: A Creative and Critical Journal* 1 (1974): 1–10. Print.

Mary Shelley's Literary Laboratory

Frankenstein *and the Emergence of the Modern Laboratory in Nineteenth-Century Europe*

MATTHEW HADLEY

> We are only just starting to take up the challenge that laboratory practices present for the study of society.
> —Bruno Latour

Frankenstein's Cinematic Laboratory

In this essay I develop the claim that the figure of the laboratory in Mary Shelley's *Frankenstein* operates as a space for the novel to disclose its own conditions of production and to autocritique its social functions and limitations. While Shelley's 1818 novel will be this essay's main focus, I begin by reading the depiction of Frankenstein's laboratory in James Whale's 1931 film adaptation. As many have pointed out in different ways, the myriad adaptations of the novel—in different genres and media, through the volumes of literary and cultural criticism, as well as in the popular conceptions of the story and characters—cast, as Chris Baldick puts it, a long "shadow" over encounters with the text. In the case of Whale's 1931 film adaptation, this shadow actually helps to highlight something crucial about the novel itself: the importance of the place of the laboratory. Shelley's laboratory is only faintly exposed, whereas the laboratories in the various film adaptations are eminently spectacular, drawing attention to the laboratory in a way that the novel does not.

The laboratory scenes in Whale's *Frankenstein* are by now so canonical that a close reading of these scenes would be superfluous. Suffice it to say that the events of the film lead to a presentation of Frankenstein's laboratory as the site to be seen *par excellence*. This space becomes a magnet for the attentive gaze, an internal space oriented around and by spectatorship and visibility. Whale's laboratory is housed in the gothic castle-like abandoned watchtower. The cold, damp stones and vaulted ceilings house numerous instruments, machines, beakers, and other contraptions that spark with frenzied activity. While otherwise secretive and kept from view, the fact that the lab is housed in a watchtower connects this space of labor to one originally created for the purpose of looking and for making sense of and policing the territory of its surroundings.

The spectacular scene of the laboratory, constructed as *the* space of visualization, provokes me to review the importance of the laboratory within and for the novel itself. The figure of the laboratory in the novel is paradoxically and retroactively made visible as a space of obscurity. This peculiar revision of the laboratory from an otherwise private, domestic, and overlooked space to one unavoidably visible—indeed the most centrally spectacular space in the film—becomes instructive for my own revision of Shelley's novel in several ways. First of all, adapting the novel to a visual medium discloses the desire (as already present in the literary narrative) to produce an estranged—and therefore instructive—image of the human. Secondly, by 1931, the laboratory was firmly established as *the* space of scientific labor, so the increased "visibility" of the laboratory in the film attests to the particular historical shifts in the practice of the life sciences. This juxtaposition of Shelley's and Whale's treatments of Dr. Frankenstein's workplace initiates a preliminary case study for the genealogy of the laboratory that I sketch below.

Despite the central importance of Victor's labor, the creation of the living human being, the crucial importance of the space of this labor—Victor's laboratory—has been consistently overlooked. Indeed, the laboratory in Shelley's novel figures so sparingly that a reader may easily read over the several brief references to where Victor actually worked. Descriptions of the two separate laboratory settings—the first for the creature, the second for the creature's aborted female companion—are furthermore strikingly scant in a novel otherwise known for its sublime settings. If the laboratory of the film is pure spectacle, operating with an intensification of the visual and imagistic, the laboratory in the novel, by contrast, emerges less as image than as a functional node within a network of spatial and social relations.

My intention here is to show how a consideration of this figure as an absent presence is crucial for a reading of the novel. I begin with a short history of this historical space, dating the emergence of the teaching lab, its institutionalized and publicly visible form, within a decade of the novel's publication. I then consider the function of lab work in the sciences by Science, Technology, and Societry (STS) scholar Bruno Latour. I show how Latour's treatment of the scientific laboratory can be articulated to theories of the space of literature. Moreover, I consider how the juxtaposition of a theorization of the scientific laboratory, and what I call the literary laboratory, discloses the similarities between both places of labor. This will lead me to show how the laboratory functions in *Frankenstein* as a way for the novel to think its own process of production, and thus, to think about the nature of both literary and scientific practices, making visible the active participation of both in the organization, regulation, and, at times, radical reconfiguration of society.

Laboratory Space: A Brief History

While the transition from alchemy to modern chemistry in seventeenth century Europe marks the first private uses of the laboratory by scientists,[1] it will take another two centuries for these spaces to migrate from the private, domestic spaces to larger institutions, public universities, and corporate laboratories (Edison's "invention factory," the massive West Orange, New Jersey, complex of laboratories, being an early example of the lab on a large scale). The laboratory since this time has been indispensible to the sciences, becoming the most important tool for the manufacture of knowledge, the production of scientific discourse, and the production of new forms, both living and nonliving. In its pedagogical use, the laboratory became the space for the production of scientists themselves who adhere to the methods of science, who know how to function as part of the laboratory spaces, who are familiar with the instruments and methods of the laboratory, and who uphold the communal processes and norms of scientific inquiry and production.

As most historical accounts of the laboratory will attest, the laboratory's origins are difficult, if not impossible, to locate. Lord Kelvin, then Sir William Thomson, published a history of the laboratory in an 1885 issue of the journal *Nature*. Reflecting on the by then well-established space, he credits the first two decades of the nineteenth century with fostering the emergence of the first modern laboratory. This is in line with the introduction to Frank James's *The Development of the Laboratory: Essays on the Place of Experiment in Industrial Civilization*, where he states unambiguously that "laboratories did not exist in the pre-industrial age," if indeed we can mark the late eighteenth and early nineteenth centuries as giving rise to industrialization (1). However, Lord Kelvin mentions that one of the first recorded public laboratories, aside from that of the Ptolemies in Alexandria during the third century BC, which "gradually sank into a place for metaphysical discussions" (Welch 495), was developed by King Frederick II for anatomy in the thirteenth century. Lord Kelvin dubs this space "the first laboratory." Since then there seems to have been a designated space for the study of anatomy, though it would not be until the sixteenth century that these spaces would have a lasting and important public role.

In terms of the history of lab practices, there are many accounts and records of the work done by experimentalists, inventors and scientists in private laboratories, and it is crucial to think of these spaces as the pre-history of what will become a more standardized and disciplined space. However, it will take a further public investment in the practice of the sciences for the laboratory to become historically visible. The emergence of the modern laboratory cannot be dissociated from its use as a space of instruction, as well as a means for the commodification of scientific labor and products. The individually owned and operated spaces were the incubators for what would slowly be centralized in the public laboratories of eighteenth and nineteenth century Europe. By the end of the 1800s, scientists working in chemistry, physics, and the life sciences (anatomy, medicine, physiology, biology, etc.) found their workshops transplanted from private dwellings to public universities. It was not until 1825, just seven years after the publication of *Frankenstein*, that Justus von Liebig would establish the first teaching laboratory soon after his appointment at the University of Giessen, thus establishing a model space for scientific work, and definitively connecting laboratory work to research, invention, experimentation and instruction (Good 557). In sum, it was the housing of the laboratory in publicly funded spaces of education (and the facilitation of the transfer to capitalist industry) that solidified the laboratory as the most important site for experiment, discovery, and invention.

In line with the relative obscurity of laboratory spaces at the onset of the nineteenth century, Shelley gives little description of the space of Frankenstein's laboratory in terms of its material configuration—i.e., where objects stand in relation to one another, how large it is, what materials are included within—which presents the difficulty of discussing a particular place without the necessary descriptive cues for constructing an image. At the bottom of a long paragraph expressing Victor's internal state, Shelley gives a cursory, one sentence description of the laboratory. Victor explains: "In a solitary chamber, or rather cell, at the top of the house, and separated from all the other apartments by a gallery and staircase, I kept my workshop of filthy creation," and the sentence continues with a second clause, attached to the first with a semi-colon; "my eyeballs were starting from their sockets in attending to the details of my employment" (33). While Shelley does not provide detailed outlines and contours of a physical space of the laboratory, she clearly elaborates the way in which Victor perceives the laboratory subjectively. There is an intensity of feeling attached to the lab, and the descriptions of the labor within are less meticulous details for how one sutures flesh to flesh, than they are the sentiments and deeply felt internal emotions produced by the operations enacted. Shelley separates the room from the other living spaces in two dimensions—horizontally by a gallery, and vertically by a staircase—yet she also includes the lab within the larger structure proper to the space of everyday life. This depiction of the laboratory discloses a place at once inside and outside the Bourgeois home. Frankenstein's laboratory is, to be more precise, situated at the literal limit of the domestic enclosure, yet taking part only at the very edge; contained yet marking the threshold between the socio-political and the interiority of the lab.

What is most interesting, however, about Frankenstein's one sentence description of the laboratory is not the many references to the isolation and solitude of laboratory labor. That is, what appears as more revealing is not the content of the description, but rather the form of its presentation. The two clauses read grammatically articulate the same thought in separate ways, the semi-colon less of a break or transition than a suggestion that the two parts of the sentence share something essential with one another. The first clause of the sentence offers only description of the lab followed by the jarring cut and suture to a description of Frankenstein's own body, "my eyeballs were starting from their sockets in attending to the details of my employment" (32). It makes sense to some extent that a description of one's working environment would lead to a description of the felt intensity of labor. However there is a suggestion in the construction of the sentence that creates an analogy between the laboratory and Frankenstein's own body—the laboratory is the place of sight, the space in which one visualizes and witnesses the secrets and processes of nature; the eyes, and therefore the head (or more precisely the brain) are the seat of vision or a repository for knowledge. Thus, Victor's mind, as a combinatory of flesh and psyche, becomes through this sentence, a laboratory in its own right, set off from yet included within the body. In line with Descartes, Shelley's depiction gives intellectual labor as problematically removed from the material world, and affords the mind a privileged status at the expense of Victor's intense suffering. If one can make this connection between the laboratory and the head (which by extension includes the brain and mind), then the image of Frankenstein's eyeballs "starting from their sockets" suggests not only eyestrain, but also a certain pressure from within. It is as if the mind overflows with the information which it has absorbed, pressing the eyes out of the sockets and threatening to break free, much as the laboratory contains or imprisons Victor himself, as if "one doomed by slavery" (31). He is separated from all otherworldly affections, yet conversely is full of an overwhelming desire to pass what is gestating within to the world without.

Latour and the Laboratory: The Body as Instrument of Literary Labor

This brief and somewhat elliptical characterization of Victor's laboratory, one that suggests an isomorphic structure between the scientific laboratory and the psyche as a place of labor, leads me to suggest that theories of the scientific laboratory might provide useful models for understanding literary production. Of the work in science studies done on the techniques and practices of the laboratory—beginning in the late 1970s—Bruno Latour's discussion of the laboratory (specifically in *Science in Action*) is instructive for my own experiment to test the fidelity between scientific laboratory labor and literary laboratory labor. While one might read this articulation metaphorically, I contend that the most profound insight comes from understanding the isomorphic and nonmetaphorical nature of the connection.

After considering the collective production of scientific knowledge through conversation and debate in a paper world (articles in journals, periodicals, etc.), Latour insists that in order to understand scientific production one must return to the place of experimentation, the laboratory to which the scientific literature points. Latour defines the laboratory most broadly as the place that produces inscriptions that will be included in a scientific paper, and thus added to a debate or struggle in process over the status of nature or reality. Because the conception of the instrument is central to his definition of the laboratory, it is necessary to draw out in more detail what Latour considers an instrument. Latour explains, "I will call an instrument (or inscription device) any set-up, no matter what its size, nature and cost, that provides a visual display of any sort in a scientific text" (68). He provides examples to elaborate further on this already somewhat abstract conception:

> For instance an optical telescope is an instrument, but so is an array of several radio-telescopes even if its constituents are separated by thousands of kilometers.... The definition is not provided by the cost nor by the sophisitication but only by this characteristic: the set-up provides an inscription that is used as the final layer in a scientific text [68].

A device or a set-up is not always an instrument, as he explains. It depends on time and history. If the readings are "black boxed"—a term Latour takes from cybernetic discourse that is "used whenever a piece of machinery or a set of commands is too complex [such that] in its place they draw a little box about which they need to know nothing but its input and output" (2–3)—then the set-up is no longer an instrument. It becomes one again, however, when it is put to use in a controversy. This goes for the separate instruments in a total assemblage that, when operating in tandem with the whole set-up to produce a reading or inscription, become instruments in their own right when their individual functions or readings come into question. There is a further advantage, he explains, to his conception of an instrument:

> It does not make presuppositions about what the instrument is made of. It can be a piece of hardware like a telescope, but it can also be made of softer material. A statistical institution that employs hundreds of pollsters, sociologists and computer scientists gathering all sorts of data on the economy *is* an instrument if it yields inscriptions for papers written in economic journals with, for instance, a graph of the inflation rate by month and by branch of industry. No matter how many people were made to participate in the construction of the image, no matter how long it took, no matter how much it cost, the whole institution is used as *one* instrument

(as long as there is no controversy that calls its intermediate readings into question). [...] At the other end of the scale, a young primatologist who is watching baboons in the savannah and is equipped only with binoculars, a pencil and a sheet of white paper may be seen as an instrument if her coding of baboon behaviour is summed up in a graph [68–9].

Now armed with the concept of the instrument, Latour can now more precisely define what he means by the laboratory: "Using this notion we can define more precisely than earlier the laboratory as any place that gathers one or several instruments together" (69).

Taking Latour's model for the scientific laboratory into the realm of literary labor, the instrument becomes the array or set-up that leads to a visual display, here transposed into literary figures and images, in the final literary text. The amorphous nature of Latour's laboratory, a point he never addresses directly, is here made even more complex in the literary laboratory. As in Latour's analysis, the production of text is only the most visible and immediate access one has to the recording processes in the laboratory. Latour moves from the world of paper into the messy and chaotic world of experimentation, invention, and production. When a reader and possible "dissenter" can participate (even if just as witness) in the creation of an image or a figure, he or she can see that the figure "has been *extracted* from the instruments in [the laboratory], *cleaned, redrawn,* and *displayed*" (65). Furthermore, it also becomes clear that "the images that were the last layer in the text, are the *end result* of a long process in the laboratory that we are now starting to observe" (65). Just as there is a world beyond that of the paper to which the figures, tables, graphs, images, or visual displays point, there is as well a world beyond paper, a specific production process, that gives rise to literature. Behind the cleaned, redrawn, and reorganized visual displays is a complex apparatus of instruments, recording devices, and machinery that we might call, for example, the family, or perhaps society in general.

Within the literary laboratory, the inscriptions from the body as instrument—those figures, images, or feelings that cannot verbalize themselves yet leave traces—are what Deleuze and Guattari in *What Is Philosophy?* call "percepts" and "affects" (something I will return to in the next section). What distinguishes art, then, is the fact that it produces ways of seeing and ways of feeling through material inscriptions. Shelley herself can be considered an instrument in that, following Latour's suggestion, the controversy surrounding the definitions of science or the human, as given through her figures and images, remain rife. Indeed, composed in a period of revolutions in the political and economic spheres, *Frankenstein* contributed to the question of the human and the role of art and science as problematics that arose in moments of profound change.

Latour's critical analysis of scientific production in the laboratory extends to an analysis of literary production within the creative writer's space of production, a space which I would argue demands to be thought of both in terms of the built environment (the network of various apparatus, spaces, bodies, and so on), but also in terms of the psychic space of the writer, the emergent imaginary realm that arises from the entire history of the experiences of a body that contributed to the production of the writer's psyche. It is to this more abstract conception of the space of literature that I will now turn.

The Space of Literature

In the penultimate paragraph of her introduction to the 1831 edition of *Frankenstein*, Shelley speaks of her novel as the "offspring of happy days," and bids her "hideous progeny go forth and prosper" (173). This playful comment has been the invitation for *Frankenstein* scholars to claim that the novel, and specifically the process of production of the creature, and I would add with and through the laboratory, allegorizes its own process of production.[2] Thus, *Frankenstein* scholars see Shelley as a type of "Frankenstein" to her monstrous book. This being the case, where or what might be Shelley's laboratory? Of course, the labor of writing (the production of the novel itself) must take place, must occur in and through a particular space of production. This is not space as empty container waiting to be the scene of a laboring body, but rather the co-creation of a laboring body with the environment in which production occurs; a setting up of the conditions of possibility. The laboratory comes into being with the scientist or the writer in a type of co-causal circuit. Shelley's laboratory might include her home, a specific room in which she wrote, an office, a study, a studio, and so on. H.G. Wells, for example, called the room in which he wrote his "cell," a term that Victor uses for his laboratory. We could call it her social network of leading radical Romantic intellectuals, not only Godwin's circle, but Percy's circle as well. We could call it the psychological space carved out by the framing of the novel, a point at which language wraps back around on itself producing an internal or enclosed world of the text. This is what literary critic Pierre Macherey refers to as the "literary space": "The 'literary space' in which the work finds its place is, finally, nothing more than the line coiled in the text" (Macherey 50). Additionally, Virginia Woolf speaks of the structure of novels as analogs to built environments in *A Room of One's Own*: "[The novel] is a structure leaving a shape on the mind's eye, built now in squares, now pagoda shaped, now throwing out wings and arcades, now solidly compact and domed like the Cathedral of Saint Sofia at Constantinople" (Woolf 71). Finally, and perhaps most immediately, the labor of writing literature takes place first within the body and mind of the writer him or herself as the primary inscriptions of experiences both on the flesh and in the memory. The body/mind becomes the central instrument in and through which these previous inscriptions are cleaned, redrawn, given form, and transferred to the page in the form of images and figurative language.

Perhaps one of the most persistent attempts to understand the production process of literature, and therefore to understand literature's very being, can be found in Maurice Blanchot's *The Space of Literature*. Blanchot's attempts to trace the contours of this "space" lead him to posit the boundaries and limits that must be placed on the interminable, the impossible, the unsayable, or the infinite if the work is to exist. The desire inherent in literature's origin to reach the absolute or totality—death for Blanchot—cannot be allowed to operate unrestrained. In order for thought to be sensible, in order for literary discourse to make sense, it must work with the conventions of language, with syntax and grammar. It must also work with and on the history of literature, its themes, figures, and modes. But even before this, Blanchot seems to be saying, the writer must restrain him or herself from the desire to say everything, to capture all of life and death in the work, or to bind the entirety of chaos itself. Even so, and perhaps ironically, the "work" for Blanchot cannot exist without this confrontation with chaos, with that which dismantles or threatens the destruction of human-made forms of thought.

Deleuze and Guattari, in line with Blanchot, speak of D.H. Lawerence's metaphor for poetry, a metaphor that Deleuze and Guattari apply to all forms of thought, as an "umbrella" that shelters people from "chaos." As they explain, "people are constantly putting up an umbrella that shelters them and on the underside of which they draw a firmament and write their conventions and opinions" (203). This transcendent "firmament," which produces the image of the infinite, or of a totality, is precisely what the artist, with the aid of chaos, struggles against. Even while the artwork might produce a totality in itself removed from the external world, its confrontation with chaos rents open those fixed opinions that become regulating truth. "Chaos" gives Deleuze and Guattari a concept of pure immanence in which forms constantly emerge and disappear, yet they insist that chaos is not disorder, nor is it nothingness, which would distinguish the concept of "chaos" as absolute immanence, a move that carries Blanchot's concept of "Death" away from its inevitable dialectical overtones. "Chaos," like Lem's Solaris, is "a void that is not a nothingness but a *virtual*, containing all possible particles and drawing out all possible forms, which spring up only to disappear immediately, without consistency or reference, without consequence" (118). This is the massive churning of the real, which is accessed from the vantage of thought's various forms. Literature, then, takes the historical forms of language and works on them, exposing them to chaos, and thus challenging fixed opinions as transitory or temporary shelters from chaos. As they explain, "poets, artists, make a slit in the umbrella, they tear open the firmament itself, to let in a bit of free and windy chaos and to frame in a sudden light a vision that appears through the rent…" (203).

Blanchot, for his part, suggests that an unwavering desire must push the writer to attempt to capture everything in language, though to make possible the production of literature, this desire must be present along with the restraint of the author, the holding back that allows for the work to emerge, which otherwise would result in a type of paralysis, the lure of the Sirens in which the poet is silenced by death. Blanchot explains the impulse or need to write as the approach towards the limits of language itself, a point at which one risks the disaster of saying nothing. He explains this in the following way:

> The need to write is linked to the approach toward this point at which nothing can be done with words. Hence the illusion that if one maintained contact with this point even as one came back from it to the world of possibility, "everything" could be done, "everything" could be said. This need must be suppressed and contained. If not, it becomes so vast that there is no more room or space for its realization [52].

Blanchot may have in mind the immediacy of an intuition of totality, in a Kabalistic sense (he does after all quote Gershom Scholem), of the moment at which the individual connects immediately to the immanence of existence. In another sense, this point may be simply the lived and living experience of the body—feelings, sensations, perceptions, affections, etc.—which, due to the complexity of their arising, become impossible to capture fully in language. The point is somehow beyond the "world of possibility." Does this mean that it is the realm of impossibility? In a sense it is, because it gives the hope to those in the realm of possibility, in the realm where things "can be done with words," that one could do and say "everything," which is of course not possible. The need (to say everything) in its realization is the production of literature—writing poetry, writing fiction. One must produce a reduction of chaos—not chaos itself but a cosmos, a microcosmos. The space of literature, what I am here calling the literary laboratory, is that conjunction that might include a frame of mind, disposition, habit, and physical place, that allows for the realization of this need.

The laboratory is the condition of possibility for the production of literary as well as scientific discourse, bringing together physical places, the human body, discourses, machinery, instruments, and so on as co-actors in production. In other words, the lab is a coordination of a host of actors and an environment in the production of a place in and through which labor occurs. The writer works on language, on images, on literary history, or history in general as, in the words of Frederic Jameson, the "raw materials" of a real material history in the production of something new (Jameson xiii). Perhaps most important, the writer works on relations—relations between humans, between humans and others, between humans and nature, and between humans and technology. Taking a political relation into the literary laboratory allows the writer to concentrate, isolate, purify, or experiment on this relationship in ways that would be impossible if situated within the complexity of the world outside, whether it be a relationship between two people, between nations, or in more speculative genres, between different species. In this sense both the scientific and literary laboratory reduce the complexity of the surrounding world, and in their autonomy experiment with materials—social, political, economic structures, affects and percepts—in a way that would simply be impossible otherwise. Thus, the laboratory of literature produces the conditions of possibility for reworking social relations.

In a 1983 essay, five years before *Science in Action*, Latour directly addresses the connection between the laboratory and its larger sociopolitical context in a way that might help flesh out the observations made above. In his essay "Give Me a Laboratory and I Will Raise the World," Latour looks specifically at Pasteur's invention of an anthrax vaccine for farm animals in 1881 as a way to understand how the products of the laboratory make demands on society as a whole, and thereby transform the lab into an invaluable space and unavoidable junction for the larger network of those concerned. The careful study shows how lab work and its products came to be necessarily incorporated into French society by "extending the laboratory itself" (150–1) out to ever expanding spheres of influence. It is through the processes of "displacements" and "translations" that the laboratory comes to radically blur the lines between inside/outside and micro/macro. In this sense, Latour's essay complicates and expands the sociological understandings of the politics of laboratory work. As he notes, Pasteur was a lousy politician and failed miserably in his attempts to participate in French electoral politics. This, however, does not mean that the labor of Pasteur was not political. In fact, Latour argues that "The congenital weakness of the sociology of science is its propensity to look for obvious stated political motives and interests in one of the only places, the laboratories, where sources of fresh politics as yet unrecognized as such are emerging" (157). This leads him to the bold statement "*Microbiology laboratories are one of the few places where the very composition of the social context has been metamorphosed*" (his italics 158).

It is on this point that Latour's essays is particularly useful in the context of *Frankenstein*. Latour attempts to convince his reader of his claims with a striking analogy between Pasteur's microbes and the emergent laboring masses at the time. This analogy transposes Latour's own theorization of the scientific laboratory into a political economic sphere in much the way that Victor Frankenstein's laboratory creation, a human being, collapses scientific laboratory work with political and ethical issues for the human subject. If the "reader isn't convinced," Latour asserts, that the laboratory is truly as powerful a force in determining the social makeup, "then he can compare the sudden moves made at the same time by socialist politicians, talking on behalf of another crowd of new, dangerous, undisciplined and disturbing forces for whom room should be made in society: the labouring masses" (158). The microbe is here related to the "labouring masses" through the way in which scientist/politicians mobilized and made visible previously invisible entities. I argue that Shelley's own literary laboratory, together with the human creature stitched together from a multitude within a scientific laboratory, makes explicitly visible what in Latour remains an underdeveloped analogy. I will conclude my essay, then, with a consideration of how this plays out in Shelley's novel.

The Creature's Reading and the Social Laboratory

The creature's narrative, describing his own experiences, acts as a juncture for the multiple levels of laboratory literature. Not only was the creature a material product of Victor's labor, and by extension Mary Shelley's own laboratory experiment, but his actions also disclose and collapse the multiple levels at which laboratory literature functions. The creature's relationship to literature is a way to understand the role of literature in the production of the human, yet also suggests the continued importance of literature as an active partner in the construction of what might be called a social laboratory in which the various monstrous and contingent products of particular sites of production might find a relevance and meaning for a larger social whole.

Nowhere is the importance of literature in the production of society and the human subject clearer than that moment in the novel when the creature becomes self-aware. At the end of his detailed account of the formative influence of the De Lacey family, for whom he felt great affection, the creature describes the other sources of profound influence. These three books that he encountered fortuitously in the woods provide the creature with a specific context, one that epitomizes the way in which an English Romantic might understand his or her relation to the rest of society and nature: *Plutarch's Lives* provides an epic account of Western history; *The Sorrows of Young Werther* gives the creature a sense of the profound depth of sentiment and feeling of a contemporary bourgeois individual; and *Paradise Lost* provides him not only with a key canonical text for the history of English literature, but also maps out for him the mythological structure, Christianity, to which much of Europe is beholden. Remembering this first literary experience, the creature explains: "I can hardly describe to you the effect of these books. They produced in me an infinity of new images and feelings, that sometimes raised me to ecstasy, but more frequently sunk me into the lowest dejection" (Shelley 86). The impact is something the creature can "hardly describe," just beyond or at the limits of signifying language. The feelings produced are importantly listed alongside the "infinity of new images" that led the creature through the entire range of human emotion—from "ecstasy" to "the lowest dejection." As a description of the creature's formation following his narrative of the De Lacey family, the idea that these books incited in him "new images" resonates with his purely voyeuristic relationship to the De Lacey's, but is also reminiscent of the way in which Deleuze and Guattari speak of literature as the production of new or intensified "affects" and "percepts," or ways of seeing.

If anything else, it is important to note Shelley's explicit move through a theory of reading and learning that resonates, as has been suggested by others, with the importance given to education and self-advancement in Rousseau, Locke, and other philosophers, as well as the centrality of enculturation for the *Bildungsroman*. The creature himself furthers this connection between viewing the De Lacey family, education, and his private reading experience: "The cottage of my protectors had been the only school in which I had studied human nature; but this book [*Paradise Lost*] developed new and mightier scenes of action" (87). Not only was the creature aware of the hovel as a space of learning, as a "school" in which he "studied human nature," the creature here implies that the books, specifically *Paradise Lost*, provided an even "mightier" insight into human nature put in terms of the book's development of "scenes of action."

Here again, as with Victor's laboratory, Shelley collapses a physical space with a psychological space; the pedagogical place of the cottage/hovel with the even more pedagogically effective mental "scenes of action" of the book. True, then, to the Romantic revolution in poetry discussed by Rancière in *The Flesh of Words*, Shelley gives the creature's experiences with real life and the literary—whether it be history, poetry, or the novel—at once in a single sentence, or in the same thought. Thus, the creature's real life experience and the literary come to be, in a sense, interchangeable with one another. The literary book merges with and becomes indistinguishable from the "book" of his own reality.

Of all the creature's experiences, the most defining moment was his discovery, and later ability to decipher, Frankenstein's lab notes. This is where the theory of reading, the power of literature as laboratory, and the nature of laboratory work all come to a head. The creature is bodily text to the lab notes' written text—both are aspects of one another—which is why the creature presupposes that Frankenstein would only need the "lab notes" in order to create another creature like him. The book here, Victor's laboratory journal, is literally that which becomes flesh. The creature, perhaps better than any other, understands and feels the "flesh" of the book in that he himself is that living flesh. Victor's laboratory notes are a book of genesis for the creature, and describe in detail the process that led to the instilling the creature with the "principle of life." Just as the body of Christ is made flesh in the scriptures, the creature is the living flesh of Victor's laboratory notes. Ironically, the laboratory notes produce perhaps the most powerful emotional response from the creature who explains, "I sickened as I read." Coming to the laboratory journal after Milton, the creature can no longer situate himself and his life's meaning within the metaphysical system of Christianity. The exposure to his origin does not, as one might expect, lead to the creature's emancipation. Rather, the creature feels excluded from a meaningful and fulfilling existence.

What the creature fails to see, what he becomes blinded to after reading Milton, is that although heaven may not apply to him, neither does the rest of the Christian system. In this sense, he cannot properly be understood as "fallen," and is not the product of an "original sin." As he himself expresses, citing a line by Percy Shelley, "I was dependent on none, and related to none. 'The path of my departure was free...'" (Shelley 86). Indeed, he has the potential for living in the world, here and now, without it being corrupted or overshadowed by a life beyond this one, even if this potential becomes foreclosed in the narrative after the fact. Interestingly, the creature's central problem is definitively not, as it is for Victor and Walton, a search for the unknown or for that which remains inaccessible to knowledge. He has the entire knowledge of his origin—all of the secrets are given to him in the journal, and there is nothing more for him to know, nothing more for him to explore or discover.

Here is a work of art that does not offer a home to a people to come, as works of art have the potential to do for Deleuze and Guattari. Rather Frankenstein's creature calls to a future world, one that does not exist, that cannot possibly exist, but one that must nevertheless be created, as Pasteur did for his microbes. There are no models or blueprints to follow to create this world that corresponds to the creature, yet however well considered, no world that restricts or prohibits the creature's ability to labor within the social laboratory will suffice. In this sense, one of the creature's central issues may be restated as precisely the loss of a space of labor, the loss or dejection from what I would call a laboratory space (Victor's laboratory, the hovel, his books). The creature's condition is one far worse than having been abandoned by heaven; the creature is abandoned by human society. When considering the ways in which laboratory work might transform society, one cannot ignore the laboratory creations that demand an altered or new context, which enact translations or displacements, as Latour would say, that show the relevance of a localized laboratory production. The importance of laboratory literature is its continued insistence, not to map the utopian relations in its own fictional or illusory world onto real social relations, nor to make these imaginary constructions necessary models for a future world. Its importance, marked by the production of literature, the reading of a novel, or the space of interaction between a writer, a reader, and a material inscription—the laboratory of literature—is a constant reminder to work to transform society by making society itself the laboratory.

Notes

1. For a further discussion of these early sites of experimentation and the upper-class manor home see Shapin.
2. David Ketterer is perhaps the most important source here who has meticulously shown, in his 1979 book *Frankenstein's Creation: The Book, The Monster, and Human Reality*, the metaphorical connection between the "novel" *Frankenstein* and Victor Frankenstein's "creature" as its guiding thread to explore the thick tapestry of the novel's allusions, influences, and historical associations.

Works Cited

Baldick, Chris. *In Frankenstein's Shadow: Myth, Monstrosity, and Nineteenth-Century Writing*. New York: Oxford University Press, 1987. Print.
Bloom, Harold, ed. *Bloom's Modern Critical Interpretations: Frankenstein, Updated Edition*. New York: Infobase, 2007. Print.
Botting, Fred. *Making Monstrous: Frankenstein, Criticism, Theory*. Manchester: Manchester University Press, 1991. Print.
Brooks, Peter. "Godlike Science/Unhallowed Arts: Language and Monstrosity in *Frankenstein*." *New Literary History* 9.3 (1978): 591–605. Print.
Butler, Marlyn. "*Frankenstein* and Radical Science." *Frankenstein*. Ed. J. Paul Hunter. London: Norton, 1996. 302–312. Print.
Davy, Sir Humphrey. *Elements of Chemical Philosophy*, Philadelphia: Bradford and Inskeep, 1812. Print.
Deleuze, Gilles, and Félix Guattari. *What Is Philosophy?* Trans. Hugh Tomlinson and Graham Burchell. New York: Columbia University Press, 1994. Print.
Gigante, Denise. "Facing the Ugly: The Case of *Frankenstein*." *ELH* 67.2 (2000): 565–87. Print.
Good, H.G. "On the Early History of Liebig's Laboratory," *Journal of Chemical Education* 13.12 (1936): 557–562. Web. 6 June 2012.
Halberstam, Judith. *Skin Shows: Gothic Horror and the Technology of Monsters*. Durham: Duke University Press, 1995. Print.
James, Frank. *The Development of the Laboratory: Essays on the Place of Experiment in Industrial Civilization*. Ed. Frank James. London: Macmillan, 1989. Print.
Jameson, Fredric. *Archaeologies of the Future: The Desire Called Utopia and Other Science Fictions*. London: Verso, 2005. Print.
Ketterer, David. *Frankenstein's Creation: The Book, the Monster, and Human Reality*. Victoria: University of Victoria, 1979. Print.

Knellwolf, Christa, and Jane Goodall. *Frankenstein's Science: Experimentation and Discovery in Romantic Culture, 1780–1830.* Burlington: Ashgate, 2008. Print.

Latour, Bruno. "Give Me a Laboratory and I Will Raise the World." *Science Observed: Perspectives on the Social Study of Science.* Ed. Karin Knorr-Cetina and Michael Mulkay. London: Sage, 1983. 141–170. Print.

―――. *Science in Action: How to Follow Scientists and Engineers Through Society.* Cambridge: Harvard University Press, 1987. Print.

―――, and Steve Woolgar. *Laboratory Life: The Construction of Scientific Facts.* Princeton: Princeton University Press, 1979. Print.

Levine, George. *The Realistic Imagination: English Fiction from Frankenstein to Lady Chatterley.* Chicago: University of Chicago Press, 1981. Print.

―――, and U. C. Knoepflmacher, eds. *The Endurance of Frankenstein: Essays on Mary Shelley's Novel.* Berkeley: University of California Press, 1979. Print.

Macherey, Pierre. *A Theory of Literary Production.* Trans. Geoffrey Wall. London: Routledge, 2006. Print.

Montag, Warren. "'The Workshop of Filthy Creation': A Marxist Reading of Frankenstein." *Frankenstein.* Ed. Johanna M. Smith. *Case Studies in Contemporary Criticism.* Series Ed. Ross C. Murfin. Boston: Bedford Books, 1992. 300–311. Print.

Moretti, Franco. *Signs Taken for Wonders: On the Sociology of Literary Forms.* London: Verso, 2005. Print.

Mumford, Louis. *Technics and Civilization.* 1934. New York: Harcourt, Brace and World, 1963. Print.

Prigogine, Ilya, and Isabelle Stengers. *Order Out of Chaos: Man's New Dialogue with Nature.* Toronto: Bantam, 1984. Print.

Ranciere, Jacques. *The Flesh of Words: The Politics of Writing.* Trans. Charlotte Mandell. Stanford: Sanford University Press, 2004. Print.

Randel, Fred. "The Political Geography of Horror in Mary Shelley's *Frankenstein.*" *ELH* 70.2 (2003): 465–91. Print.

Shelley, Mary. *Frankenstein.* Ed. J. Paul Hunter. New York: Norton, 1996. Print.

Sterrenberg, Lee. "Mary Shelley's Monster: Politics and Psyche in *Frankenstein.*" *The Endurance of Frankenstein: Essays on Mary Shelley's Frankenstein.* Ed. George Levine and U. C. Knoepflmacher. Berkeley: University of California Press, 1979. 143–171. Print.

Thomson, Sir William, "Scientific Laboratories." *Nature* 31 (1885): 419–13. Print.

Welch, William. "The Evolution of Modern Scientific Laboratories." *Annual Report of the Board of Regents of the Smithsonian Institution.* Washington: Government-Printing Office, 1985. Print.

Whitman, Frank. "The Beginnings of Laboratory Teaching in America." *Science.* August 19, 1898. 201–6. *JSTOR.* Web. 16 June 2011.

Woolf, Virginia. *A Room of One's Own.* New York: Harcourt Brace, 1989. Print.

Ecotopian London
Morris's Geography of Conservation
Margaret S. Kennedy

> "Progress is the realisation of Utopias"—Oscar Wilde, "The Soul of Man Under Socialism"

> "And Science—we have loved her well, and followed her diligently, what will she do? I fear she is so much in the pay of the counting-house ... that she is too busy, and will for the present do nothing. Yet there are matters which I should have thought easy for her; say for example teaching Manchester how to consume its own smoke, or Leeds how to get rid of its superfluous black dye without turning it into the river, which would be as much worth her attention as the production of the heaviest of heavy black silks, or the biggest of useless guns"
> —William Morris, "The Lesser Arts"

In 1890, William Morris published *News from Nowhere*, transferring his longstanding ideas about Socialism, craftsmanship, and ecology into a narrative. His optimistic vision captured the public imagination and convinced critics of the practicality of his ideas. The book's "singular charm" won over reviewers (Johnson 339),[1] despite its relatively flat characters, and created a new genre, the ecotopia. Departing from popular science fiction, such as Richard Jefferies's *After London, Wild England* (1885) and H.G. Wells's *The Time Machine* (1895), dystopias critiquing faith in progress and the monstrous city, Morris's ecotopia challenges the belief that the city is inherently corrupt. Like his contemporaries, Morris questions the ability of science to rescue civilization, but rejects the Victorian trope of the city as an alienating abyss of filth. He creates a sustainable London, an urban ecology, through agrarian living. "Nowhere" is emphatically retrograde in its rural sensibility, yet fits squarely in the science fiction tradition by de-familiarizing London, producing strangeness through a process of rehabilitation that condemns human mastery of the environment. SF often functions as a diagnosis of contemporary problems, becoming a call to action by mapping possible alternatives (Suvin *MOSF* 12). If most SF depicts a dystopian world perverted by technology, Morris maps a geography of conservation, a blueprint for a sustainable place. Nowhere conserves handicraft, and as a result, the environment, suggesting how pollution may be reversed. Guest hopes, "if others can see it as I have seen it, then it may be called a vision rather than a dream" (228). Nowhere, or "no place," conceptualizes a possible future by sowing eco-consciousness intended to bloom into a cleaner, healthier England.

Morris called *News from Nowhere* a "utopian romance," but it is arguably science fiction, as Guest travels to an almost alien future. While technology is a feature in much SF, it is not a requirement of the genre. Rather, it depends on "cognitive estrangement" and the constructed future, though strange, being a possibility through human agency, thus neither mimetic nor fantastical.[2] Morris creates a recognizable London, but produces feelings of estrangement by reviving an agrarian past where humans live in harmony with an all-inclusive environment, not as masters that dominate it. Utopia is "the sociopolitical subgenre of science fiction" (Suvin "Counter Projects" 88), and for Morris it becomes the vehicle of eco-socialism. Morris's England, an ecotopia where craftsmanship and conservation intersect, rejecting modern toil in favor of medieval work, could will into existence a utopian design.

Morris problematizes SF's connotation with a technological future, arguing for back-to-the-land strategies as a legitimate alternate reality, in the process throwing into high relief contemporary environmental attitudes. Morris eliminates advanced technology from Nowhere, distinguishing between handicraft and science and dispelling the myth that increased technology can improve our welfare. Throughout his work, Morris differentiates between technology as we typically define it—advanced machinery, for instance—and *techne*: "an art, skill, or craft; a technique, principle, or method by which something is achieved or created," or "a product of this, a work of art" (OED). *Techne* points to the practical application of art, rather than the aesthetic creed of art for art's sake. Lecturing on a utopian future, Morris urges, "Let us remember that even savages live, though they have poor tools, no machinery, and no co-operation, in their work: but as soon as man begins to use good tools and work with some kind of co-operation he becomes able to produce more than enough for his own bare necessaries" ("Dawn of a New Epoch" *WMAS* 152). Morris emphasizes the role of community over machinery in achieving subsistence. Florence Boos calls Morris's prose style "the rhetoric of fellowship" in its accessibility ("An Aesthetic Ecocommunist"), and his style also mirrors his eco-consciousness: an ecosocialism encouraging fellowship with the land.

Certain key ideas emerge in Morris's lectures that *News from Nowhere* invokes, particularly scaling down production modeled on a feudal past. He believed an agrarian economy rooted in art could cure social ills and regain harmony with the environment, explaining that the arts, in their real meaning, "are surely the expression of reverence for nature" ("Architecture in Civilization" *WMAS* 60). In "Art Under Plutocracy," a lecture concerned with the gap between rich and poor, Morris connects the health of the land with the health of the people, arguing "the happiness of life is sickening in the house of civilization" (*WMAS* 119). The modern ecocritic Wendell Berry theorizes "health," the feeling of belonging to the community, a sense of place, and the satisfaction of a job well done, is opposed to "dis-ease," the consciousness of the division between our bodies and the world, or uneasiness about our separation from the natural world precipitated by industrialism (144).[3] Morris's oeuvre offers an early foray into these concepts, condemning "the sickness of the world" caused by reckless decadence and exploitation of the earth as a resource while producing cheap, excess goods ("The Art of the People"). Agrarian living, an overall reliance on the land, promotes health. Morris's philosophy is predicated on acknowledging realist nature, which Kate Soper theorizes as

> nature as matter, as physicality: that 'nature' whose properties and causal processes are the object of the biological and natural sciences. To speak of "nature" in this conception is to speak of those material structures and processes that are independent of human activity (in the sense that they are not a humanly created product), and whose forces and causal powers are the necessary conditions of every human practice, and determine the possible forms it can take [132–2].[4]

Human beings do not determine the environment; rather, human beings and their lifestyles are determined by the environment. Realist nature is democratic in that it reduces the human, in Aldo Leopold's famous phrase, to "plain member and citizen" of the ecosystem (204). Morris, a Social Democrat, erases class distinctions and, effectually, species distinctions, by recognizing the value in all creatures.[5]

Subsistence living does not imply drudgery. Morris frequently distinguishes between "useless toil" and "useful work," stressing the importance of beauty, equated with sustainability. An object is beautiful "if it is in accord with Nature, and helps her; ugly if it is discordant with Nature, and thwarts her; it cannot be indifferent" ("The Lesser Arts" *WMAS* 2). Useless toil "makes the thousand and one things which nobody wants," fulfilling sham desires to fuel commerce, wasting resources in the process, while pleasurable labor satisfies humanity's fundamental needs ("The Art of the People" *WMAS* 21). Morris's ecosocialism breaks down class barriers by dignifying handicraft, resting on the assumption that "it is the nature of man, when he is not diseased, to take pleasure in his work," identifying "cultivating the earth" as "the most necessary and pleasantest of all work" ("Useful Work *versus* Useful Toil" *WMAS* 128, 138), a sensibility made clear in *News from Nowhere*, when farm work is sought out as a respite from stationary or indoor occupations. Participating in the harvest restores health.

Continually differentiating between needs and wants, Morris argues health is encouraged by scaling down: "Simplicity of life, begetting simplicity of taste" ("The Lesser Arts" *WMAS* 15). As Boos explains, "By simplicity [...] Morris meant something like sustainability, self-sufficiency and abstention from conspicuous consumption" ("Ideals of Everyday Life" 160). "The Lesser Arts" contends an appreciation of beauty encourages the preservation of the environment.[6] If we value the beautiful, we will wish to preserve the environment, an aesthetic version of intrinsic value theory, which urges humans not to view the environment as a resource, but something to be benignly enjoyed. Art raises consciousness. Attacking capitalism, Morris advocates sustainable living, where wealth, like health, depends on cultivating the land. He defines wealth as "what Nature gives us and what a reasonable man can make out of the gifts of Nature for his reasonable use. The sunlight, the fresh air, the unspoiled face of the earth..." ("Useful Work *versus* Useless Toil" *WMAS* 131). Wealth, then, is determined by comfort (subsistence living) instead of capital.

"[B]lindness to the natural beauty of the earth" is equated with carelessness, while the appreciation of beauty cultivated by art is the earth's "only possible guardian" ("The Prospects of Architecture in Civilization" *WMAS* 60). Concepts in common with Victorian Natural History, such as "seeing" rather than looking and wonder at ecological webs, permeate *News from Nowhere*. The "short-sightedness" of humanity is a recurring thread in Morris's lectures and his ecotopian novel where he emphasizes aware vision, the naturalist gaze, which reveals natural wonders while critiquing science. Technology should eliminate pollution, rather than cause it: "Science duly applied would enable [people] to get rid of refuse, to minimize it, if not wholly to destroy, all the inconveniences which at present attend the use of elaborate machinery, such as smoke, stench, and noise; nor would they endure that the buildings in which they worked or lived should be ugly blots on the fair face of the earth" ("Useful Work *versus* Useless Toil" *WMAS* 140). Science becomes problematic when it recklessly manipulates the environment, ignoring the symbiosis between human beings and their habitat. A certain amount of pollution is inevitable—all animals impact the earth; our duty, however, is to "minimize" our impact.

In *News from Nowhere*, these concepts of meaningful work and dependency on and observance of natural law cultivate a sense of place, in an "actual" place. Utopia refers both to *eu-topos* (good place) and *ou-topos* (no place), and despite using "Nowhere" in his title, Morris re-maps actual England into a "good place" by constructing meaningful relationships with local environments. In the spirit of learning "to love the narrow spot that surrounds our daily life" ("Art and the Beauty of the Earth" *WMAS* 91), Morris considers how to resuscitate and preserve the health of London, as opposed to simply retreating into a rural or imagined setting. Morris's significant intervention into environmentalist thought was his promotion of an urban ecology: *rus in urbe*, bringing the country to the city. In "Art and the Beauty of the Earth," Morris insists, "We must turn this land from the grimy backyard of a workshop into a garden.If that seems difficult, or rather impossible, to some of you, I cannot help it; I only know that it is necessary" (*WMAS* 93). "Garden" indicates rehabilitation and conservation while conflating country and city.[7] His cities encompass rural elements—livestock, horse-drawn vehicles, farming, etc.—creating an *urban* pastoral, or an urban ecology, which reconciles man-made, artificial elements with the natural landscape. Here manifests the type of science Morris desires, cultivating land in a sustainable way: *techne*, or manual tools, rather than machinery.

Morris's "Society of the Future" is "a society conscious of a wish to keep life simple, to forego some of the power over nature won by past ages in order to be more human and less mechanical, and willing to sacrifice something to this end. It would be divided into small communities varying much within the limits allowed by due social ethics, but without rivalry between each other, looking with abhorrence at the idea of a holy race" (*WMAS* 183). The terms "citizen" and "nation" do not exist in Nowhere. In this cosmopolitan view, the people conceive of their places seamlessly connecting to "the outlands" or other areas; they are aware of their place in the earth as a whole, not separated by the imagined borders of "England" per se.[8] Dissected into what Martin Delveaux calls "mini-cities," Nowhere combines "traditional agricultural practices and de-urbanisation/reforestation with modern, pollution-free use of science in transport, energy and telecommunication, revealing a hybridity between pre- and post-industrialism" (77). Nowhere does not regress into a feudal past, but improves on the model. While the city becomes a community center, there is no evidence of urban sprawl (cancerous growth).

Morris's urban ecotopia proves the possibility of dwelling in the city, and is thus literally an "ecopolis," fitting Paul F. Downton's modern definition of a sustainable, ecological city: "an attempt to return to the human scale in city making, to return to the idea of city as community, and to make the city the centre of restorative activity rather than destruction, in dynamic balance within itself and with the nature of the land that supports it" (4). Indeed, he acknowledges his debt to Morris, "paraphrasing" his concerns about "how we live" and "the way we might live" (7). The ideal city is a web that interconnects with other webs. Morris presages E.F. Schumacher's economic ideal, "small is beautiful": "Small-scale operations, no matter how numerous, are always less likely to be harmful to the natural environment than large-scale ones, simply because their individual force is small in relation to the recuperative forces of nature" (37). Schumacher identifies the "economics of giantism" as a product of 19th century thinking (79), and could easily be quoting Morris when he recommends an agrarian economics oriented "towards the threefold ideal of health, beauty, and permanence" (121), "a direction that shall lead [the economy] back to the real needs of man" (169). Morris's eco-socialism thus laid important groundwork for contemporary environmentalism, as well as offering a counter-discourse to Victorian faith in technology's limitless potential for progress.

More than merging country and city, urban ecology wholly deconstructs binary thinking (self/Other; nature/culture). Clara, one of Guest's guides, asks of the Victorians:

> Was not their mistake once more bred of the life of slavery that they had been living?—a life which was always looking upon everything, except mankind, animate and inanimate—"nature," as people used to call it—as one thing, and mankind as another. It was natural to people thinking in this way, that they should try to make "nature" their slave, since they thought "nature" was something outside them [200].

Victorians attempted to harness nature to fuel their large-scale industries. Nowhere renders the term Nature obsolete. Environment is regarded as a habitat, so much part of the human experience it cannot be conceived or discussed separately from it. Realist nature reveals human beings as part of an ecology, including plants, animals, and land. Proper cities build a community that comprises all creatures, satisfying Leopold's definition of "a land ethic," which "enlarges the boundaries of the community to include soils, waters, plants, and animals, or collectively: the land" (204). A sustainable community requires "simplicity" or back-to-the-land ways of living to limit harm to the ecosystem.

Such a geography of conservation emerges in *News from Nowhere*, which narrates the optimistic vision of William Guest as, returning home from a meeting of the Socialist League, he is instead transported to 21st century London, journeying through sustainable places along the Thames. Various guides (presumably Guest's descendants) navigate him through alien concepts such as "shopping" without money. Nowhere, completely decentralized, lacks government and formal education systems, deregulating trade and institutions such as marriage. Dick, the waterman, his lover Clara, and his grandfather, Old Hammond, "lecture" on these socialist principles and the proper relationship to the land, while Guest answers questions about his "planet," as Victorian England's concepts of wealth, the nation, and civilization are equally foreign.[9] Guest is schooled in the eco-consciousness, the type of practical knowledge valued in Nowhere, that revived the environment. Recovering from his first feeling of "delicious relief caused by the fresh air and pleasant breeze," Guest experiences "mere measureless wonder" (45). In Nowhere, people continually wonder at the individuality of each season and the abundance of the land. The woods become a schoolroom, teaching people to see not

Nature, an idealized or subjective landscape, but realist nature, an interface between the human and non-human. Guest adopts an "archeological natural-history" mode (55), a way of "seeing" the environment's actual impact, which produces for him the alienating effect that characterizes SF. Nowhere, as potential England, is not an invented place with imagined conditions; the naturalist gaze reveals realist nature to Guest for the first time, and the combined effect of Nowhere's future setting and Guest's past vision are continually unsettling.

The novel opens on the railway, iconic of Victorian progress and technology, where Guest is "stewing discontentedly" "in that vapour-bath of hurried and discontented humanity, a carriage of the underground railway" (43). "Vapour," a familiar Victorian key word for miasma, suggests both the smoke from the railway and smoggy conditions more generally, and as Morris uses it here, a sense of dis-ease: anxiety and depression caused by disharmony with the environment. Living in pollution pollutes the mind. Guest suffers from the actual smog *and* its cause: capitalist industry. As he exits the carriage, into the post-industrial future of Nowhere, he experiences "an indefinable kind of look of being at home and at ease" (171). Transported to 2003, Guest experiences health for the first time on the shore of a renewed Thames. The soap-works, the lead-works, and other industries with "smoke-vomiting" chimneys have disappeared (48).

As Norman Talbot puts it, Guest is "baptized in the new Thames" (43), made possible by the purified water, suggesting both the water's transformation and its transformative powers. The Thames, full of salmon and clean enough to bathe, presents a stark contrast to Dickens's *Our Mutual Friend*, a novel deliberately brought to mind by Morris's revision of Boffin, a recognizable figure of "the degrading effects of class-based wealth in nineteenth-century literature" (Donaldson 30). Dick, the waterman who first befriends Guest, acknowledges the connection, telling Guest, "we only call him Boffin as a joke, partly because he is a dustman, and partly because he will dress so showily" (60).

Boffin literally becomes a "Golden Dustman" (60), but rather than made rich by the copious waste of London, wealth is determined by sufficient livelihood. Guest frequently marvels at what he regards as fancy dress; self-adornment is the norm in Nowhere, as everyone has free access to quality materials. Each laborer—be it dustman, historian, reaper—contributes equally to the landscape, eliminating professional hierarchy. Morris showcases the unglamorous profession of a dustman to emphasize this point, as well as to juxtapose dis-eased Victorian England with a healthy future, allowing the reader to see realist nature more clearly.[10] Laura Donaldson also explores the ennobling of Boffin, asking, "If the figure of Boffin in *News from Nowhere* embodies Morris's goals for the transformation of nineteenth-century cultural and literary values, the question remains: transformed from what?" (29).[11] Donaldson posits Morris's "artistry of reversal"—converting the sordid scavenging of the river in a filthy boat into Guest's wholesome journey to the harvest—"ultimately enlarges to include all dimensions of society" (37), introducing a clear polemic.

Boffin's function is primarily symbolic, since being a dustman at all is a contradiction.[12] There is no waste (dust) in Nowhere, as Old Hammond explains, "The wares which we make are made because they are needed: men make for their neighbors' use as if they were making for themselves, not for a vague market of which they know nothing[…]. Nothing can be made except for genuine use" (127). As men now know precisely what they want, they "are not driven to make a vast quantity of useless things," allowing them the time to make useful goods with care and enjoyment (127). Conspicuous consumption, what Morris calls a wasteful "fever" in his lecture "The Society of the Future" (*WMAS* 185), is eliminated in this economy, which moves from large-scale manufacturing to cooperative craftsmanship.

Morris frequently argues that the division between the classes is that of "waste and want" ("The Art of the People" *WMAS* 33). Laborers work to pay tribute to the rich, denied the use of the goods they make; commerce functions to create goods for the wealthy to waste, producing a false demand. A clear disservice to laborers, this system also renders the rich helpless. Hammond laughs "at that silly nineteenth-century fashion […] of ignoring all the steps by which their daily dinner was reached, as matters too low for their lofty intelligence" (94). He scoffs at being "civilized" if that means neglecting physical work, upending the definition of a gentleman as one who doesn't dirty his hands. Accruing monetary wealth becomes irrelevant: "The reward of labour is *life*," Hammond tells Guest (122). Morris's conservation ethic relies on craftsmanship, which by obeying realist nature, or understanding the determining influence of the environment, operates on a more proportionate scale to satisfy "real" needs.

Differentiating between *techne* and technology, Hammond

denounces 19th century machinery for increasing the burden of labor and glutting the market with useless goods. Civilization, or "organized misery" (126), is antagonistic to realist nature. If to be savage is to reject mass-manufacture, which distances human beings from their environment, Hammond happily accepts the label. Tools that facilitate our subsistence and our art are in a different class than the factory, steamboat, etc., that mass produce or operate on a large scale. In "The Soul of Man Under Socialism," Oscar Wilde insisted, "At present machinery competes against man. Under the proper conditions machinery will serve man" (1183). While SF is characteristically preoccupied by the fear of technology overcoming humankind, Morris creates Wilde's conditions in Nowhere, condemning not only technology that usurps handicraft, but technology that destroys the integrity of the environment. Abolishing manufacturing is necessary for the health of the ecosystem: "whatever coal or mineral we need is brought to grass and sent wither it is needed with as little as possible of dirt, confusion, and the distressing of quiet people's lives" (102). In his version of SF, Morris proposes a new paradigm, where technology is carefully evaluated, only utilized if a job cannot be adequately or comfortably performed by hand. Dick explains, "this is not an age of inventions. The last epoch did all that for us, and we are now content to use such of its inventions as we find handy, and leaving those alone which we don't want" (192).

Thus factories become "banded-workshops; that is, places where people collect who want to work together" (81). Surprised, Guest sees "'no smoke coming from the furnaces' […]. To which Dick replies, "'why should you see smoke?'" (82). Morris did not dismiss science altogether, but felt our energies needed to be redirected to invent cleaner, sustainable technologies, what we would call "alternative energy" today. "Force-barges" operate with an unspecified clean fuel (186), which Morris leaves to posterity to invent. This smarter manufacturing, or *techne*, is in fact created by science and satisfies needs as well, or better than, big industry.

These "banded-workshops" run on cooperation. As everyone will work to provide for him/herself, agrarianism further destroys the difference between laborer and employer, or the class system generally. Hammond explains that the "means of the fructification of labour, the land, machinery, capital, means of transit, &c.," were taken out of the idle hands that exploited unpaid labor and put into the hands of the workers (153). Hammond describes the commons theory, the availability of public land as opposed to private, enclosed property. Morris believed everyone owned the land, or rather that no one did.[13] Eliminating notions of ownership, if everyone is granted access to the land, the primary cause of dis-ease is eradicated. The Revolution, set in 1952, is successful because a universal strike makes the wealthy powerless: "thousands of middle-class families, who were utterly dependent for the next meal on the workers" (149), became frantic trying to support themselves with no practical knowledge. The public, recognizing their reliance on the worker, and the environment by extension, is forced to capitulate.

Eco-socialism allows one to meet his/her basic needs, working the land for subsistence, not wages. The land is never exploited as a resource, but the workers in Nowhere are aware of its determining impact on their lives. Marx's "freedom to fish" means the freedom to meet one's needs through the land, which is impossible if land is privatized.[14] Morris is vitriolic against a system where farm laborers are not allowed to work the land for themselves; following the whims and instructions of their employer, they were often thwarted in maximizing the potential of the land, weakening the harvest for all. Thus, urbanites and rural laborers alike could be denied the ability to meet their subsistence through the land. Morris builds a community democratizing art, weaving a web of cooperation and dependence. Utopia, really ecotopia, requires an agrarian model—a radically altered perception of humanity's place in the ecosystem—to produce ideal, universal conditions.

Hammond summarizes England's historical progress: moving from an imperfect feudalism to the even less desirable capitalism, "it is now a garden, where nothing is wasted and nothing is spoilt, with the necessary dwellings, shed, and workshops scattered up and down the country, all trim and neat and pretty" (105). Hammond specifically calls to mind Morris's use of "garden" as metaphor for urban ecology. A garden becomes emblematic of cultivating the land for livelihood, intervening into the landscape without subduing it. This is a far cry from the picturesque gardens of the 18th century, well-manicured properties meant to be admired from a respectable distance. "Trim," a word Hammond uses above, comes to signify the Victorian garden philosophy. It suggests care, generally meaning orderly, but it could also be a pejorative term, resonant of restraint and bourgeois taste. Michael Waters explains, "[I]n many contexts, 'trim' contrasts with 'tumbledown,'" and since Morris frequently uses trim to describe interiors, it serves "as a paradigm of the relations between people and nature under ideal conditions" (17), the "happy union of house and (formal) garden" (18). A garden, then, is not a wild space, but a shared space, the *rus in urbe*. However, Morris also employs "trim" negatively to indicate unnecessary manipulation of the landscape. Guest notices that woods lose their "gameskeeperish trimness, and were as wild and beautiful as need be, though the trees were clearly well seen to" (183). Morris makes a distinction between dominating the land like a gamekeeper—sculpting the environment—and necessary intervention. A garden, essentially a small-scale farm attached to the home, is independent of the forests. This suggests a separation between land used for cultivation, and woods and similar spaces that should be conserved. Morris prefers wildness, though acknowledging necessary maintenance such as removing dead branches or cutting back overgrowth. He clearly resists idealizing the environment, and such recognitions of the reciprocal relationship with land ground his use of realist nature.

In a sense, to till a garden is to make land a "home," a version of Heideggerian "dwelling," a term appropriated by ecocritics to mean living practically within the environment, coexistence, and duty and responsibility to the earth (Garrard 108).[15] To dwell is to be, and to let be; it is symbiosis with the earth. Morris repeatedly uses the words "dwelling," "dwelling-place," and "dweller," indicating his residents do not simply live in a particular location, but participate in its ecosystem. Hammond explains, "The spirit of the new days, of our days, was to delight in the life of the world; intense and overweening love of the very skin and surface of the earth on which man dwells" (158). Dwelling, or eco-consciousness, expands our appreciation of the world and creates an ecology that humans are part of, rather than apart from.

Most significantly, Morris's *novum* is London, England's capital city, described as "a pleasant country place—pleasanter, indeed, than the deep country was as he had known it" (44). Though Guest travels up the Thames, his journey shows no significant differentiation between the city and country. He is continually struck by the healthiness he encounters everywhere, especially in the "country" people (63), a designation Dick does not understand. Every place is rural. The Revolution triggered an "exodus of the people from the town to country" (199), mixing together their respective knowledges. Nowhere combines the best of both worlds: agrarian principles with culture (art, music, literature and science). Hammond details this transition: "the difference between town and country grew less and less; and it was indeed this world of the country vivified by the thought and briskness of town-bred folk which has produced that happy and leisurely but eager life of which you have had a first taste" (104). Morris, a native Londoner, would certainly appreciate valuable urban qualities separate from an industrial or decadent lifestyle. Conserving the environment does not require abandoning the city. *News from Nowhere* suggests that human beings can dwell anywhere if their architecture grows out of the earth instead of reinforcing separation of human beings and the environment. When Ellen, Guest's love interest, arrives at the Old House near the hay-fields, she "laid her shapely sun browned hand and arm on the lichened wall as if to embrace it, and cried out, '[...] How I love the earth, and the seasons, and the weather, and all things that deal with it, and all that grows out of it, –as this house has done!'" (220). The house blends into the landscape, becoming an emblem of dwelling. Ellen's attractiveness stems from her love of the earth, her sun-tanned limbs bespeaking physical labor coupled with intelligence.

When Guest describes the architecture in Nowhere, it seems alive: "not only exquisitely beautiful in itself, [...] it bore upon it the expression of such generosity and abundance of life" (62). "Green" dwellings blend into the earth. Architecture becomes an organism, not only beautiful, but useful: "Each house stood in a garden carefully cultivated, and running over with flowers. The blackbirds were singing their best amidst the garden trees, which [...] seemed to be all fruit-trees" (77). Though "running over with flowers," these are predominantly kitchen gardens, indicating food is profitably grown in the city as well as the country. By building this harmonious architecture within his ecopolis, he reminds us that community includes the non-human.

Like other SF writers, Morris depicts "a realistic irreality" (*MOSF* viii). Subtitle aside, is *News from Nowhere* Romance or Realism? Morris's realist nature clearly determines the lifestyle of Nowhere, and in important ways, Morris resists idealizing tendencies, despite creating an ideal place. Nathanael Gilbert discusses the landscape of the novel in relation to landscape in art, particularly painting, that creates a recognizably national, English countryside while subverting the social reality of labor and class division. Gilbert makes important observations about Morris's conception of the environment, what he terms a "landscape of resistance." What Morris resists is the tendency to simply repeat conventional descriptions of landscape, or to idealize nature:

> Instead of creating a romanticized version of the rural landscape of the nineteenth century that conceals or misrepresents the conditions of the laborers within it, he projects this image of an agricultural landscape, albeit an English landscape, into the future where, in the wake of social revolution, nothing need be concealed. Things are what they seem to be: women and men happily work together in a summer meadow for the sake of work itself [27].

In a sense, Morris's novel is forgivably ideal by virtue of being a utopia, but it is "envisioned" as a desirable possible future, rather than "idealized" in the sense of whitewashed. His urban ecology forms the *ideal* relation to the environment, which as realist nature is not *idealized*.

Yet, *News from Nowhere* remains SF because, through time travel, it participates in a possible future, producing cognitive estrangement *through* realist nature. Guest must come to understand humanity's ecological role, and bring this knowledge back to 19th century England to warn against exploitative, unsustainable industry. Morris both resists fantasy, a completely unattainable or supernatural future, and dystopia by rejecting technology as society's cure. Morris joins in the distrust of technology, but suggests it could be used selectively to create a better future, even if it resembles a pre-industrial past. Morris mixes generic romance (medieval fiction) and Romanticism (radical literature inspired by legend and folklore to protest industrialism and elitism), but ultimately creates SF by rooting past concepts in the future. Humanity does not need to colonize a new planet; the potential for ideal conditions exists. Chris Baratta suggests SF "can provide the foundation for a new environmental awareness, one that is needed for a new understanding of not only how humanity is connected to the natural world, but also to what created our disconnect" (5). While Morris pinpoints capitalism, large-scale industry, and anthropogenic arrogance as the cause of this dis-ease, if SF, at heart, is a call to action, *News from Nowhere* shifts the paradigm to be what we could do to make things better rather than write apocalyptic fiction about dystopian futures bred of "our current anthro-dominated commodification and destruction of the natural world" (5). Both time and the mode of re-seeing (the naturalist gaze) generate the sense of strangeness necessary to the SF genre and allow the unique character of realist nature to come through.

Morris hoped his utopia would be actualized. He proclaimed,

"Nothing can make me believe that the present condition of your Black Country yonder is an unchangeable necessity of your life and position: such miseries as this were begun and carried on in pure thoughtlessness, and a hundredth part of the energy that was spent in creating them would get rid of them" ("The Beauty of Life" 42). "News from" implies this "utopian romance" is a harbinger, presaging or forecasting the future. While the name "Nowhere" indicates this place does not exist, and may perhaps be impossible, it can also suggest this London does not exist *yet*, and will not come into being until humanity achieves eco-consciousness.

Notes

1. While Ernest Callenbach's 1975 novel gave the name to the genre, Morris's *News from Nowhere* is really the first ecotopia, defined by "the recurrent theme of living in harmony with nature, which ... contributes to a pollution-free environment" (Delveaux 76).

2. As Suvin notes, this distinguishes SF from escapism. SF should not be defined in terms of science or the future, but "as a fictional tale" determined by a new place, or "locus," that is "*radically or at least significantly different from the empirical times, places, and characters* of 'mimetic' or 'naturalist' fiction," while remaining a possibility (*MOSF* viii).

3. Indeed, John Ruskin deconstructs the word "disease" in "Of Kings' Treasuries" (1867), yoking physical and mental health. Conspicuous consumption instigates disease—literally the lack of ease—as the consumer relentlessly pursues unnecessary goods and diversions which continually defer lasting satisfaction. Ruskin diagnoses capitalism as the toxin infecting society and this concept frequently recurs throughout the Victorian period, notably in the works of Edward Carpenter, a prominent socialist. His book, *Civilisation, its Cause and Cure* (1889), influenced Socialist philosophy at the fin de siècle; the "cure" referred to is agrarianism. While his ideas coincide with Morris's, Morris reached a wider audience.

4. Soper thus places humanity outside of nature while insisting on the symbiosis between human and non-human.

5. See Peter C. Gould's *Early Green Politics*, particularly Chapter 3, for a fuller discussion of Victorian Socialism in the 1880s. He shows how the brotherhood of Socialism includes all sentient life and their belief that respect towards animals promotes respect among men.

6. Kathleen Maloney, following E.P. Thompson, calls this "the education of desire" (45), from material desire to real needs.

7. For further reading, see Michael Waters's *The Garden in Victorian Literature* (Chapter 8), Carole G. Silver's *The Romance of William Morris* (Chapter 6), and Alex Shishin's essay "Utopian Ecology: Technology and Social Organization in Relation to Nature and Freedom."

8. According to Benedict Anderson, the imagined community, such as a nation or religious sect, is socially constructed, reliant on imagined relationships between its members, rather than face-to-face contact. Morris creates a new type of imagined community, not founded on capitalism and consumerism, but on coexistence transcending national borders. Morris's vision evokes the notion of "act locally, think globally." In "Imagining the Future: Mercier's 'L'An 2440' and Morris' 'News from

Nowhere,'" Gregory Ludlow notes, "Unlike much xenophobic utopian literature of the past, Morris' vision of his peaceful, restructured society of the twenty-second century is not restricted to the domestic scene but has international ramifications as well. In his world of the future the whole system of rival and contending nations has disappeared, along with the inequality between individuals in society" (30).

9. The lecture format is a distinctive feature of SF.

10. Both Gregory Ludlow and Norman Talbot point to Dickens's literary presence in Morris as a means of contrast and critique. Interestingly, Morris takes a page out of Edward Bellamy's book, as in Bellamy's utopia *Looking Backward* (1887), West opens a Dickens's novel for comfort, only to be struck "by force of contrast" with "the strangeness of my own present environment" (Chapter XII, 87).

11. Donaldson argues that as Morris's Boffin is the writer of "reactionary novels," Morris's intent is to *critique* Victorian realism. Since Dickens's introduces Boffin in his pursuit of knowledge—hiring Wegg to read to him—Donaldson suggests Morris hopes to transform the Victorian novel, typically preoccupied with realist portrayals of social problems, which becomes obsolete once society is transformed.

12. Unless, of course, we view "dust" as the common Victorian euphemism for "dung," which the future Londoners suggestively store in the old Parliament buildings.

13. Morris articulates another socialist platform here. The Free Trade in Land movement at mid-century and the Land and Labour League founded in 1869 campaigned to transfer land from the state or private holders to the laborers as commons.

14. Marx's *German Ideology* (1845). See also Tony Fitzpatrick.

15. Heidegger's use of "*bauen*," to dwell, means to preserve and protect the earth, in addition to laying down roots ("Building Dwelling Thinking").

Works Cited

Anderson, Benedict. *Imagined Communities*. London: Verso, 2006. Print.

Baratta, Chris. "Introduction." *Environmentalism in the Realm of Science Fiction and Fantasy Literature*. Ed. Chris Baratta. Cambridge: Cambridge Scholars, 2012: 1–8. Print.

Bellamy, Edward. *Looking Backward 2000–1887*. Ed. Matthew Beaumont. Oxford: Oxford University Press, 2009. Print.

Berry, Wendell. "Health as Membership." *The Art of the Commonplace: The Agrarian Essays of Wendell Berry*. Ed. Norman Wirzba. Emeryville: Shoemarker & Hoard, 2002: 144–158.Print.

Boos, Florence S. "An Aesthetic Ecocommunist: Morris the Red and Morris the Green." *William Morris: Centenary Essays*. Ed. Peter Faulkner and Peter Preston. Exeter: University of Exeter Press, 1999: 21–46. Print.

_____. "The Ideal of Everyday Life in William Morris' *News from Nowhere*." *The Literary Utopias of Cultural Communities, 1790–1910*. Ed. Marguérite Corporaal and Evert Jan van Leeuwen. Amsterdam: Rodopi, 2010: 141–170. Print.

Carpenter, Edward. *Civilisation, its Cause and Cure*. London: Swan Sonnenschein, 1906.

Delveaux, Martin. "From Pastoral Arcadia to Stable-State Mini-Cities: Morris's *News from Nowhere* and Callenbach's *Ecotopia*." *The Journal of William Morris Studies* 14.1 (Autumn 2000): 75–81. Web. 15 July 2013.

Donaldson, Laura. "Boffin in Paradise, or the Artistry of Reversal in *News from Nowhere*." *Socialism and the Literary Artistry of William Morris*. Ed. Florence Boos and Carole G. Silver. Columbia: University of Missouri Press, 1990: 26–37. Print.

Downton, Paul F. *Ecopolis: Architecture and Cities for a Changing Climate.* Collingwood: Springer and CSIRO, 2009. Print.
Fitzpatrick, Tony. "The Resourceful Past: William Morris, Socialist Romanticism and The Early Fiction of H.G. Wells." *The Wellsian: Journal of the H.G. Wells Society* 32 (2009): 36–53. Print.
Garrard, Greg. *Ecocriticism.* New York: Routledge, 2008. Print.
Gilbert, Nathanael. "The Landscape of Resistance in Morris's *News from Nowhere*." *The Journal of William Morris Studies* 16.1 (Winter 2004): 22–37. Web. 15 July 2013.
Gould, Peter C. *Early Green Politics: Back to Nature, Back to the Land, and Socialism in Britain, 1880-1900.* Sussex: The Harvester Press, 1988. Print.
Heidegger, Martin. "Building Dwelling Thinking." *Basic Writings.* Ed. David Farrell Krell. San Francisco: HarperCollins, 1993: 343–363. Print.
Johnson, Lionel. *Academy.* 23 May 1981, Rpt. in *William Morris: The Critical Heritage.* Ed. Peter Faulkner. London: Routledge & Kegan Paul, 1973. Print.
Lawton, Lesley. "Lineaments of Ungratified Desire: William Morris's *News from Nowhere* as Utopian Romance." *Anglophonia* 3.3 (1998): 113–123. Print.
Leopold, Aldo. *A Sand County Almanac.* Oxford: Oxford University Press, 1968. Print.
Ludlow, Gregory. "Imagining the Future: Mercier's 'L'An 2440' and Morris' 'News from Nowhere.'" *Comparative Literature Studies* 29.1 (1992): 20–38. JSTOR. Web. 15 July 2013.
Maloney, Kathleen. "Studying the Past, Envisioning the Future: Teaching History via William Morris's *News from Nowhere*." *The Journal of William Morris Studies* 17.2 (Summer 2007): 41–53. Web. 15 July 2013.
Morris, William. *News from Nowhere and Other Writings.* 1891. Ed. Clive Wilmer. London: Penguin, 2004. Print.
_____. *William Morris on Art and Socialism* [*WMAS*]. Ed. Norman Kelvin. New York: Dover, 1999. Print.
Schumacher, E.F. *Small Is Beautiful: Economics as If People Mattered.* New York: Harper Perennial, 2010. Print.
Shishin, Alex. "Utopian Ecology: Technology and Social Organization in Relation to Nature and Freedom." *Local Natures, Global Responsibilities: Ecocritical Perspectives on the New English Literatures.* Ed. Laurenz Volkmann, Nancy Grimm, Ines Detmers, and Katrin Thomson. New York: Rodopi, 2010: 55–63. Print.
Silver, Carole. *The Romance of William Morris.* Athens: Ohio University Press, 1982. Print.
Soper, Kate. *What is Nature?* Oxford: Blackwell, 2004. Print.
Suvin, Darko. "Counter-Projects: William Morris and the Science Fiction of the 1880s." *Socialism and the Literary Artistry of William Morris.* Ed. Florence Boos and Carole G. Silver. Columbia: University of Missouri Press, 1990: 88–97. Print.
_____. *Metamorphoses of Science Fiction.* New Haven: Yale University Press, 1979.
_____. *Positions and Presuppositions in Science Fiction.* Kent: Kent State University Press, 1988. Print.
Talbot, Norman. "A Guest in the Future *News from Nowhere*." *Socialism and the Literary Artistry of William Morris.* Ed. Florence Boos and Carole G. Silver. Columbia: University of Missouri Press, 1990: 38–60. Print.
Waters, Michael. *The Garden in Victorian Literature.* Aldershot: Scolar Press, 1988. Print.
Wilde, Oscar. *The Complete Works of Oscar Wilde,* 5th ed. HarperCollins, 2003. Print.

PART THREE

RE-VIEWING DAMAGED WORLDS THROUGH QUESTS

Underworlds of Despair and Hope in Cormac McCarthy's *The Road*

Justin T. Noetzel

In Cormac McCarthy's Pulitzer-Prize winning novel *The Road*, a father and his young son march through the charred and desolate shell of the post-apocalyptic world on a quest for hope. Using sparse but powerful language, McCarthy describes this world as a "barren, silent, [and] godless" landscape (4) and a "wasted country" (6) with "dust and ash everywhere" (7). Most of the countryside has been burned out of existence, leaving only the charred stumps of trees and gray ash blowing across dead fields and cracked roadways. When they pass through cities, they find that the previously bustling settlements have become places of death and evidence of a civilization petering out of existence. In one mostly burned town, they encounter the ash and dust-covered detritus of the pre-apocalyptical world, including "cars in the street caked with ash" and "[a] corpse in a doorway dried to leather" (12). Throughout the novel the father and son march relentlessly towards the coast, where they hope to find sustenance and salvation, but they find only a "gullied and eroded and barren" land (177) before "dead gray sands and a cold and desolate ocean devoid of all animal life" (215). Everything that they experience is only a lifeless and infected version of its former self, and they exist in a perpetual state of cold and gray desolation.

The Road is a story of almost universal destruction, and McCarthy matches the novel's jarringly simple title with sparse language and a narrative of ceaseless movement. The unnamed and archetypal father and son climb through ruined forests and march along crumbling roads towards the coast, and only a few buildings remain standing in this American wasteland. But, because of the vast destruction that has been wrought in this world, these man-made structures have become sources of potential danger. The father scavenges for supplies in these buildings, but his son maintains a strong fear of all enclosed spaces. The son is afraid to enter man-made structures because his whole life has been lived on the open road—he is comfortable camping with his father in the wilderness, but he is deathly afraid of the evil that hides inside houses and other buildings. The apocalypse in *The Road* not only destroys much of the human population and the constructed world, but also throws the essential human concepts of interior and exterior, native and foreign, and civilization and wilderness into disjunction. The boy is comfortable only out of doors, and he sees the hidden danger that lies within buildings as uncanny—his native existence is situated in the remains of the natural world, and he equates interiority with death.

This fear of enclosed spaces courses through McCarthy's narrative, and the boy's humanity suffers each time he and his father encounter the evil that is hidden inside buildings. They reach the novel's metaphorical and literal pit of despair when they find a cellar full of slaves, men and women who are stored like cattle to provide food and pleasure for their cannibal tormentors. The father and son narrowly escape this underworld of despair, but the father is worried that an indefinable "something" is stolen from the boy after witnessing such a hellish underworld. Such experiences also assault the reader's own humanity and conceptions of the home, but in order to propel his narrative into a more hopeful trajectory, McCarthy balances the novel's subterranean imagery. *The Road* presents opposing and balanced versions of what exists beneath the surface, because the wanderers soon encounter a much different underground space, a hidden bomb-shelter that houses innumerable food-containers and other household comforts. This bunker is an underworld of hope, and it provides the necessary revitalization to strengthen the father and son so that they can continue their journey. Not only does this shelter feed and clothe the two desperate individuals, it also allows the father to re-inscribe in his son the love for interior spaces that was an essential part of human culture before the apocalypse. In the underworld of hope, the father recreates a "home" for his son and renews in him a fire and faith in humanity that drives him for the rest of the novel. The father and son emerge from this bunker reborn and ready to continue their journey.

"Darkness coming fast": Creation and Destruction

The son's fear of enclosed spaces arises from his lack of experience living indoors, and McCarthy juxtaposes his birth with the destruction of civilization. The father remembers the sight and sensations from this destruction in flashbacks from the night his wife's water broke: "a long shear of light and then a series of low concussions.... A dull rose glow in the windowglass" (52). On this same night the parents watch the cities burn around them, and the son is born a few days later. As the mother and father behold their son for the first time, all that remains of civilization is "the gathering cold [and] the fires on the horizon" (59). Because civilization is destroyed through an apparent nuclear holocaust, the boy who was born as the world burned around him has no memories of living indoors. The son is perpetually afraid of houses and all other human-created buildings because the apocalypse at the time of his birth has disengaged him from what philosopher Gaston Bachelard calls in *The Poetics of Space* "the hierarchy of the various functions of inhabiting":

> Over and beyond our memories, the house we were born in is physically inscribed in us.... After twenty years, in spite of all the other anonymous stairways, we would recapture the reflexes of the "first stairway," we would not stumble on that rather high step. The house's entire being would open up, faithful to our own being... In short, the house we were born in has engraved within us the hierarchy of the various functions of inhabiting. We are the diagram of the functions of inhabiting that particular house, and all the other houses are but variations on a fundamental theme [14-15].

The concept of inhabiting, from the Latin verb "habitare," to dwell, is central to human existence, but it is bound to a specific room, building, or place. The boy has no concept of a bedroom or a living room, and no "first stairway," because all of the sleeping and living that he has ever known has been outdoors. As Erik Hage states, the boy is a pure and blank slate: "born after the devastation, he has no sense of the... structures that preceded this life" (143). The boy was forced out of his house and onto the road before space could inscribe itself within him, and so he does not possess the loving connection to this "fundamental theme" that his father does. Furthermore, the boy's essential lack of human experience brings him into conflict with his father, because the man lived most of his life within the "functions of inhabiting." The son believes that interior spaces can only contain violence, but the father remembers his own past and hopes that they might find salvation behind doors and inside walls. When they come across the father's boyhood home, he is excited to explore his former abode, but the son remains fearful because of the terror that might be hidden inside. The man walks from room to room soaking in the memories of the place, including the Christmases spent in front of the fire and "the dreams of a child's imaginings" located in his old bedroom (McCarthy 26–27). The boy's fear of enclosed spaces overrides his father's nostalgia, and in the old bedroom he reveals his anxiety: "I'm scared… I'm really scared" (27).

The first tragedy in the novel is the fact that the father has many memories and dreams that the son cannot even comprehend: "Sometimes the child would ask him questions about the world that for him was not even a memory" (53–54). All that the son knows are "decaying cities and buildings, rusted cars and tools, [and] weathered trains and boats" (De Bruyn 782). The father, on the other hand, strains with all of his will to hold onto the memories that he still possesses. The memories and sensations connected with the natural world are of the utmost importance, because he knows that he will never again see birds flying through the air or taste a peach fresh from the tree (McCarthy 18). He recalls the pleasantness of a day at the lake with his uncle as "the perfect day of his childhood [and] the day to shape the days upon" (13), and this memorial structure is of the utmost importance in a burning and crumbling post-apocalyptic world. The deteriorating society around the man is a constant reminder of the fragility of his own past, and the glow from a forest fire one morning reminds him of the "flaring and shimmering" sun on an overcast day (31). This rare sight stirs up a memory that the father had long forgotten, and it inspires him to try to make a list of such sensations in his head and structure his memory so that he can recall such inspiring events and spectacles. The father clings with all of his might to the memories of his childhood home and the other relics of his history, but the son possesses a profoundly different life experience and sees his father's house as just another building that might hide evil men. The boy's entire life consists of living outdoors and moving from one place to another, and in his conception of the world, buildings are nothing more than spaces for evil to reside and trap prey. The interior spaces in *The Road* represent the vastness of the unknown, and all too often, they house an evil that the son is afraid to comprehend.

The importance of the home as the source and foundation for humanity is one of the central notions of modern space and place theory. Bachelard further equates the home with the one who dwells there: "Our soul is an abode. And by remembering 'houses' and 'rooms,' we learn to 'abide' within ourselves.... [Houses] are in us as much as we are in them" (xxxvii). The young boy in *The Road* does not have any life experience with houses and rooms, and consequently, his ability to inhabit the world and abide contentedly within himself is irreparably damaged. Similarly, geographer Yi-Fu Tuan describes the cosmic structure that is centered on the dwelling in his text *Space and Place: The Perspective of Experience*: "home is the center of an astronomically determined spatial system. A vertical axis, linking heaven to the underworld, passes through it. The stars are perceived to move around one's abode; home is the focal point of a cosmic structure" (149). The home is an essential place for human existence, not only because it is where we lay our heads or eat our meals, but also because it is the center of the mythical relationship between creation and destruction, and between life and death. The boy, therefore, has lived his entire life without this center, and this glaring absence has instilled within him a deep desperation and fear. Even the buildings and houses that he has seen from the outside exist in various states of ruin. Dylan Trigg notes that "functional buildings and meaningful places enable us to bind our past and present to the space that surrounds it," but this spatial identity and memory is irrevocably fractured when these buildings fall into disuse and disrepair (quoted in De Bruyn 781). Since the boy has no memory of a functional and life-giving home to begin with, he lacks the spatial identity his father possesses.

The boy's fear of interior spaces is potentially crippling precisely because of the need to enter and investigate houses and other buildings in order to survive. The father does not feel the same fear that the boy does, because he has a frame of reference and foundation for the ideology of inhabiting in the dwellings of his childhood. The father retains his spatial identity and remembers his life before the apocalypse, the past when interiority was associated with comfort and security. This identity and memory empower him to cautiously scavenge inside dilapidated houses and other structures and retrieve for his son whatever he can find to help their survival. Ben De Bruyn recognizes the "tension between recognition and estrangement" that exists between the father and the son (781), so that even when they reach the father's childhood home, the boy is fearful of what might be hiding inside. The father understands what they need to do to survive, however, and through his exploration he exhibits what John Cant calls a "determined pragmatism in the face of potential danger" (272). The father seeks salvation inside these houses because they are all that remain of civilization in the world. As he searches for food or useable goods, the father also searches for the objects that can reconnect him with the lost past of humanity. In one small town that the wanderers encounter, the boy is worried that they will meet "the bad guys," but the father knows that they have to take a chance and explore: "We'll have to take a risk. We need to find something to eat.... We have to look some more.... We have to keep looking" (McCarthy 79–80).

The small bits of food, clothing, and tools that they recover from buildings provide a meager amount of sustenance and comfort for the man and the boy, but they are all-too-quickly used up or stolen. These objects also represent "something," a concrete manifestation of the objective world and humanity's inhabiting past. The father and son cling to the possession of all of the things that they find in the novel, because in the absence of sufficient food and permanent shelter, they are forced to confront the threat of nothingness. The father knows how much of the human experience his son is already missing, and so the menacing nihilism of the post-apocalyptic world is especially dangerous. Thomas S. Hibbs describes how such a vacuum of belief threatens to consume the whole of civilization, including "democratic ideals such as individual rights and human dignity[,] the pursuit of happiness, [and] the possibility of progress" (5). Although institutions such as the government and the economy are long extinct in *The Road*, the danger of a complete destruction of all human rights and happiness still lurks. In one harrowing passage, the man feels this encroaching nihilism when he awakes to a night of "sightless and impenetrable" blackness (McCarthy 15). When he stands up from his makeshift bed of old blankets and a tarp, he totters in the "cold autistic dark with his arms outheld for balance," and he took "great marching steps into the nothingness, counting them against his return" (15). As the night surrounds him in pure blackness, his arms soar and search for "something nameless in the night," something upright and stable that offers support and structure in this world of ash and ruin (15). McCarthy's tortured prose and sentence fragments in this passage reveal how close the father is to the precipice of nothingness. His entire world, except for his son, is a severe darkness in which only the strongest will for survival and the most potent hope can provide orientation.

The father's preoccupation with balance and seeking the upright resonates with his nature of inhabiting, because his pre-apocalypse dwellings were supported by upright walls and columns. The son, however, would not understand such metaphors of existence. In a world still reeling from global disaster, the father seeks order and direction, not just in his southward march for survival but also on the spiritual dimension. He must protect his son and instill faith in the boy that "something nameless" knows and that there is light and hope after the long dark night of the soul. McCarthy's passage above also echoes Tuan's discussion of the importance of the home, which lies at the heart of an "astronomically determined spatial system" (149). The father's driving force in his endless march along the fractured and disintegrating landscape is hope for the discovery of a true homeland for his son, something the boy has never experienced. The father has an indomitable will for survival, what John Cant describes as the "vitality that burns within the ardent heart" (271). He is also the "virile, heroic warrior, whose distinguishing mark is a creative and courageous boldness" (Hibbs 17), who arises to battle the vacuum of nihilism. With this creativity he constructs a lantern out of discarded farm equipment, and with this boldness he shoots in the head a man who is holding his son hostage. His uncompromising will overcomes the son's fear of the enclosed, as it must, as they search for a new homeland.

"The crushing black vacuum of the universe": Despair

The inner turmoil of the father and son in *The Road* are matched by the structure of the narrative and the symbolically traumatized landscape. John Cant explains this connection by stating that "movement of the travelers and the movement of the text are one," and the episodic marching and resting in the novel combine to form the complete journey and mirror McCarthy's chapter-less prose of fragmental paragraphs (267). Similarly, Kenneth Lincoln describes the writing as "a postholocaust grammar of scree, shards, smoke, fractals, bits and pieces of charnel, dead flesh and sallow bone" (165). The novel's charred roadside corpses and disintegrating buildings and signs mirror the trauma that the man has faced and his ongoing battle against nothingness. Lawlessness and depravity reign supreme in the novel, and the epicenter of this culture of violence is a "once grand house" that remains "tall and stately with white doric columns across the front," where even the windows remain unbroken (McCarthy 105). This house appears at first glance to offer some hope of salvation, but its true nature as the darkest vision in the entire novel soon becomes clear. Immediately the boy registers his fear of the structure, telling his father again and again that they should not enter the building: "Papa let's not go up there... I don't think we should go up there" (106). McCarthy builds on the boy's ominous tone by noting that "Chattel slaves had once trod those boards bearing food and drink on silver trays" (106). As they enter the home, they are greeted with the long forgotten splendor of a foyer with a black-and white-tiled floor and a broad staircase leading up to the second story (107). They move further into the house and find a pile of clothing, blankets, and sleeping bags, but with each step, the boy's fear grows—he goes from holding his father's arm to hanging onto his hand, and the text notes that the boy is "terrified" (107).

The relative innocence of the house's exterior belies the sinister secret that lies hidden inside, because the father and son find a padlocked hatch on the pantry floor. The boy is almost in tears as he begs his father to leave the home, but the man presses on and unlocks the hatch. As they descend into the basement, the man's senses are assaulted by the horrific scene that unfolds: "Coldness and damp. An ungodly stench. The boy clutched at his coat.... Huddled against the back wall were naked people, male and female, all trying to hide, shielding their faces with their hands.... The smell was hideous" (110). The father and son immediately realize the hell into which they have descended, and the sight of a man lying on a bloody mattress "with his legs gone to the hip and the stumps of them blackened and burnt" confirms that this damned cellar is merely the food pantry of the cannibals who dwell above. This fortified subterranean room represents the epitome of the boy's fear of the enclosed, and it is the most terrifying moment in the novel. The father and boy spend only a matter of seconds enduring the "ungodly stench" of the cellar, because they are terrified by this small band of sub-human people imprisoned in limbo on the very precipice of hell. The reader is as frightened as the two wanderers during this episode, especially when the father notices the home's inhabitants returning. These "bad guys" represent the most deformed and demonic depths of human degradation that the apocalypse has wrought on civilization, and if the man and boy are caught, they will be subject to the horrors of "cannibalism, slavery, starvation and torture" (Kollin 170).

This cellar represents the underworld of despair in *The Road*, a place where the dregs of humanity simply wait for death at the hands of their cannibal tormentors. McCarthy's depiction of this underworld contains echoes from Bachelard, who writes: "the cellar… is first and foremost the dark entity of the house, the one that partakes of subterranean forces. When we dream there, we are in harmony with the irrationality of the depths" (18). Bachelard furthers his analysis of the dark power of the cellar by referring to the depravity concentrated in the underground space in stories like Edgar Allan Poe's "The Cask of Amontillado": "these tales are the realization of childhood fears… [and such stories] of criminal cellars leave indelible marks on our memory" (20). The rational and hopeful world is in danger of extinction throughout *The Road*, and nowhere more powerfully than within the plantation house. It is appropriate that the smell of the cellar is ungodly because this pit is truly God-forsaken, and the hideous shrieks that the father later hears echoing from the house are those of hell's tortured. The underworld that the father and his son encounter is, as Bachelard describes, "buried madness [and] walled-in tragedy" (20).

There is no escape from this hell for those trapped in its depths. In addition to the padlocked door and the feral humans who live in the house above, the walls of this underworld have "the entire earth behind them" (20), so the only option for the basement dwellers is death. These post-apocalyptic chattel are frightening to the father and son for many understandable reasons, but on a metaphorical level, they represent the opposite of hopeful wandering—the imprisoning of despair. Whereas the father and son march across the landscape through the forest and on the road, these people have been consumed by the earth and are stuck in a limbo while simply waiting for death. These lost souls in *The Road*'s underworld of despair have been stripped of their humanity. The father and son must escape this cellar and continue moving in order to live, and they must also fight to resist losing their autonomy and identity into the smoking and lifeless landscape as so many others have. McCarthy describes the many charred corpses that have met their final rest on the roadside in grisly detail, including the "mummied dead everywhere… [s]hriveled and drawn like latterday bogfolk" (24).

The preponderance of violence, like that which the plantation house encloses, is one of the strongest undercurrents in the writing of Cormac McCarthy. For example, Vince Brewton writes about the changing landscape of violence in McCarthy's novels and argues that Lester Ballard in *Child of God* becomes increasingly violent as he "occupies a series of downwardly mobile dwellings" such as rented shacks, jail cells, and caves in the earth (124). The correlation between descending quality of habitation and ascending capacity for horrible acts is also present in *The Road*, a world where Ballard's "crescendo of horror" would probably allow him to thrive. The commonality of such ferocity and evil is exactly what the father and son must fight along their journey. Instead of escalating in violence as they move from one dwelling to another, they keep a low profile and avoid confrontation. Similarly, *The Road* parallels McCarthy's *Blood Meridian* in the movements of each novel's characters. Steven Shaviro describes how *Blood Meridian* features "restless, incessant horizontal movements, nomadic wanderings [and] topographical displacements," and both novels depict "the ceaseless repetition of violence" amidst a "no-place of desolation" (as qtd. in Brewton 131). Because of the nomadic wandering in *The Road* and the mostly horizontal movement, the father and son's departures into the underground take on enhanced significance. In the plantation home's cellar the danger is heightened—not only is the cellar an interior space, it is also an underground interior space, a hell from which escape is barely an option.

Throughout *The Road*, McCarthy surrounds his characters with the sensation of an inevitable descent toward chaos and extinction. While viewing his tent early in the text, the father sees it as "the pitch of some last venture at the edge of the world. Something all but unaccountable" (McCarthy 48). In the basement of the plantation house, the father and son come as close as they will ever be to falling into complete nothingness. Although they survive, the father recognizes the supreme disorientation such a traumatic experience has on their journey. In the darkness of the forest outside the plantation house, he realizes that he has "no idea what direction they might have taken" as they fled, and he worries that his mind is betraying him (115–116). The wanderers are able to continue their journey, but the father soon experiences a metaphysical absence to complement his unknown spatial trajectory. A few days after surviving the cannibals' cellar, he has an ominous vision of the "absolute truth of the world": "[t]he cold relentless circling of the intestate earth. Darkness implacable.... The crushing black vacuum of the universe. And somewhere two hunted animals trembling.... Borrowed time and borrowed world and borrowed eyes with which to sorrow it" (130). Once again, the narration breaks down as the father meditates on the unthinkable and leans towards despair with the thought of two hunted animals trembling in the face of crushing and implacable nothingness.

"Warm at last": Hope

The man and boy escape with their lives from the underworld of despair, but the father is worried about the psychological trauma that such horrific visions impose on his son. McCarthy's sparse narration again matches the desperate and searching mood of the action when the father thinks, simply, "*something* was gone that could not be put right again" (136, emphasis mine). The father fears that their short visit into the depths of man's depravity has forever scarred his son, and when they find a locked underground bunker in the yard of another house, the boy is again intensely afraid of its contents. The father's indomitable will for survival counteracts this fear, however, because he knows he must provide for his son. As the text notes early on, the boy is the father's entire world, and the father's insatiable yearning for a better life for his son is his sole reason to struggle for survival in such a harsh world (5-6). The boy is the father's warrant and justification for belief, and the man must find a way to restore the fatal loss in his son that occurred in the forsaken basement. The man restores this loss by reaffirming the boy's hope and reiterating what their mission is. At many points along their journey, the father reminds the boy of their mantra as some of the only good guys who are left in this post-apocalyptic world: they are fighting for survival amidst a world of desolation, and the central tenet of their goodness is that they would never stoop to the degradation of cannibalism, not in any circumstance, even if they were on the precipice of starvation (128–129). Such paternal reassurances are important, because the father worries that irreversible damage has been done to the boy because of the horrors in the cellar and the numerous and nightmarish roadside images. In one of the novel's most horrific spectacles, the father and son see the blackened and headless corpse of a baby suspended over a campfire where its monstrous cannibal-parents recently enjoyed a meal (198).

It is precisely because of this unwavering strength and this unquenchable drive towards hope that the father is able to provide for his son. Despite the narrow escape at the plantation house, he investigates the next house with as much thoroughness as he can muster. Just when he begins to think that "death was finally upon them" and that he should find a secluded place where their bodies will not be disturbed or found by the bad guys (129), he uncovers a locked plywood door buried in the yard. Even though the man is perpetually on the brink of starvation throughout the novel, he also has precisely honed and almost animal-like senses. This sensory ability gives him a finely attuned connection to the natural world around him, as glimpsed when he feels "the earth itself contracting with the cold" through his feet (261). He can also sense changes in the weather and approaching danger, as well as small undulations in the ground on which he strides. In fact, McCarthy's landscapes are "as powerfully rendered as the language of the fiction" (Jarrett 134), and the charred land and buckling blacktop in The Road are almost primary characters. The father is able to discover a basket-full of apples in an old orchard because he walks barefoot across the grass (McCarthy 120–121), and in doing so he interacts with this landscape-character and engages in a discourse of sensual appreciation. The father is also able to discover the door buried in the yard not by plotting it on a map or visually locating it in the landscape, but by experiencing the place through a more "intimate" or "sensuous geography" (Warde 132) by means of his internal sense of balance and the nerve endings in his feet.

The father's "multi-sensory mapping of space" (133) allows him to locate the door, and with his fearless determination he convinces his son that they need to explore what is below. The man knows that his son is frightened and thinking about their harrowing descent into the cannibals' pantry, but he explains what they need to do to survive: "I think there may be things in there and we have to take a look.... This is what the good guys do. They keep trying. They don't give up" (McCarthy 137). The boy recognizes his father's courage and follows him down the rough wooden stairs, and in the concrete bunker below they find a miraculous domestic blessing. They climb down into an old bomb shelter, a buried paradise with concrete walls, an enclosed piece of sanity and domestic comfort that stands in stark contrast to the horror that the two wanderers found in the previous subterranean space. In this underworld of hope the father cannot help but exclaim "Oh my God" over and over again, and these words act as a prayer of thanksgiving for what is bestowed upon them (138). With one glance the father sees "Crate upon crate of canned goods. Tomatoes, peaches, beans, apricots. Canned hams. Corned beef. Hundreds of gallons of water in ten gallon plastic jerry jugs. Paper towels, toiletpaper, paper plates. Plastic trashbags stuffed with blankets" (138). He tells his son, "I found everything. Everything" (139). The boy has trouble comprehending the seemingly infinite treasure in this vault, asking his father if this bounty from the vanished world is real and why it is here (139). The boy is confronted with a glimpse of humanity that he has never before experienced, and the sudden and miraculous revelation of this underground paradise leaves him at a loss for words.

Before entering the bunker, the boy has a dysfunctional notion of topophilia, the love of a space or place and its value for man that Gaston Bachelard discusses in *The Poetics of Space*. The boy sees interior spaces as the refuge for evil, not "the felicitous space" that man loves and that must be "defended against adverse forces" (Bachelard xxxv). The brief time these two spend in the bunker teaches the son how to love man-made spaces and how to exist as an inhabiting being. The bunker is a beloved space, like a warm bed or a comforting nook in Bachelard's estimation, because it is "a haven that ensures... one of the things [man] prizes most highly—immobility" (137). As opposed to the immobility of being trapped, which happens all too often in *The Road*, the security and comfort in the underworld of hope allow the father and son to relax and enjoy life. This time of recreation reveals the bunker's different spatial makeup when compared with the rest of the novel's settings. Whereas most of the action in *The Road* occurs in places of indifference, crumbling highways or ruined buildings that are all cut from the same cloth, the bunker possesses an unmatched power and vitality in the novel. While outside, the father and son must continually make progress on their journey, but the bunker provides a restful and re-humanizing respite from that incessant motion.

This buried paradise is the exact opposite of the cellar of the damned—it provides shelter and sustenance and gives the boy a glimpse of humanity that he has never experienced. This underworld of hope and salvation allows the father to bestow forgotten sacramental blessings on his son and to teach him to embrace topophilia. After the father puts the son to bed with the previously unimaginable pillow and blankets, he methodically goes through the supplies in the bunker (141–142). With this sorting and organizing action the father begins to inhabit the space and prepare it for his son's dwelling. He later instructs the son on how to use the chemical toilet, cooks for him, and bathes him. The son indulges in his bath, telling his father that he is "Warm at last" (147).

With this purifying water the father christens the son into the world of inhabiting, and he also converts the boy into a believer who will maintain hope and struggle for his own survival. In the process of cooking warm and plentiful meals, daily bathing, and washing the boy's laundry, the father reinvigorates his son and replaces the "something" that was stolen in the plantation cellar. These sacramental actions and the additional comfort from checkers, Coca Cola, and chocolate bars help to banish the stain of the underworld of despair and renew the boy's hope.

The bunker is also a location for the revitalization of memory and meaning. Throughout the father and son's journey, the man repeatedly consults the tattered fragments of a roadmap that he hopes will lead them to their desired coastal destination. Each attempt at reconnoitering his position, however, also leads to further deterioration of the map. As Anthony Warde notes, this disintegration reflects the map's "decreasing ability to serve as a means of understanding and negotiating space" (125). It has become an object of dis-orientation, because "the lines, names and symbols on the map refer not to the blasted and borderless landscape across which the man and boy move, but to a social and political order that has long since disappeared" (Warde 125). As the map falls apart and loses its objective connection to the world, the man's psyche reels and he is plagued by semantic breakdown. "He tried to think of something to say but could not," the narration reveals in one of the darker moments (McCarthy 88). As the man struggles to preserve his memory and keep his son's hope for the future alive, he is plagued by a repeated feeling of loss and emptiness in which the world is "shrinking down about a raw core of parsible entities" and the "names of things [are] slowly following those things into oblivion" (88). In this oppressively gray world, colors no longer exist. In an atmosphere choked with dust and ash, birds no longer fly through the air and crops do not grow on the ground. With the immense death and destruction that occurs each day, things waste away and are gone, words and meanings are forgotten, and the cycle of semiotic devolution leaves fewer and fewer things in the world.

The man's despairing and frightened view of the world here is reminiscent of Hibbs' description of Nietzschean nihilism as "the moral state in which the highest values devalue themselves, human aspiration shrinks, and the great questions and elevating quests of previous ages no longer have any resonance in the human soul" (6). The bunker is a place to fight this contraction and extinction, where the father teaches the son both history and survival. The father teaches his son to value himself and to understand what aspiration truly is, and he must restore the idiom, the meaning of community, for his son. Their relationship in the bunker is a good representation of what John Cant refers to as the boy's "learning both practical and moral lessons by observing his father's endeavors" (275). When the boy learns the proper order for eating his meals and how to make coffee, he is, in effect learning the "rhythms of life" (Bachelard 65) that only exist elsewhere in the novel within the father's deepest memories. When the son asks what he should eat first when they sit down to bountiful breakfast, the father begins to inscribe in him the idea of domestic peace by telling him to eat whatever he likes (McCarthy 145). The father also has to teach him the basic methods of pre-apocalypse human consumption: "You put the butter on your biscuits. Like this" (145). For the first time in his life, the boy experiences the satisfaction and contentment of a full stomach, a bath and a haircut, new sweaters and socks, and the swaddling embrace of new blankets.

This underworld of hope allows the father and son to receive respite from the permanent dispersal of their endless quest. For an all too brief time, it becomes a true home for the pair. In Bachelard's philosophical understanding, the bunker becomes a true home and "body and soul," and it maintains them "through the storms of the heavens and through those of life" (7). As Warde notes, however, the bunker is "an industrial Eden whose goods can be consumed but not renewed" (134), and so the father and son cannot bask in its warm embrace for long. When they finally leave the vault, it appears as "a grave yawning at judgment day in some old apocalyptic painting" (McCarthy 155). The two wanderers survive a brief visit to hell and pass through unnumbered horrors in their travels, and so McCarthy's imagery here is entirely appropriate. After a few days' rest in the underground paradise, they emerge reborn and ready to find their way to a promised land where they can create a real and permanent home of their own. Because the two wanderers become spiritually reinvigorated, they can continue their journey. The boy remains wary of interior spaces and does not want to spend the night inside a house later in their journey (205), but he relents because he recognizes the help that buildings can provide through the food, clothing and hot water that they contain (212–213). In the bunker the father instills hope in goodness into his son so that they can persevere and complete their quest.

In the world of *The Road*, civilization is deconstructed and boiled down to its very essence. Most people are gone, words have lost their meaning, and all that remains is an elemental sense of good and evil. The father emphasizes this idea for his son, teaches him that they are the good guys, and models the behavior of the good before and after their time in the bunker. The most important action the good guys can do is to keep hope alive by, as the father characterizes this action, "carrying the fire" (83). The father maintains that carrying the fire is real, even in the few last words to his son, telling him at the novel's end: "It's inside you. It was always there. I can see it" (279). Cant argues that this fire represents "civilization being passed from father to son" (270), but it is also a more personal matter to the man and his boy. De Bruyn enhances this metaphor by describing it as the "ancestral fire, the fire of lexification and human world-making" (784). This fire represents the cultural and familial inheritance that the boy receives just before his father dies, and Yi-Fu Tuan explains the mythic importance of the sacred ancestral fire: "Rootedness was an ideal of the ancient Greeks and Romans," and each family nurtured their own sacred fire which, if worshipped and cared for properly, elevated the ancestors to "protecting gods" (153). Furthermore, the sacred fire was the symbolic heart of the family and the literal center of the home: "Duty and religion required that the family remain grouped around its altar; the family was as much fixed to the soil as the altar itself" (153). By continuing to carry the fire, the son will preserve and translate the memories, words, and culture of his ancestors and his father. In order to perpetuate his own survival, he must find more of the good guys so that he can create a new community and family on whom he can bestow his own legacy. The hope that the sacred fire keeps alive connects the father and son with their ancestors and also with the mysterious creators of the bunker, and it is the son's warrant to keep the fire burning throughout his life.

Early on in the text, the son sees a solitary young boy wandering along the road, and he remains worried about this boy throughout all of his own tribulations. At the very end of the novel, the boy asks his father if he remembers the boy and if he thinks the boy has survived. The father again reminds his son of the power of hope, because he believes that the boy is all right (McCarthy 281). When the son persists and asks who will take care of the boy, the father delivers a simple answer that is also his core metaphysical belief: "Goodness will find the little boy. It always has. It will again" (281). In this moment, as the man lies on the ground bleeding from a fatal arrow-wound, he reminds the boy how they have survived for so long. The father's unyielding refusal to give in to despair and nothingness, coupled with his undying hope in something good, drove him in his endless march along the novel's road. In this quest, his entire reason for remaining alive was to take care of his son and teach him that goodness still exists. The boy learned what hope is during their time in the domestic bliss of the bunker, and he follows this teaching at the novel's end. "You need to keep going," the man tells the boy just before he dies. "You don't know what might be down the road. We were always lucky. You'll be lucky again. You'll see" (278). The son accepts his inheritance of hope and goodwill, and he continues to carry the fire after his father dies. He has a strong memory of the man as well as the comfort that a home can provide, so he is finally ready to join the community of other "good guys" at the novel's conclusion.

Works Cited

Bachelard, Gaston. *The Poetics of Space*. Trans. Maris Jolas. Boston: Beacon Press, 1994. Print.

Brewton, Vince. "The Changing Landscape of Violence in Cormac McCarthy's Early Novels and the Border Trilogy." *Southern Literary Journal* 37.1 (2007): 121–143. Print.

Cant, John. *Cormac McCarthy and the Myth of American Exceptionalism*. New York: Routledge, 2008. Print.

De Bruyn, Ben. "Borrowed Time, Borrowed World and Borrowed Eyes: Care, Ruin and Vision in McCarthy's *The Road* and Harrison's Ecocriticism." *English Studies* 91.7 (2010): 776-789. Print.

Giles, James R. *The Spaces of Violence*. Tuscaloosa: University of Alabama Press, 2006. Print.

Hage, Erik. *Cormac McCarthy: A Literary Companion*. Jefferson, NC: McFarland, 2010. Print.

Hibbs, Thomas S. *Shows About Nothing: Nihilism in Popular Culture from The Exorcist to Seinfeld*. Dallas: Spence, 1999. Print.

Jarrett, Robert L. "The Rhetoric of McCarthy's Fiction: Style, Visionary Landscapes, and Parables." *Cormac McCarthy*. New York: Twayne, 1997: 121–153. Print.

Lincoln, Kenneth. *Cormac McCarthy: American Canticles*. New York: Palgrave Macmillan, 2009. Print.

McCarthy, Cormac. *The Road*. New York: Vintage, 2006. Print.

Kollin, Susan. "'Barren, silent, godless': Ecodisaster and the Post-abundant Landscape in *The Road*." *Cormac McCarthy: All the Pretty Horses, No Country for Old Men, The Road*. Ed. Sara L. Spurgeon. London: Continuum, 2011: 157–171. Print.

Tuan, Yi-Fu. *Space and Place: The Perspective of Experience*. Minneapolis: University of Minnesota Press, 2005. Print.

Warde, Anthony. "'Justified in the World': Spatial Values and Sensuous Geographies in Cormac McCarthy's *The Road*." *Writing America into the Twenty-First Century: Essays on the American Novel*. Ed. Elizabeth Boyle and Anne-Marie Evans. Newcastle upon Tyne: Cambridge Scholars, 2010: 124–137. Print.

The Silence of the Subaltern
The Rejection of History and Language in Amitav Ghosh's The Calcutta Chromosome

Shayani Bhattacharya

> "Every city has its secrets," the voice began, "but Calcutta, whose vocation is excess, has so many that it is more secret than any other"
> —Ghosh, *The Calucutta Chromosome*

The primacy of quest narratives, from Arthurian Romances to J.R.R. Tolkien's *The Lord of the Rings* and beyond, is largely due to the adventure that leads to the discovery of both the object of the quest and the self. The successful completion of the quest not only rewards the Knight/quester with the object of discovery but s/he (mostly he) gains self-knowledge. Thus the idea of a quest is based on the trope of discovery through knowledge. The winner of the Arthur C. Clarke Award, Amitav Ghosh's sole science-fiction thriller *The Calcutta Chromosome: A Novel of Fevers, Delirium and Discovery* (1996) is also a quest narrative that is ultimately an investigation into the nature of knowledge. However, Ghosh's novel turns the notion of the quest on its head by not only showcasing the impossibility of knowledge but also subverting the possibility of gaining the object of the quest. The revelation at the end of a quest does not bear fruit in *The Calcutta Chromosome* because, through a rejection of language, the quest ends mired in silence and secrecy.

Amitav Ghosh uses the quest narrative in the form of science fiction to pose a challenge to the inevitable primacy of westernized constructions of knowledge and rational inquiry. According to Ghosh's alternative form of knowledge, "to know something is to change it" (Ghosh 91). Therefore, knowledge not only becomes mutable but also an impossible pursuit. Perhaps what is most interesting about this novel is the usurpation of knowledge, and scientific knowledge, commonly the property and domain of the white male, by the colored female, Mangala. If Gayatri Chakravorty Spivak questions the subaltern's ability to speak, I would like to argue that Ghosh's novel emphatically centers the subaltern from the margins, thus allowing for the much-needed space for the subaltern's speech. However, in this novel, the subaltern speaks through silence thereby rejecting the primacy of language—a discourse that according to Hélène Cixous regulates the phallocentric system.[1] Just as Spivak locates women as subaltern, so too in Ghosh's narrative, the subversion of western episteme is invested in the subaltern female. Cixous' call for the adoption of non-linear and cyclical forms of writing (that privilege experience over patriarchal language) is paralleled in Ghosh's non-linear, heteroglossic narrative that ties together different continents and centuries in the span of two days. As the nature of knowledge that is premised on discoveries, proof and authorship is turned on its head, I argue that the quest in this novel is not just a quest for scientific discoveries or medical miracles, but rather for understanding the mutability of knowledge and the power of silence through the real and imagined spaces of the city.

The novel begins with the idea of discovery and quest, when the AVA/IIe computer dredges up an old LifeWatch ID card that starts the data analyst, Egyptian émigré Antar, on a quest for the Calcutta chromosome. Set in the near-future in New York City, within the confines of a tenement building somewhere near Penn station, the non-linear narrative moves from the backwaters of Renupur, to the teeming din of 1995 Calcutta, from the British cantonment in Secunderabad, to New York and an obscure nameless hamlet in Egypt. Narrated through multiple flashbacks and retellings by different speakers, the quest for the Calcutta chromosome follows Antar's former colleague, LifeWatch employee L. Murugan, as he heads to Calcutta to piece together the "real" story behind Ronald Ross' Nobel winning discovery of the transmission of malaria through mosquitoes. According to Murugan's theory, Ross had been guided every step of the way to serve the experimental purposes of a group that Murugan enigmatically dubs the "counter-science" group. For the counter-science group, led by Mangala, an uneducated sweeper woman, and her assistant Laakhan, a dhooley-bearer, silence is a religion.

For them the end result of this malarial research was not finding a cure for malaria, but rather using the malarial parasite to cure syphilis and via that route achieve "interpersonal transference," and therefore immortality. In his quest to uncover this secret history, Murugan encounters Urmila Roy who works as a reporter for the *Calcutta* magazine. The two of them, along with ex–Hindi film actress Sonali Das, hurtle through the city as they attempt to catch up with Mangala and Laakhan in their latest avatars before the next "crossing" and their transference into new bodies. When Antar is chosen as the recipient of this counter-knowledge and aided in "crossing over" by Tara (Urmila as the latest re-incarnation of Mangala), the different narrative threads connect the different places and tie together over a hundred years of events and people.

Empirical Episteme and Its Subversion

The classic quest trope of the Knight/quester who becomes the receptacle of the bounty of the quest is subverted in *The Calcutta Chromosome*. The classic quest usually ends with the quester having gained the object of the quest. Initially this quest seems to be L. Murugan's; as a repository of information on Ronald Ross, Murugan seeks to put together the "real" story behind Ronald Ross' Nobel winning breakthrough. But as he admits to Urmila, "[i]t can't be me" (259). He is deemed worthy of only putting the pieces of the puzzle together. He is neither afforded the knowledge of the resolution, nor is he destined for the prize. The quest could have been Ronald Ross'; but despite getting the Nobel, "Ronnie" is not the quester because he is not even aware of the true quest. The object of the quest, therefore, is the subversion of knowledge, the creation of "a single perfect moment of discovery when the person who discovers is also that which is discovered" (260). Even though Urmila becomes the object of the quest, the quest is ultimately Mangala's—an entity who does not and cannot hold a single form/identity.

Since the novel begins with the LifeWatch card that appears on AVA's inventory, Ghosh sets up an oddly symbiotic relationship between AVA and her human operator Antar. AVA's "stimulated urge for self-improvement" leads her to ask a litany of questions. However, this drive is not motivated by the need to *know*, but rather to create a memory bank of information for the consumption of the International Water Council. Despite her simulated "human" features, AVA's "curiosity" is based on a compendium of information that is without any lived experience. Juxtaposed with the "limbo of AVA's memory" is the lived experience of Antar, which allows the information about the card and LifeWatch to be reconstructed through memory and not a digital database. Thus in designating memory as the repository of information/knowledge, Ghosh (like Cixous) privileges personal experience and memory over empirical forms of knowledge, like the database of the International Water Council. The Council (for which Antar works) "saw themselves making History with their vast water-control experiments: they wanted to record every minute detail of what they had done, what they would do..." (6). This stranglehold over knowledge, the record keeping and meaning making under the repository of one established institute is broken by the unofficial history that is delivered to Antar by Murugan in a variety of forms. Thus the novel from the onset sets up a contentious relationship between empirical knowledge and alternate forms of knowledge that question the primacy of westernized modes of scientific research, rationale and dissemination of information.

Murugan's quest for the truth behind Ronald Ross' discovery is in effect a search for the secret history of the indigenous group behind that discovery, which in turn becomes a quest for immortality through the Calcutta chromosome.[2] This quest is set against the much-documented historical backdrop of malarial research during the mid-nineteenth century. As Murugan tells Antar "[r]emember this was the century when old Mother Europe was settling all the last unknowns: Africa, Asia, Australia, the Americas, ... And this was just about the time when the new sciences like bacteriology and parasitology were beginning to make a splash in Europe" (50). This institutionalization of western scientific research and knowledge is evident not just in the history of such research but also in Ronald Ross' own personal minute records of his research process. Murugan observes that through his records and diaries, Ross "wants everyone to know the story like he is going to tell it; he's not about to leave any of it up for grabs" (46). Thus, not only is the repository of information controlled and owned by empirical, western forms of knowledge, but also the dissemination and record of the same is in the domain of the western male. Additionally, this record is shown to be rigid and constricted, as in the case of Murugan, whose publications on the alternate history of Ronald Ross' research is ridiculed and disregarded by American academia. Before starting on his quest, Murugan writes an article titled, "Certain Systematic Discrepancies in Roland Ross' account of Plasmodium B." When this article is roundly criticized by major journals the undaunted Murugan writes a second revised version, "An Alternative Interpretation of Late 19th Century Malaria Research: Is There a Secret History?" However, his hypothesis of "Other Mind: a theory that some person or persons had systematically interfered with Ronald Ross' experiments to push malaria research in certain directions while leading it away from others" (32-3) is once more rejected by American academia. The parodic titles of Murugan's articles not only serve as Ghosh's jibes at the pompousness of academia, but also work to reflect on the rigid and constricted nature of western episteme. The indomitable Murugan then shares the unusual history of his findings with Antar in an unconventional narrative format before embarking on his eastward journey.

In pursuit of his research Ross is firmly entrenched in the hierarchy of knowledge wherein knowledge cannot belong to nor acknowledge the subaltern.[3] Though Ross works closely with his Indian malarial subjects, Murugan reports that Ross disregards the human aspect; not caring to know their names, faces and details of their lives. This marked disinterest showcases the power of knowledge as invested in the white man who sees the subaltern as a voiceless chorus. This colonialist understanding of the world, argues Uppinder Mehan in his article "Postcolonial Science, Cyberpunk and *The Calcutta Chromosome*," "sees the colonies as devoid of any meaningful science and as the possessors of only ancient technologies" (Mehan 2). But Ghosh, in creating an alternate history of Ronald Ross' discovery and by centering the decentered subaltern in this new history, challenges not only the veracity of history, but also the understanding of knowledge as fixed and institutionalized. Diane M. Nelson in her essay "A Social Science Fiction of Fevers, Delirium and Discovery: 'The Calcutta Chromosome,' the Colonial Laboratory, and the Postcolonial New Human" claims, "the book argues against the assumption that modern laboratories exist only in the 'First World' and that only rich white men 'do' science" (Nelson 254). The novel, therefore, critiques the construction of the colonies as spaces of darkness and primitiveness, which privileges the colonizers' conceptualization of science, rationale and reasoning as the only viable model. In a fantastic turning of the tables, Ross, who believes himself to be in complete control of his research, does not realize that "all the time it's he who *is* the experiment on the malaria parasite" (Ghosh 69). His myopic colonial vision keeps him from recognizing the obvious manipulation by Mangala and Laakhan, attributing each of his breakthroughs to some "Fat Cat way up in the sky" (69).

The novel therefore not only rejects the primacy of westernized forms of empirical knowledge, but also poses its own alternate model of knowledge through counter-science. The "impossibility of knowledge"[4] that Murugan identifies as the philosophy of the "counter-science" group, is predicated on the idea that the limitations of knowledge must be recognized—"knowledge couldn't begin without acknowledging the impossibility of knowledge" (91). Mangala's quest for knowledge is for knowledge itself, not institutionalized record or academia. This rejection of dissemination of knowledge and the accolades that follow such records, is not just because western forms of knowledge and science refuse to acknowledge the validity of research. Rather Mangala and Laakhan by-pass the trappings of research, awards, grants and publications and thus move beyond the empirical to think about the nature of knowledge and its scope outside the research lab. Thus the idea of empirical, fixed knowledge that must be made public and preserved is subverted by this strain of knowledge that is fluid.

> Thinking of it in the abstract, wouldn't you say that the first principle of a functioning counter-science would have to be secrecy? The way I see it, it wouldn't just have to be secretive about *what* it did (it couldn't hope to beat the scientists at that game anyway); it would also have to be secretive *in* what it did. It would have to use secrecy as a technique or procedure. It would in principle have to refuse all direct communication, straight off the bat, because to communicate, to put ideas into language would be to establish a claim to *know* which is the first thing that a counter-science would dispute… With the idea that knowledge is self-contradictory; to know something is to change it, therefore, in knowing something, you've already changed what you think you know so you don't really know it at all: you only know its history. Maybe they thought that knowledge couldn't begin without acknowledging the impossibility of knowledge [91].

This different, non-standard and unique approach that eludes standard techniques of research exposes the inadequacy of western knowledge and episteme. Like the Borgesian *aleph*, this redefined concept of knowledge is accessible to all because it appears to be stored in a common bank that everyone can dip into. Like the *aleph* not everyone is worthy of it, and hence it changes and mutates, becoming accessible only to the chosen few. Only someone like Mangala makes possible the subversion of the concept of knowledge as a repository of western civilization. Murugan explains to Urmila that because Mangala was "completely out of the loop, scientifically speaking," it was possible for her to be unfettered by conventional research norms "she wasn't carrying a shit-load of theory in her head, she didn't have to write papers or construct proofs" (209).

Mangala's science does not concern itself with research leading to a cure, but rather she explores the nature of the disease. Ghosh mentions that Mangala's cult is as unknowable as a disease and this bond resonates in Mangala's quest. The organic and changeable nature of the disease is symbolized in the Calcutta chromosome. Different from the chromosome that determines the nature of the DNA, the Calcutta chromosome is unique and mutates, thus becoming extremely difficult to categorize. Resisting empirical forms of documentation this chromosome represents a kind of understanding that depends on the suspension of the conceptualization of knowledge as fixed and constant. Mangala's experiments with the disease, and in turn the chromosome, therefore celebrates the fluidity and mutable nature of knowledge, thus subverting the fixed and constricted notions of Western episteme.

Reclaiming the Decentered Subaltern

Gayatri Chakravorty Spivak's sustained critique of class-consciousness and subjectivity modeled on western constructs is developed in her seminal essay "Can the Subaltern Speak?" The essay illustrates Spivak's concern "to excavate the disempowered and silenced voices of the past from the material and political context of the present" (Morton 58). She discusses the idea that "the ventriloquism of the speaking subaltern is the left-intellectual's stock-in-trade" which, in a bid to represent the subaltern, inevitably ends up not just appropriating their voices, but also effectively silencing the subaltern (Spivak 28). Spivak's contention challenges the conceptualization of civilization and development according to western constructs. By extension, she questions the understanding of language as a clear and transparent system of communication. She dispels this by discussing how language controls and dominates, thereby obfuscating social and political inequalities. The critical vocabulary that is required to articulate the experiences and histories of those who are historically exploited and marginalized is absent. Spivak suggests that "[i]f, in the context of colonial production, the subaltern has no history and cannot speak, the subaltern as female is even more deeply in shadow" (32). Given the predisposition to privilege men in historical discourse, Spivak explores how literature allows for an alternate site to investigate the role of women in the social text of postcolonial

India. Amitav Ghosh's novel becomes one such site where the subaltern poses a challenge to Ronald Ross' privileged discourse. Positioned in the margins, Mangala represents the subaltern, the "fringe people, marginal types; they're so far from the mainstream you can't see them from the shore" (Ghosh 92). The margins are essentially decentered, indefinable and therefore in flux. The fluidity of this space allows for it to be a space of change and difference and thus the source of subversive power.

The subaltern at the margins of society also inhabits the margins of "civilization." Ghosh's narrative, which spans the breadth of three continents—Asia, Africa and North America—is ultimately about his own birthplace and his nostalgia for the melting pot that is Calcutta (or as one should put it *was* Calcutta). Calcutta, in this novel, is not the erstwhile capital of British India or the bustling metropolis of the twentieth century, but rather a space of mysteries and secrets. In the words of Phulboni, (as quoted in the epigraph here) the successful Bengali writer in the novel, the secrecy of Calcutta becomes the epitome of the subversive power of silence that Mangala wields. The muggy rainy afternoons which obscure vision, the dark ill-lit potters' alley crammed with unfinished clay idols in Kalighat, the conspicuously inconspicuous Ronald Ross memorial, the curtained alcove in the Dilkhusha Cabin, the old abandoned "site of the Robinson Hotel" all showcase the inscrutability of the city where Murugan seems unable to make any headway. Ghosh transforms the perception and understanding of urban Calcutta by making visible its invisible and unknown corners and the inhabitants of those corners. Murugan's discovery of the prostitutes and their colorful perfumed domain above the squalor and stench of the everyday bustle of Free School Street; the secluded and inconspicuous Ross Memorial, tribute to Ross as well as the cult of Mangala Bibi, next to the busy thoroughfare of Harish Mukherjee Road; the din of the Dilkhusha cabin cut out by the curtained booth that Murugan and Urmila occupy; the dark workshops off of potter's alley in Kalighat where artisans secretly make idols of Mangala Bibi hidden behind the recognizable faces of the Hindu deities; and the site of the Old Robinson Hotel that remains shrouded in darkness while the lights blaze and illuminate the rest of Robinson street—all effectively construct the world of the city anew for the reader.

James H. Thrall, in "Postcolonial Science Fiction? Science, Religion and the Transformation of Genre in Amitav Ghosh's *The Calcutta Chromosome*," discusses how Ghosh lays out the city's colonial heritage and its postcolonial transformation in literally concrete terms. The urban landscape is moored to specific geographical reference points that are repositories of colonial grandeur, like the Wicket Club, former colonial mansions and the Presidency General Hospital (P.G. Hospital). However, when Ghosh juxtaposes these spaces with the dark alleyways and infamous red light areas, he brings the secret and unknown parts of the city in direct contact with the luminous sections. The novel simultaneously makes room for the inhabitants of these dark and secret corners of the city, the "fringe people," to lay claim to and control these spaces of colonial history. Mangala and Laakhaan, emerge out of the ubiquitous railway system that had enabled the British to control India and its resources. The two subaltern figures not only adopt the railways as their home and use it to penetrate one of the British bastions of scientific research in India (D.D. Cunningham's laboratory in the P.G. Hospital), but they also wield the railways as a weapon to maintain the secrecy of their cause. Claire Chambers, in her essay "Networks of Stories: Amitav Ghosh's *The Calcutta Chromosome*," discusses Martin Leer, who addresses the novel's intricate relationship with the railway network in his "Odologia Indica." Leer explains how "[r]ailway stations ... function as the sites where characters and stories appear from and disappear into; centres which connect parallel worlds, a kind of real-world Internet portals" (qtd. in Chambers 52).[5] Thus through the dexterous manipulation of the railways (that connect the periphery to the center), the subaltern manage to manipulate the hierarchical relation between the two.

Mangala's knowledge and control over the laboratory[6] displaces the American scientist turned missionary Elijah Munroe Farley and, eventually, D.D. Cunningham (the director of P.G. Hospital) himself from his own laboratory. Laakhan in turn dexterously uses the railways, a symbol of progress and privilege, the stronghold of the colonists and the upper class, to first eliminate the upper caste stationmaster of Renupur and then best the British linguist J.W.D. Grigson.[7] In both instances Laakhan manages to triumph because of his marginal location. In Renupur his status as a social pariah forces him to live along the railway tracks far away from the habitations in the village, which allows him to gain complete knowledge and understanding of the imperial invention and use it for his own ends. Similarly, in Secunderabad, his location in the outhouses/servants' quarters near the railway tracks, far away from the colonial bungalows of the British army officers, gives him access to the railway lines and therefore provides the means for besting

Grigson. In his 1995 avatar of Romen Halder, Laakhan opens up the site of a colonial mansion under renovation to the hordes of indigents from Nepal so that the once exclusive European premises becomes the domain of the homeless subaltern. Ghosh describes the "hallway was full of people ...cooking, eating, sleeping, feeding their children," thus inhabiting the bastion of the colonial past with the subaltern and reclaiming the space of exclusion. By opening up spaces that were restricted and inaccessible to the subaltern, the novel displaces the fixed binary between the center and the margins.

The people on "the fringes" are not only repositioned in the center but the center itself is decentered. Those who are disregarded by Ross as a voiceless chorus—the lab assistants, the volunteers, and later in the twentieth century, the khukri-wielding gorkhas, the taxi drivers, the gap-toothed street-urchins—are grouped in a nameless and almost faceless mass. Though not afforded any names and often deprived of speech, they nonetheless form the matrix of the city. Ghosh's novel does not relegate this subaltern mass to form the backdrop of his narrative, but rather manipulates the historical figures of Ross and his fellow British officers, social personages like Sonali Das and middle class intellectuals like Murugan and Urmila, to act as the chorus for the subaltern's song. Laakhan emerges as the hero of the experiment who links together the whole story of Mangala bibi. His many chameleonesque avatars become symbolic of the faceless mass, the members of which (in the eyes of the hierarchical elite) are interchangeable for one another. Laakhan and his subaltern compatriots dexterously use this anonymity to manipulate the hierarchy.

The Subaltern's Silence

The reconstruction of the city as a reclaimed space of the subaltern is made possible not only through the centering of the figures of Mangala and Laakhan, but also through the rejection of language and the adoption of silence. The idea of silence as a necessity for secret-keeping is always a paradox because the status of the secret exists in its telling. To be a secret it must be identified as such and therefore necessarily the silence must be broken, but in the case of *The Calcutta Chromosome* this notion of secrecy is turned on its head as silence nurtures and mutates the secret, the proliferation of which occurs in its hiddenness.

> That which is hidden has no need of words to give it life; like any creature that lives in a perverse element, it mutates to discover sustenance precisely where it appears to be most starkly withheld—in this case, in silence... Mistaken are those who imagine that silence is without life; that it is inanimate, without either spirit or voice. It is not; indeed the Word is to this silence what the shadow is to the foreshadowed, what the veil is to the eyes, what the mind is to the truth, what language is to life... [Ghosh 22–5].

Thus, the notions of silence and darkness, which are seen as backward or regressive, are celebrated to subvert the stranglehold of western registers of knowledge. The celebration of silence is necessarily a rejection of language. Chambers argues that throughout his writing, Ghosh is preoccupied with the notion that language is not a neutral reflection of reality, but in fact irrevocably shapes our view of reality (Chambers 53–5). The counter-science group, by adopting the code of silence and indirect communication, therefore rejects the traditional lines of communication entrenched in hierarchical language that robs the subaltern of speech. The secrecy of Mangala that culminates in her refusal to articulate her discoveries, showcases the redundancy of language for those who are excluded from the privilege of language. Additionally, the rejection of language also suggests its limitations and the impossibility of revealing anything fully.

The pursuit of silence is contradictory in literature since it depends on language.[8] This problematic relationship manifests itself in a complex relationship in Phulboni's speech on literature where he forges an inextricable bond between language and silence. Ghosh's celebration of silence is also a reference to the inaccessibility of the written language to the subaltern. The novel critiques the exclusionary tactics of the written word and the dissemination of documented forms of knowledge. Chambers suggests a third appendix to the function of silence in the narrative, as "the only appropriate response to incidents of great trauma and suffering." She argues that Ghosh's preoccupation with silence might be an "ethical response to the economic and social gags of colonialism. Ghosh's creation of a space for silence in this novel may come as a reminder that we should not 'speak for' the subaltern, but rather recognize, with Spivak, the unrepresentable aspects of the Other's experiences" (57). Ghosh's rejection of conventional documentation privileging silence, allows for the subaltern to claim spaces made unavailable to them. The strictures of the written word gag the subaltern by constructing knowledge as repositories of Western civilization. When the subaltern in the novel reject these constructions and adopt silence they showcase the inadequacy of language to encompass their experience.

Silence and the Narrative

The postmodern anxiety about the impossibility of representation and the failure of language easily translates here into a narrative that reflects this anxiety through its intertextuality, heteroglossia, cyclicality and multiple authorial voices. The tripartite structure of the beginning, middle and end is totally subverted in *The Calcutta Chromosome* because the revelation at the end comes almost simultaneously with the beginning. The novel ends with Antar reading/watching the file on the Calcutta chromosome, which takes the reader to the beginning of the novel, thus encompassing the narrative in a recurring loop. This loop connects the end with the beginning, thus subverting the hegemony of a linear narrative. "Only way to escape the tyranny of knowledge is to turn it on itself. But for that to work they have to create a single perfect moment of discovery when the person who discovers is also that which is discovered" (Ghosh 260). As the narrative unfolds on the pages, and the reader reaches the end of the novel, the threads across continents and centuries are pulled together and Antar becomes the recipient of the information with the end tying in neatly with the beginning. Non-linear narrative time is mirrored in the multiple selves of the protagonists, as Chitra Sankaran discusses:

> Also, there is a fluidity in the conception of Mangala Bibi as both a sweeper on the one hand and as a goddess worshipped by the masses on the other. This sense of overlapping selves can be further witnessed in the figure of the Nepali boy who chases Murugan on his arrival in Calcutta. The boy turns out to be the young servant of the celebrated film star Sonali. But later he is found performing rituals at Romen Haldar's building that is under renovation. Again, he can be traced to the fishmonger who sells fish to Urmila Roy and deliberately provides clues on Cunningham/Ross through a photocopy of a nineteenth-century government Gazette used to wrap Urmila's fish [Sankaran 110–11].

The multiplicity of the characters is simultaneously reflected in the heteroglossic city, which appears to act as the repository of the human race with its British military officers, long-forgotten Anglo-Indian landladies, khukhri wielding Gurkhas, job-seeking vagabonds from the heartland of Northern India, street urchins, Sikh taxi drivers, exotic filmstars, the new-age Bengali "woman of substance," and the Calcutta-born Tamil

NRI Murugan. At the heart of this excess is the figure of Laakhan. Alternately Lokhkhon, Lakshman and Lutchman, the identity of Laakhan and the role that he plays drives the greater part of the quest.

This overwhelming mixture resonates in the multiple voices of the narrative, which amplify the heteroglossia of the city. This heteroglossia is structured in the way Ghosh intersperses the metanarrative with dialectical English, turns of phrases and a style characteristically associated with Indian English ("umbrella-headed minister," "cabbage-head," "Urmi-pishi Kirmi-pishi"). Ghosh also invokes a variety of narrative styles distinctive to each segment of the narrative. The sections concerning the period of the British Raj, resonate with the tone akin to literature from and about the period, evident in the writings of the likes of Mulk Raj Anand, Khushwant Singh, William Dalrymple and Ghosh himself. Phulboni's narrative alludes to the very popular and often pulp genre of Bengali horror fiction (popularly referred to as "ghost stories" or *bhooter golpo*), while the Murugan narrative has the frenetic pace of a thriller. When discussing the history of malarial research, Murugan veers from his chatty boisterous style to a pseudo academic register of speech ("it must be noted however..."). The different registers of speech of the likes of Buddhu Dubey (the station master Phulboni encounters in Renupur), Urmila's family and Urmila herself when talking to the taxi drivers are examples of the heteroglossia that challenges the hierarchical privilege of the master narrative voice. The changing styles and voices infuse fluidity into the otherwise rigid colonial English language, thus robbing the metanarrative authorial voice of its hierarchical privilege, and instead making room for a heteroglossic orchestra of voices.

Similarly, authorship is obfuscated and the source of the narration gets blurred in Phulboni's narrative. The narrative begins with Urmila acting as the narrative voice, however, when the chapter changes, it continues seamlessly in third person narration. Thus the voice of one character (Phulboni) gets appropriated by another (Urmila) and finally becomes part of the metanarrative. This is mirrored elsewhere in the text when AVA reconstructs Murugan's file on Farley. The obfuscation of narrative voices allows for the transference of narrative impetus between characters, thereby making it impossible to concretize the source of information. This maneuver therefore is commensurate with the "counter-science" group's rejection of authorship and recognition.

The narrative with its heteroglossia and different narrative voices also poses a challenge to the notion of authorship premised on creativity and originality. Urmila's recollection of Phulboni's story of the woman who was saved from drowning challenges the authority of Phulboni, and subsequently that of the author, making Phulboni wonder whether:

> a story come[s] to be in the words that I conjure out of my mind or does it live already, somewhere, enshrined in mud and clay—in an image, that is, in the crafted mimicry of life?... It was Phulboni who was no longer sure which had happened first [the story or the incident] or whether they were all aspects of the coming of that image into the world [Ghosh 194–5].

Thus the obfuscation of the source of the story subverts the original claim of authorship. This obfuscation is made manifest through the multiple authorial presences of Murugan, Ross, Farley, Grigson, Phulboni and Ghosh, which in turn allow for intertextuality. Chambers claims that Ghosh's "allusions to a wealth of stories from different cultural tradition[s] represent an attempt to challenge the 'claim to know' of western scientists such as Ross." Ghosh, she argues, "counteracts the rigidity of scientific discourse with complex layers of stories" (Chambers 42–3). She states that the use of the nodes within a network structure allows Ghosh to escape from the idea of a center and periphery.[9] This intertextuality references to different documents and situates the master narrative as part of a larger discourse. Simultaneously, the network of texts establishes the narrative as one of many, thus robbing it of its privileged status.

History as Fiction

The multiplicity of narrative voices, the heteroglossia of the city, the challenge posed to the authority of narrative and knowledge questions the endeavor of documentation and narrative. Since language is the corner stone of both, the suspicion of language aids in the suspicion of history and the construction of an alternative history. Linda Hutcheon introduces the concept of historiographic metafiction whereby the 19th century separation of history and fiction is countered. She discusses self-reflexive novels, which problematize historicity and thereby erode the confidence in the empirical epistemological process associated with history. Historiographic metafiction problematizes the closely structured and self-sufficient worlds created by 19th century realist fiction and history writing. It demystifies the heroic and falsifying view of history by blurring the line between history and fiction. Historiographic metafiction, therefore, uses history to rewrite and rethink the past in order to open it up to the present, thus keeping it from being conclusive. It refers to other texts because the past can be known only through the mediation of other texts (Hutcheon 105-23). So history is a constructed document authored by an individual, and hence open to questioning and interpretation. Also, because history is a construct of language and language is suspect, the novel rejects the notion of both history and language, thereby parodying it. By drawing attention to the way in which institutions (International Water Council, histories of scientific research in the West) and individuals (Ross) construct and disseminate their knowledge as history, and therefore truth, the novel questions the empirical truth status of history by showcasing it as fiction that belongs to the domain of the western male.

Murugan's very Americanized (somewhat parodied) and unique retelling of the Ross saga robs history of its empirical, objective weight. For instance, when talking about Ross' sudden decision to foray into malarial research he says that Ross, instead of saving for the power lawnmower, throws his chips into the ring. The anachronistic turn of phrase appropriates from history its pedantic tone and "truth" quotient. This recognition comes about because of an understanding of the limitations of language. The novel examines the idea that narratives, even such apparently factual ones as histories, are "not at all transparent either in terms of language or structure" (105).

Though a product of language itself, Amitav Ghosh's complex narrative attempts to reject the tyranny of language. The novel marries the postmodern suspicion of language and representation in order to question the veracity and authority of history to attain the desired effect of challenging and subverting colonial history. A sharp critique of knowledge that is enslaved to western constructs, the novel showcases the subalterns' celebration of their peripheral status through the rejection of language. The impossibility of knowledge necessarily indicates a lacuna, and this lacuna is appropriated by the subaltern and effectively dismantled in order to challenge the very core of knowledge and its dissemination through language. Interlaced with silence, the novel showcases the limitations of language, as Mangala's discovery remains a secret. The final step of the interpersonal transference remains embedded in the smoke and the din of the drums in the Robinson street mansion. Through the effective rejection of language and history, those who remain faceless, nameless and voiceless in the city are endowed with the

152 PART THREE: RE-VIEWING DAMAGED WORLDS THROUGH QUESTS

power of knowledge. It is the subaltern who are not only celebrated but also immortalized.

Notes

1. For Hélène Cixous' discussion on the *écriture féminine* that privileges experience over language and showcases the need for non-linear cyclical writing see "The Laugh of the Medusa."
2. For Uppinder Mehan's discussion of the three-fold quest of Murugan see "Postcolonial Science, Cyberpunk and *The Calcutta Chromosome*."
3. See James H. Thrall's "Postcolonial Science Fiction?" where he discusses the roots of colonialism in science fiction by critiquing the way rationality is so often represented as mastery of advanced technology.
4. Murugan's identification of a knowledge that recognizes its own "impossibility" draws both on postmodernist thought and on a strain of Hindu thought which indicates that recognizing that one does not know everything is the first step towards knowledge" (Chambers 41–2). See Claire Chambers' "Networks of Stories: Amitav Ghosh's *The Calcutta Chromosome*" for her analysis of a passage from the Upanishads that resonates very clearly with the novel both in its creation for a space of coexistence of conventional knowledge and its mysterious antithesis, "not-knowledge," and in the connection it makes between knowledge and immortality.
5. Chambers extends this argument to draw parallels between the grid of the railway system and the network of the World Wide Web, which is a more subtle form of hegemony and control. See Chambers 52–3.
6. Mangala's control over the research process is evident from her knowledge and manipulation of the sample slides when Farley visits the lab. In fact, she holds court next to the lab, conducting ritualistic experiments on syphilitic patients in the outhouses of the hospital, despite the presence of a *sahib* (master, foreigner). She gleefully watches as Farley makes his panicked escape after she allows him to see her breakthrough in malarial science. Having effectively gotten rid of Farley, Mangala mysteriously manages to displace Cunningham from his own lab and installs Ross in P.G. Hospital to continue her experiments on him.
7. As evident from Phulboni's supernatural experience in Renupur, the young Laakhan, persecuted by the upper caste station master for his caste status, uses the railway employee's own tools (the railway and the signal lamp) against him to both kill the man and escape with his life. When J.W.D. Grigson, cushioned by his white supremacist's knowledge that catalogues a whole nation into neat categories, tries to box and label Laakhan—"I have got all you natives figured: I know exactly where every single one of you belong" (Ghosh 82)—Laakhan manages to turn Grigson's curiosity against him by once more using the Railways as a prop.
8. Chambers discusses George Steiner and Michael Wood who claim that the ultimate, yet impossible, aim of literature is silence
9. See Chambers' discussion of Gerard Genette's use of architextuality and its relation to Kristeva's definition of intertextuality. She examines how Ross' diaries and memoirs are transformed by Murugan's investigation into Managala and Laakhan. She discusses Foucault's statement of a book as "a node within a network" meaning that it cannot be separated from its literary influences and historical context. Additionally she reads the novel as hypertextual in the sense of hyperlinks as discussed by Theodor H. Nelson, which links texts non-hierarchically (Chambers 44).

Works Cited

Chambers, Claire. "Networks of Stories: Amitav Ghosh's *The Calcutta Chromosome.*" *ARIEL* 40.2-3 (April-July 2009): 41-62. *Academic OneFile.* Web. 11 April 2013.

Cixous, Helene. "The Laugh of the Medusa." Trans. Keith and Paula Cohen. *Signs: Journal of Women in Culture and Society* 1.4 (1976): 875-93. *JSTOR.* Web 7 July 2013.

Ghosh, Amitav. *The Calcutta Chromosome: A Novel of Fevers, Delirium and Discovery.* New Delhi: Penguin (Ravi Dayal), 1996. Print.

Hutcheon, Linda. "Historiographic Metafiction: The Pastime of Past Time." *A Poetics of Postmodernism: History, Theory, Fiction.* London: Routledge, 1988. Print.

Mehan, Uppinder. "Postcolonial Science, Cyberpunk and *The Calcutta Chromosome.*" *Intertexts* 16.2 (Fall 2012): 1-14. *Project MUSE.* Web. 10 May 2013.

Morton, Stephen. *Gayatri Chakravorty Spivak: Routledge Critical Thinkers.* London: Routledge, 2003. Print.

Nelson, Diane M. "A Social Science Fiction of Fevers, Delirium and Discovery: 'The Calcutta Chromosome,' the Colonial Laboratory, and the Postcolonial New Human." *Science Fiction Studies* 30.2 (July 2003): 246-66. *JSTOR.* Web. 17 April 2013.

Sankaran, Chitra. "Sharing Landscapes and Mindscapes: Ethics and Aesthetics in Amitav Ghosh's *The Calcutta Chromosome.*" *History Narrative and Testimony in Amitav Ghosh's Fiction.* Albany: State University of New York Press. *Project Muse.* Ebook. Web. 12 May 2013.

Spivak, Gayatri Chakravorty. "Can the Subaltern Speak?" *The Post-Colonial Studies Reader.* 2d ed. Ed. Bill Ashcroft, Gareth Griffiths and Helen Tiffin. London: Routledge, 2006. Second Edition. Print.

Thrall, James H. "Postcolonial Science Fiction?: Science, Religion and the Transformation of Genre in Amitav Ghosh's *The Calcutta Chromosome.*" *Literature and Theology* 23.3 (September 2009): 289-302. *Humanities International Complete.* Web. 18 May 2013.

A Case of Terraphilia
Longing for Place and Community in Philip K Dick's Do Androids Dream of Electric Sheep?

Susan M. Bernardo

> Rather than writing stories about doom, perhaps we should take doom for granted and go on from there. Make the ruined world of ash a premise.... And make the central theme of the story an attempt by the characters to solve the problem of postwar survival.
> —Philip K. Dick, "Pessimism in Science Fiction" (1955)

Philip K. Dick followed his own advice in his 1968 novel, *Do Androids Dream of Electric Sheep?*, since disaster is a precondition of the narrative. World War Terminus has made Earth a planet-wide fallout zone from which healthy people emigrate to Mars. Oddly, though, some who are qualified to relocate, choose to stay. Early on the novel brings up the question of why anyone would choose to stay on Earth, or, in the case of the renegade androids who leave Mars, head for Earth. Early in the novel the narrator gestures toward an answer to this question, "Perhaps, deformed as it was, Earth remained familiar, to be clung to. Or possibly the non-emigrant imagined that the tent of dust [from the fallout] would deplete itself finally" (Dick 17), but this speculation only pushes the reader to look for a fuller explanation not only of why some remain, but also to examine how those who remain deal with such cataclysmic environmental change and what those adaptations reveal about humanity's link to Earth and other beings.

As the experiences of the characters unfold in the novel we see that they live in a complex system of accommodations to a ruined world and try to create/approximate senses of place and community. The novel depicts both the debased planet and the individuals whose links to others and the environment are tenuous at best. People need acts of will and imagination to carry on. Underlying this pursuit of connections is terraphilia—a term I use to indicate a sense of a deep bond with and loyalty to the Earth—that is necessary for anyone to attempt to move forward and remain on a wrecked planet. Two artists, Richard Cabe and Susan J. Tweit, also use the term terraphilia and provide the following definition on their website: "An intrinsic affection for and connection to the Earth and its community of lives. Without this connection, we are lonely, lacking, no longer whole." Their formulation most helpfully includes both the ideas of lack and community.

Dealing with environmental and cultural losses creates a nostalgic longing that itself results from destruction of the customary links to others in the broadest sense, encompassing all that is non-human and that provides the conditions in which humanity is possible. The concern about the negative results of human alienation from the environment goes back at least to the Romantics who saw industrialization as a culprit, and Marx's views in the first volume of *Capital* about the alienation of labor (Chapter 716). Carl Jung writing in the 1950s and the start of the 60s echoes both Marx and the Romantics, but also claims that people need a sense of place and permanence: "A community is based on personal relationships. No community can evolve where people can easily move households from one place to another" and "I am fully committed to the idea that human existence should be rooted in the earth" (155–156). For Jung, it is separation from others and from the environment that cause neuroses in people. Part of the problem manifests itself in what he sees as the inability to link with other people even at the basic level of serious conversation (139). The lack of connection extends beyond the individual or even the community for Jung. He says, "Man feels himself isolated in the cosmos. He is no longer involved in nature and has lost his emotional participation in natural events, which hitherto had a symbolic meaning for him" (79). Though he is not anti-technology or against the modern idea of progress, Jung clearly sees that humankind has suffered a loss that is fundamental since people can no longer make sense of the world that created them.

Similarly, Ursula Heise believes that humanity's destructive behavior results in alienation in another way. She sees humanity's loss in terms of species. In talking about extinctions of species in "Lost Dogs, Last Birds, and Listed Species: Cultures of Extinction," she points out that

> such extinction stories function as a means of representing turning points in human cultural histories, in which the loss of a particular species stands in both for a broader sense of the vanishing of nature and the weakening of human bonds to the natural world. As these stories unfold, part of human identity and culture itself seems to be lost along with the disappearance of a nonhuman species [69].

Heise's direct link of species loss to human loss can act as a commentary on Philip K. Dick's *Do Androids Dream of Electric Sheep?* In a 1976 essay, "Man, Android and Machine," Dick wrote, "By more modern views we are overlapping fields, all of us, animals included, plants included. This is the ecosphere and we are all in it" (223). This broad sense of links is at work in the novel. Though Dick apparently locates the sense of loss in Deckard's individual psychological struggle, that struggle itself, as both Jung and Heise would indicate, is a symptom of a larger issue. The book explores how people try to readjust in the face of cataclysm not just by adapting to a new, diminished world, but also by finding ways to create substitutes for the most important missing elements: ties to place, a sense of community, and a rudimentary understanding of the lives of the non-human, all in an attempt to hang onto some vestige of human culture and society.

One of the key plot elements and apparent ironies of Dick's novel *Do Androids Dream of Electric Sheep?* is the drive that Mars-based androids have to make their way to Earth—a dying, inhospitable planet that physically well humans most often choose to leave. Critics have explored the androids' lack of empathy in detail,[1] but the terraphilia that the androids suffer has not gotten much attention. Neither the androids nor the humans on Earth have immediate experience of unbuilt nature or fully functioning society. They acquire their views of Earth, society, and nature through information, from history to catalogues and media shows. The common ailment of both the humans and androids then is a terraphilia that can have no consummation because the world for which they long does not exist. Simulation and substitution are the ways they deal with this deficit and manage to create a sense of place from an initially broad idea of space and environments.

Rather than empathy alone being a determiner of humanity, the novel presents this very human struggle to recover a sense of belonging and human culture as the core of Deckard's questioning. While in his capacity as a bounty hunter he retires renegade androids in order to protect the hegemony and survival of humanity using an empathy test to sort android from human, his actual personal focus is less on empathy than it is on a need for connection in the broader sense of community and links to place. Both community and place are problematic concepts, however, since in post–World War Terminus San Francisco people live as near as they can to each other, but still inhabit mostly empty buildings. Their interactions are limited to short conversations, like the one Deckard has with his neighbor on the roof of the building they live in, or work-oriented contacts. Deckard may fit in broadly as a human among other humans, but their links to each other are weak. For example, the opening of the novel, which focuses on him and his wife, Iran, shows the reader the strain of living in a depopulated world. Iran uses her mood organ to dial depression, because, as she says: "'And I heard the building, this building; I heard the—' She gestured. 'Empty apartments,' Rick said," and she adds, "'I realized how unhealthy it was, sensing the absence of life, not just in this building but everywhere, and not reacting—do you see? I guess you don't'" (Dick 5). If empathy is a key human characteristic, one cannot practice it in isolation. The alienation that Iran feels, in this sense, undermines the emphasis the novel places on empathy in the form of the Voigt Kampff test that Deckard administers to suspected androids to find out whether they are human and can experience empathy. The novel also includes the key example of Phil Resch, a bounty hunter Deckard meets as he pursues Luba Luft, one of the escaped Nexus-6 androids. Resch exhibits reprehensible behavior and a lack of decency when he shoots Luba, not really because she is an android, but because she is an android who managed to irritate him. Being human is no measure of character or even a guarantee of a capacity for empathy. Furthermore, both Deckard and his boss, Harry Bryant, know that the Voigt Kampff test can also wrongly tag mentally ill human beings as androids (38). Therefore, empathy cannot be the sole indicator of humanity since some of the humans in the book have difficulty experiencing connection, or even well centered individuality, because of their physical and emotional distance from each other.

In contrast, the androids seek to return to Earth in order to have some individual freedoms and to cease functioning as tools or companions to the people to whom they have been assigned, not to join with humanity. An ad asserts: "Either as a body servant or tireless field hands, the custom-tailored humanoid robot—designed specifically for Your Unique Needs, For You Alone—given to you on your arrival [on Mars] absolutely free…" (17; Dick's emphasis), making clear that androids are incentives to human colonization of the red planet. When an interviewer questions a recent immigrant to Mars, Mrs. Klugman, she says, "'Having a servant you can depend on in these troubled times…I find it reassuring'" (18). Clearly those who leave Earth feel a need for even simulated, non-human beings in their midst. The fact that that relationship effectively enslaves the androids does not concern colonists such as Mrs. Klugman, since she sees the android as non-human. The irony of course is that the simulated human can bring such comfort, thus helping to simulate a sense of community on Mars. Precisely because the Rosen Corporation intends to create androids who can fit in with humans, the company includes intelligence in the beings it makes, thus making their commodification more cruel.

One of the androids who escapes from Mars, Pris, helps expand the reader's understanding of their desire to leave Mars and need to blend in with what is left of human society on Earth. When Pris moves in to the all-but abandoned building where John Isidore resides, she tells him "'it's [Mars] an awful place. This'—she swept the room, the apartment, in one violent gesture—this is nothing. You think I'm suffering because I'm lonely. Hell, all Mars is lonely. Much worse than this'" (150). At Isidore's bewildered reply that androids keep people company on Mars—the ads clearly have influenced his perspective—Pris tells him that "the androids are lonely too" (150). Isidore, who does not at this point know that Pris is an android, proves to be one of the best listeners in the novel despite his low status as a "chickenhead," or person with significantly reduced mental capacity. His impulses, set against those of various others, appear to be the most compassionate, the most human and humane. He tries to revive conventions of neighborly behavior when he scrounges around to find a food gift (unfortunately decayed margarine) to present to Pris when he knocks on her door and introduces himself. Just as he mimics the remnants of human society with spoiled food, and thus exposes the poor state of human social interaction, Pris illuminates the breakdown of society on Mars when she refers to the brisk black market in what she calls pre-colonial fiction: "'There's a fortune to be made in smuggling pre-colonial fiction, the old magazines and films. Nothing is as exciting. To read about cities and huge industrial enterprises, and really successful colonization'" (151). In addition to referring to science fiction and film, Pris's statement reveals that fiction and film are two of the arts that provide a window into a world that perhaps never was, but could act as a basis for daydreaming and creating goals, though these goals would be unattainable on any large scale. In the absence of physical examples of fully functioning cities and societies, the arts, the novel hints, can help to provide solace and substitution. What they cannot provide is restoration since that would require will, time, and the impossibility of replication of the way things were and worked prior to cataclysm. The androids themselves serve as an example of an attempt at replication. The Nexus–6 series of androids, and especially the doubling of Rachel/Pris, illustrate what Baudrillard terms "the obliteration of the original reference." He points out that "In a series, objects become undefined simulacra of one another" (Baudrillard *Simulations* 97).

Neither androids nor humans live in or create the worlds Pris alludes to, but some androids do try to reconstruct elements of human society and recreate themselves as part of human society. The android who shot Deckard's colleague, Dave Holden, for instance, poses as a low-functioning human, a so-called "anthead," and has a job at the Bay Area Scavengers Company. When Rick encounters this dangerous android, Polokov, the android is masquerading as a Soviet cop called Sandor Kadalyi. He not only almost fools Rick—what helps to give Polokov away is the odd firearm he carries—but actually does fool Rick's boss (by posing as a colleague over the phone), who instructs Rick to let this visitor tag along as he retires the Nexus–6 renegades. In posing as a Soviet bounty hunter, Polokov takes on the role of one who retires androids, mirroring Deckard and representing a system set up to kill him and others like him. Though Deckard does figure out that the cop is really Polokov, his initial concern is not about verifying this tag along's identity, but about whether he would have to share the bounty with him. Once reassured on that point, he is content to wait for Polokov/Kadalyi as long as the delay does not let the trail go cold.

For Rick, the money represents a way to be able to afford to replace the electric animal he has, a sheep. When he reveals to his neighbor that his sheep is a machine, his neighbor compassionately tells him that he will not share that information with anyone else in the building, thus making clear for the reader that those who do not have a biological creature risk scorn. As Sherryl Vint points out in "Speciesism and Species Being in *Do Androids Dream of Electric Sheep?*" one of the major ironies of the novel is that for all the emphasis on the importance of having a live animal, the characters and society in the book do not actually have any real emotional bonds with their animals (116). Molloy agrees when she states, "Even though the animal may be elevated to the level of the sacred, the overriding system of exchange affords meanings to animals that are primarily intended to prescribe the social relations with humans" (114). The animals, however, are not only status symbols. They also represent the need that humans have to try to recreate a world that they think existed prior to World War Terminus, a world in which humans supposedly had links with creatures. Both the gradual and accelerated extinctions of species, however, work against the notion that people had forged real bonds with other species even prior to World War Terminus.

Animals have their greatest importance in the novel as a way for Deckard to work through his own limitations, questions and prejudices. The episode with the toad toward the end of the novel when Rick is in the deserted area north of San Francisco makes clear that he wants to believe in the possibility of an appreciation for other species because that appreciation is part of being able to have connections with other people. His discovery of the toad occurs just after he fuses with Mercer without the assistance of an empathy box. At the start of the novel Iran points out that he has never really gotten the knack of fusion, so his unassisted link here is unusual. Even when he gets the toad home and Iran discovers that it is an electric animal, he states that electric things have their life, too—his view of who or what counts has broadened beyond humans (fully functioning and damaged), to androids, and to other types of being. Facts have nothing to do with his revelation, since Buster Friendly and His Friendly Friends reveal that Mercer and Mercerism are frauds put forward by the government and film industry. Buster and his android friends, whom the government allows to remain on Earth because they provide much-needed twenty-four hour entertainment, go so far as to locate an aging alcoholic former actor, Al Jarry, who substantiates their information since he acted the part of Mercer in some short films (Dick 209). Significantly, the exposé airs at the same time that the androids torment a spider while they are gathered in Isidore's apartment. Even though Isidore is upset because of the torture, he insists that Mercerism will last despite the damaging news (211). Belief also sustains Deckard since that is what drives any possibility of getting past any of the malaise of the world he lives in. In constructing a belief in others Deckard not only avoids solipsism, he also gestures toward a world in which all have a place, all fit in and have a role and command the respect of others. The novel certainly does not imply the creation of a utopia or the restoration of the past, but does indicate that nostalgia and unease help engender hope at least for individuals to link with others in microcosmic community.

Even before the pivotal toad encounter, Deckard faces both the power of simulacra and the hope for community in the form of Luba Luft. As he attends a rehearsal of Mozart's *The Magic Flute* with Luba playing the role of Pamina, he realizes how much he enjoys opera. Despite the limited success of the rehearsal, we read, "What a pleasure; he loved *The Magic Flute*" (Dick 97). The narrative also speaks of the space of the opera house in terms that mingle biological, geological and constructed forms. The chapter begins with "In the enormous whale-belly of steel and stone carved out to form the long-enduring opera house…" (97), thus situating Rick in what appears to be at once the story of Jonah, the story of the plight of whales, the mingling of biological form with industrial materials, and art's tenacity. The scene he sees, as Patrick McCarthy points out, highlights the figure of Papageno, decked out in bird feathers as he tries to catch birds. Though Papageno is a threat to the animals, he and Pamina sing of harmony, friendship and sympathy. These concepts combined sound like a sense of belonging and community. As McCarthy translates the German lyrics "Only the harmony of friends eases all hardships and without this sympathy there is no joy on earth" (348). The rehearsal of the opera itself acts as a beginning of Deckard's shift in perspective. He comes to the venue happy to hear an opera with which he is familiar, but the reader hears only that Deckard had heard recordings of great opera stars, not that he has been to performances. Being in the presence of the unfolding of the opera, even with the quirky misstep he notes—"The Moor's slaves—in other words the chorus—had taken up their song a bar too soon" (Dick 97)—still affects him. In part his response is a repetition, but it is a repetition with a difference. When he hears Pamina and Papageno sing, the narrator tells us that "the words [about the magic bells]…always brought tears to his eyes, when and if he happened to think about it" (97), but this time his thoughts turn negative. He thinks that "in real life no such magic bells exist" (98), and also thinks about Mozart dying young. Because he comes to the theater in order to retire an android, his own emotional response darkens, but he does wait until there is a break in the rehearsal to confront Luba. Deckard, like Jonah who tries to flee rather than do the job God has assigned him, experiences reluctance to do the task he faces.

As he investigates her at the opera house, Deckard learns that the androids have succeeded in building part of a parallel society on Earth. When he interviews Luba Luft to try to test her capacity for empathy, she calls a policeman who turns out to be working for an android-infested police force rather than the one that employs Deckard. Many of those who work at the parallel institution do not realize that it is not the "real" thing. Many critics point out how crucial Deckard's talk with Luba is,[2] but most gloss over the oddity of the second police organization. The androids essentially choose to hide in plain sight by replicating the very institution that seeks to discover and eliminate them. Beyond the idea that this other police force may indicate a weird degree of self-loathing, it also indicates that the androids would create a society that is based on laws and regulated behaviors. They want an orderly world. Since the main character of the novel's agenda is to root out androids who are trying to pass as human in order to preserve actual (though sometimes damaged) humanity, the androids' institutional simulation serves not only as a mirror of human society, but also as a protection against it. The fact that Luba calls the android-based force when Deckard begins questioning her also tells the reader and Deckard that the androids are far more embedded on Earth than anyone had suspected. Deckard's police force is no longer dealing with various renegade individuals or small groups of recently arrived androids. The androids use this other police station as a clearinghouse for returned androids, so it acts as a hub for them. The book does not actually deal with any systematic approach to trying to dismantle the other force, however, as Deckard lurches toward his existential crisis and begins to have doubts about the validity of his job as a result of the Luba Luft episode.

The other major simulation in the novel comes through the use of the empathy box that even the most degraded humans, such as John Isidore, have and use. The empathy box allows for a connection with other human beings through the link to the figure called Mercer. Use of the empathy box serves as the perfect example of a blurring of the line between the concocted and the real. Users often experience physical pain and lacerations as they climb the hill while rocks fly towards them, sometimes hitting them. Some people actually fuse with Mercer. An early example in the book involves Isidore who brings the reader through

Mercer's experiences, especially those that involve his ability to raise animals from the dead. Mercer's narrative includes his ostracism from society brought on by others' intolerance of his strange talent. The message is that people have not only helped to destroy other species, but they have also actively resented the idea of restoring the lost. Embedded in Mercer's story is a much deeper exposé than Buster Friendly's debunking of Mercerist fusion. People have dismantled society and abandoned hope through intolerance of difference—both difference among humans and difference across species. The concocted narrative is as close to truth as any critique of humanity can get in the novel. As Vint points out, the degrading power of capitalist prerogatives is a key part of the destruction of society in the book: "The unstable boundary in the novel between real and artificial animals suggests how living nature can become, like the commodity, a dead thing that only seems to have life and which dominates the human rather than being connected to humanity through social relations" (119).

The episodes in the novel involving the Rosen Corporation's owl, the critically ill cat and the tormented spider all support Vint's statement. They also provide a way for the reader to see different attitudes about the acceptance of others among characters in the novel. When Deckard visits the Rosen Corporation to try to be sure that the Voigt-Kampff test for empathy will actually work when he encounters the Nexus–6 androids he needs to pursue and retire, Rachel Rosen, as a representative of the corporation and an android herself (though she initially is unaware of her non-human status) tries to bribe him by offering him an owl. This is extraordinary, since as Rick knows from his almost obsessive reading of the *Sidney's* catalogue—which lists animals, their availability and current price—that owls are extinct. Because of the scarcity of the creature/commodity Rick is actually tempted, but more importantly, he is willing to believe that there just may be an actual owl in existence—either one that miraculously survived World War Terminus, or one the Corporation has somehow created as a biological animal.[3] The episode exposes both the lengths to which the Corporation will go to manipulate the law and protect their investment in the Nexus–6 androids and Rick's otherwise well-hidden optimism. The commodity status of animals in this scene is a given.

As a contrast to Rick,[4] the novel presents J. Isidore's handling of a sick cat. He thinks it is an electric animal, but as the driver of the van for Mr. Sloat's veterinary clinic, the Van Ness Pet Hospital (though they treat electric animals, the van looks like it comes from a regular vet), he does everything he can to try to help it. Isidore feels compassion for the animal's suffering. While everyone around him sees Horace, the cat, as either a commodity, part of a business transaction, or a status symbol, Isidore sees only a being in pain that needs help. In a later scene, because of Isidore's capacity for empathy, and in opposition to his need for inclusion in a society that has branded him a chickenhead, he cannot bear to watch Pris's cold treatment of a spider he finds. Though he wants to be part of a group, he cannot stand the capacity for sadism that her mutilation of the spider reveals. As she coldly snips one leg after another from the arachnid, ostensibly so she and her android comrades, Irmgard and Roy Baty, can see how many legs it needs in order to move, Isidore protests and stops the spider's suffering by drowning it (Dick 211). As N. Katherine Hayles points out, "J.R. perceives the heat energy rushing from the room, as if the room's physical decay sprang directly from her lack of empathy" (433). She adds that this shows that his ability to separate inside from outside worlds is seriously distorted. Though her psychological reading of Isidore is perceptive, the "distortion" also indicates the importance of the links between the person and the animal. Both Rick and Isidore's reactions to animals, or offers of animals, reveal their need to create connections to others—whether to impress others or feel more a part of society. The commodifying tendency that critics identify in the novel indicates not only a shift in the way characters view others, but also permeates the way they view places.

For Isidore the con-apt building where he lives has a non-life of its own that the novel describes as the ineluctable growth of kipple—the process of decay, the breakdown of objects:

> He lived alone in this deteriorating, blind building of a thousand uninhabited apartments, which like all its counterparts, fell, day by day, into greater entropic ruin. Eventually everything within the building would merge, would be faceless and identical, mere pudding-like kipple piled to the ceiling of each apartment. And, after that, the uncared for building itself would settle into shapelessness...[Dick 20].

When Rick realizes that he has to head to the con-apt building to retire the remaining Nexus–6 androids, he thinks about its location in an abandoned area and realizes this "a good place to hide. Except for the lights at night.... Phototropic, like the death head moth" (180). It is an area that he at first sees as on the fringes of the society that remains and significantly thinks of the lights in terms of a creature. Strange areas link with absent animals for Deckard. He clearly has some sensitivity to place as a key part of the challenge of facing the androids. This all but abandoned building shows the reader Deckard's first direct encounter with Mercer. Mercer appears to him to help him in his encounter with the android who is Rachel Rosen's double, Pris. Mercer tells Rick that he is in the building because of Isidore and warns Rick that one of the androids is actually behind him (221). This instance of special intervention helps prepare Deckard for his subsequent fusion as well. Depopulated spaces become extraordinarily meaningful for Rick, though he initially has trouble maneuvering in and understanding these areas.

Rick sees the unpopulated desert area he heads to after retiring the last of the escaped Nexus–6 androids as strange. He initially tries to understand it in terms of goods. When he sees the long view of the landscape as he approaches it in his hovercar he thinks it looks like "a shipping room when all the merchandise has left," and only secondarily thinks "crops grew here and animals grazed. What a remarkable thought" (228). Both men's notions of place involve absences of people and other creatures, and in the case of kipple, the absence continues to expand. The voids that Berman links to the androids when he says "The androids are always marked by absences, which stand in contradistinction to the human characters" (93) holds true on a psychological level, especially in the spider episode, but there are clearly larger absences in the novel and the humans are not immune to experiencing these gaps. Both Rick and Isidore's ideas also reveal the need to reach for what the absences gesture toward: a nostalgia for those who used to live in bustling apartment buildings, or a pastoral landscape that supported animals. A sense of place requires connection, history and memory. Both Rick and Isidore have some sense of how their society worked, how humans and the world were prior to World War Terminus. Dick's use of narrative indirect voice to bring the reader into Rick's and Isidore's thoughts also expands our understanding of their odd subject positions in relation to a sense of place and community.

Even if neither man had a direct recollection of a fuller place, imagination can be a powerful force. As Laurence Buell points out "the fact that the imagination hasn't been there and maybe never will hardly lessens the intensity of such storied or imagined places to induce longing and loyalty" (73). This imaginative power also acts as a comment on the attraction of pre-colonial fiction discussed earlier. In Dick's novel the power of imagination is the unspoken element in Mercerist fusion. Mercerism, after all the existential angst Rick experiences and the bleak depression that both Iran and Isidore know (she through dialed depression and he through the descent into what he calls the tomb world) combined with the blankness of the destroyed earth, stands as a bulwark against complete dissolution of connection to others and the world. Richard Viskovic asserts that "Mercer's story offers a glimpse of hope in the half-life existence of the people waiting for death and degeneration on the dying earth" (181). Though Mercerist fusion appears to be an escape from the grimness of the fallout environment, it offers both links to others and the trial of climbing and feeling the pain of being pelted by rocks. Thus, Mercerism is not some Marxist opiate of the masses. The suffering acts both as individual and collective penance, though not as atonement, and as a physical reminder of one's actual existence. Feeling both attachment and sensation—even if it is painful part of the time—are essential to being consciously alive. The positive feelings that people share via the use of the empathy box are part of the conglomerate of linked consciousness. Thus it takes more than physical presence to constitute identity and community, but physical awareness is part of the mix.

Dick explains how the idea that a meaningful link to another person is fundamental in his 1972 essay, "The Android and the Human." He says:

> The world of the future, to me, is not a place but an event. A construct, not by one author in the form of words written to make up a novel or story that other persons sit in front of, outside of, and read—but a construct in which there is no author and no readers but a great many characters in search of a plot. Well, there is no plot. There is only themselves and what they do and say to each other, what they build to sustain all of them individually and collectively, like a huge umbrella that lets in light and shuts out the darkness at the same instant [205].

The de-emphasis on place and event in this passage does not, however, negate the idea of a sense of belonging. Dick's formulation recenters people so that the link to another person is what matters most. The umbrella image, of course, metaphorically begins to re-create place as a zone of safety and solace. In the novel, Deckard needs to share his experiences with someone with whom he feels safe. Though he thinks of talking about his experiences with his injured colleague, Dave, he actually speaks with Iran.

Even though the start of the novel seems to indicate that they are emotionally distant from one another, Rick and Iran need and care about each other. The novel opens and closes with the couple. At the start Rick worries that Iran will not be able to snap out of the depression she has scheduled on her mood organ and at the close of the narrative she supports him when he tells her about finding the toad. When it turns out to be mechanical she orders electric flies for it. She earlier supports his purchase of the doomed goat that Rachel Rosen murders, though she initially wished she had been more involved in the decision to purchase the animal. It is Iran who points out that they should share their joy about the goat with others. She listens to him as he had listened to her about her need to experience depression. In essence, they share their sense of alienation and their need for community. As a parallel to her depression statement, we read that Rick thinks he has become "an unnatural self" (Dick *Do Androids Dream* 230) after he has retired the Nexus-6 androids. Importantly, she sees that he needs to recover from the events of the day, but does not simply tell him to rest. She also watches him sleep because she is concerned that he might have nightmarish fears as he sometimes does, which cause him to "spring to a sitting position" (243). Her worry tells the reader both that Deckard has been haunted in the past—even before the major task of retiring the Nexus-6 androids fell to him—and that she wants to help him through his angst. In this sense, she acts as the metaphorical umbrella of Dick's statement.

    Deckard has come to realize that not only his android-destroying job, but also his need for connections to others, are at the root of his negative epiphany about his own unnaturalness. That word is extraordinary in the world of the novel, since the idea that anyone truly knows what constitutes natural being is ludicrous. The term is problematic even in a less environmentally compromised world. That he has his revelation in a bleak landscape prevents a reader from thinking that there could be restoration of the Earth, but at the same time insists that his experience is absolutely valid for him. His revelation is not just that one should respect other beings. The idea of that respect is rooted in a sense of place, a connection to the Earth: "Life which we can no longer distinguish. Life carefully buried up to its forehead in the carcass of a dead world" (238). The dead world of this passage acts as a host would in relation to a growing parasite. The symbiotic link is fundamental, whether or not it is comfortable for either participant.

    Similarly people's odd relationships with the machines they use—most importantly the empathy box and the mood organ—indicate not only a level of self-alienation, but also the idea that simulations help bridge the gaps people feel. As Sims says of *Do Androids Dream of Electric Sheep?*, the novel "shows us that technology can be used as a guide to return the survivors of World War Terminus to the humanity that they have abandoned for solipsistic individualism" (68). In other words, machines are not the problem in the novel. They act as symptoms and partial solutions for humanity's malaise. Beyond machines and their capacity to assist in creations and simulations, belief, and acts of will that lead to a conversion toward community, influence Deckard. The arts as well technology help to steer him a direction that aids in his need to reimagine what it is to be more fully human.

In the end there can be no revival or recreation of the past, but that does not keep the characters in the novel from harboring a longing for that which they know only as ghost remnants or traces, as the examples of Isidore's margarine gift, and the spider, toad, and owl episodes indicate. The shadow of something just out of reach that simulacra (both androids and animals) represent is both a consolation and a cause of unease because people live in an in-between state that has not fully accepted simulacra as genuinely helpful. Iran's conversation with Rick about her need to dial depression is an early instance of that unsettled state. Since we learn that colonizing Mars, though it may sound like a good idea in the ads, is actually not a good alternative to living on Earth, there is no external place that can help. Without a developed sense of place and a connection to the planet that make possible the idea of community, no one can feel content. This is what Rick discovers when he finally makes the accommodation to the electric toad. He begins to see that there is something worthwhile even in simulacra. He also sees that the role of will and power of collective desire that expresses itself through Mercerist fusion, which Deckard experiences without the empathy box, can bring some relief from the strain of living in a scarred environment.

No matter how miserable the condition of Earth has become, terraphilia remains and functions as the foundation for humanity. Simulacra, the arts, and experience, combine to leave the reader and Deckard with the hope that people can find a way to imagine community and begin to attempt to create it.

Notes

1. For example, see Barlow, Galvan, Sims and Heise's "From Extinction to Electronics."

2. See Rossi's essay.
3. On the importance of animals, especially birds in the novel see Molloy.
4. For discussions that focus on doubling throughout the novel see Warrick and Francavilla.

Works Cited

Barlow, Aaron. "Philip K. Dick's Androids: Victimized Victimizers." *Retrofitting Blade Runner: Issues in Ridley Scott's Blade Runner and Philip K. Dick's Do Androids Dream of Electric Sheep?* Ed. Judith Kerman. Bowling Green, OH: Popular Press, 1991. 76–89. Print.

Baudrillard, Jean. *Simulations*. Trans. Paul Foss, Paul Patton and Philip Beitchmen. New York: Semiotext[e], 1983. Print.

Berman, Michael. "Images of Absence in P.K. Dick's *Do Androids Dream of Electric Sheep?*" *Literature and Aesthetics* 16.2 (2006): 75–94. Print.

Buell, Lawrence. *The Future of Environmental Criticism: Environmental Crisis and Literary Imagination*. Malden, MA,: Blackwell, 2005. Print.

Cabe, Richard, and Susan J. Tweit. "Terraphilia." Salidamillworkwww. Online. 20 June 2012.

Dick, Philip K. "The Android and the Human." *The Shifting Realities of Philip K. Dick: Selected Literary and Philosophical Writings*. Ed. Lawrence Sutin. New York: Vintage, 1995. 183–210. Print.

_____. *Do Androids Dream of Electric Sheep?* New York: Del Rey, 1996. Print.

_____. "Man, Android, and Machine." *The Shifting Realities of Philip K. Dick: Selected Literary and Philosophical Writings*. Ed. Lawrence Sutin. New York: Vintage, 1995. 211–232. Print.

_____. "Pessimism in Science Fiction." *The Shifting Realities of Philip K. Dick: Selected Literary and Philosophical Writings*. Ed. Lawrence Sutin. New York: Vintage, 1995. 54–56. Print.

Francavilla, Joseph. "The Android as *Doppelgänger*." *Retrofitting Blade Runner: Issues in Ridley Scott's Blade Runner and Philip K. Dick's Do Androids Dream of Electric Sheep?* Ed. Judith Kerman. Bowling Green, OH: Popular Press, 1991. 4–15. Print

Galvan, Jill. "Entering the Posthuman Collective in Philip K. Dick's *Do Androids Dream of Electric Sheep?*" *Science Fiction Studies* 24 (1997): 413–429. Print.

Hayles, N. Katherine. "Schizoid Android: Cybernetics and the Mid-Sixties Novels of Philip K. Dick." *Journal of the Fantastic in the Arts*. 8.4 (1997): 419–42. Print.

Heise, Ursula K. "From Extinction to Electronics: Dead Frogs, Live Dinosaurs, and Electric Sheep." *Zoontologies: The Question of the Animal*. Ed. Cary Wolfe. Minneapolis: University of Minnesota Press, 2003. 59–81. Print.

Heise, Ursula K. "Lost Dogs, Last Birds, and Listed Species: Cultures of Extinction." *Configurations* 18 (2010): 49–72. Project Muse. Web. 2 April 2012.

Jung, C. G. *The Earth Has a Soul: C.G. Jung on Nature, Technology and Modern Life*. Ed. Meredith Sabini. Berkeley, CA: North Atlantic Books, 2008. Print.

Marx, Karl. *Capital. Volume 1.*Trans. Ben Fowles. New York: Penguin Books, 1976. Print.

McCarthy, Patrick A. "Do Androids Dream of Magic Flutes?" *Paradoxa* 5. 13–14 (2000): 344–352. Print.

Molloy, Claire. "Dreaming of Electric Sheep and Negotiating Animality." *Of Mice and Men: Animals in Human Culture*. Eds. Nandita Batra and Vartan Messier. Newcastle upon Tyne: Cambridge Scholars, 2009. 106–120. Print.

Rossi, Umberto. "The Android Cogito: *We Can Build You* and *Do Androids Dream of Electric Sheep?" The Twisted Worlds of Philip K. Dick: A Reading of Twenty Ontologically Uncertain Novels.* Jefferson, NC: McFarland, 2011. 143–172. Print.

Sims, Christopher. "The Dangers of Individualism and the Human Relationship to Technology in Philip K. Dick's *Do Androids Dream of Electric Sheep?*" *Science Fiction Studies* 36 (2009): 67–86. Print.

Vint, Sherryl. "Speciesism and Species Being in *Do Androids Dream of Electric Sheep?*" *Mosaic* 40.1 (2007): 111–126. *Academic OneFile.* Web. 5 March 2009.

Viskovic, Richard. "The Rise and Fall of Wilbur Mercer." *Extrapolation* 54.2 (2013): 163–182. Print.

Warrick, Patricia S. "Mechanical Mirrors, the Double, and *Do Androids Dream of Electric Sheep?*" *Mind in Motion: The Fiction of Philip K. Dick.* Carbondale: Southern Illinois University Press, 1987. 117–132. Print.

Discursive Transgressions and Ideological Negotiations
From Orwell's 1984 to Butler's Parable of the Sower

Keith Elphick

The Dystopian Construct: Creating a Nightmare

The dystopian novel has traditionally been regarded as a work that serves as a warning or cautionary tale of what the future *could* become if a society refuses to alter its detrimental path. Unlike the utopian novel, which is removed and "suspend[ed] from real time and space," dystopian authors make direct allusions to the history of their present society in the hope of enlightening readers to its instability (Baccolini 114). Once dystopian authors identify the pernicious elements of a society, their goal then moves from warning readers of their destructive nature to educating them. While it is important for these authors to maintain a direct connection with the present society being critiqued, the dystopian author often has to foresee that society's future and portray its debased and highly damaged position to readers. This process not only creates a setting that is a complete horror, but also a plot that is capable of engulfing readers in the chaotic world of the dystopia.

While scholars have traced the origins of the dystopia genre to publications written well before the twentieth century, the World Wars, development of nuclear technologies, and violence associated with conflicting political regimes set the stage for a text as disconcerting as George Orwell's *1984*. Since its 1949 publication, the seminal novel has undoubtedly established itself as the foundational text of the genre and the portrait of complete social nightmare. Critics from all fields of literature, including science fiction, modernism, postmodernism, and realism, find that Orwell's amalgamation of dystopian elements into one novel has set a foundational standard for the genre. Reflecting on the effect *1984* had on the dystopia, Chad Walsh writes: "[*1984*] is something close to the complete dystopia. Most of the horrors that other books have predicted are here combined and synthesized into 100 per cent nightmare" (107). Unlike *Brave New World* and *We*, *1984* abandons readers at the end of the novel in a state of horrified paralysis, leaving them without any imagined possibility for future action. The only image that readers are left with is O'Brien's terrifying description of the Party's idealized society: "A world of fear and treachery and torment, a world of trampling and being trampled upon, a world which will grow not less but *more* merciless as it refines itself" (Orwell 341–42). It is Orwell's refusal to conclude his novel with any corpuscle of hope that establishes it as such a seminal publication in the dystopian genre, for he understands that a false sense of optimism in the world of Oceania would undermine the novel's powerful message.

While dystopian novels like *1984* do portray a version of the future that is utterly terrifying to those who read it, that horrifying picture is all that is provided explicitly. Dystopian authors achieve their goal of reawakening citizens to their own troubled social structure and do establish what writer Kim Stanley Robinson deems an "underlying metaphorical purpose," but they often offer no solutions to combat the problems causing social debasement; the message is, as Robinson states, an embedded metaphorical one (xi). Ultimately, the hyperbolized "bad places" depicted in these texts cause such devastation, change is inconceivable.

The Emergence of a New Discourse: The Critical Dystopia

Thankfully, a future like Orwell's *1984* did not, or has not *yet*, occurred. No authoritarian regime like Big Brother has taken control of society and no ideology as violent and despotic as Oceania's Innerparty has infiltrated our psyches. This is not to say that because *1984*'s Innerparty, or a regime similar to it, has not dominated present society it cannot or will not ever happen. The classic dystopian structure, like *1984*'s, serves its most fundamental purpose: articulating a warning that awakens the social consciousness to the societal problems of the prospective future.

Although *1984* has continued to act as the undisputed model text for complete dystopian nightmare, the past thirty years have produced a new dystopian subgenre that strays from the classic pattern found in *1984, Brave New World,* and *We.* Unlike the authors of the dystopia genre, the authors of critical dystopias attempt to provide answers to the unchallenged problems in dystopian novels like *1984*. While solidified step-by-step instructions for solving the environmental problems associated with mass materialism will not be found in these novels, the characters in many critical dystopias painstakingly struggle to *adapt* to and *better* the problems facing them in these texts' microcosmic societies. While the adjective "optimistic" has perhaps too strong a connotation to describe this subgenre of dystopian studies, there is a sense of hope and unity in these novels that has kept it apart from the despair engulfing the classic dystopias. Critic Tom Moylan has deemed the critical dystopia's ability to maintain a "utopian impulse," while "linger[ing] in the terrors of the present," one of this genre's key attributes (199). In addition to the critical dystopia's ability to balance despair and hope, one will also find the authors of this genre consistently working through alternatives in order to retain a belief in future possibility.

Since a definition for the critical dystopia does not exist, literary scholars have provided criteria by which one can analyze a text to determine its *critical* potential. Critics frequently cite Moylan, Sargeant, and Baccolini for their works regarding the history of the dystopia and the emergence of the critical dystopia. In his prestigious work *Scraps of the Untainted Sky,* Moylan provides a synthesis of both utopian and dystopian characteristics to formulate a working definition of the critical dystopia: "[They] teach their readers not only about the world around them but also about the open-ended ways in which texts ... both elucidate that world and help to develop the critical capacity of people to know, challenge, and change those aspects of it that deny or inhibit the further emancipation of humanity" (199). In her article "Gender and Genre," Baccolini furthers Moylan's working definition of the critical genre, writing that these texts "maintain a utopian core" and "help to deconstruct tradition and reconstruct alternatives" (qtd. in Moylan 188). She also finds that the critical dystopia will usually "negate state ideals, preserve radical actions, and create a space in which opposition can be articulated and received" (188). Scholar Lyman Tower Sargent offers a definition of the critical dystopia that places emphasis on a publication's historical moment. He purports that the critical dystopia is "a non-existent society ... normally located in [the] time and space that the author intended a contemporaneous reader to view as worse than contemporary society but that normally includes at least one eutopian enclave or holds out hope that the dystopia can be overcome and replaced with a eutopia" (qtd in Moylan 195). For all the latter scholars, the critical dystopia is a work that refuses the imagined, idyllic, and unthreatened society of the utopia while not becoming hopelessly suffocated in the violent, debilitating, and pessimistic world of the dystopia.

Although the definition of the critical genre remains elusive, partly because of the genre's tendencies to blur the borders of differing literary genres and respond to problems as they arise in their social context, the "critical" component denotes a tenacious analysis of the novel's social structure that moves its characters into the sphere of action. Unlike traditional dystopias and anti-utopias, the critical dystopia partners analysis with action; characters attempt to change or to alter the systemic variables causing turmoil within the microcosm. In contrast to the anti-utopias, or the dystopian novels accompanying *1984*, the characters within critical dystopias do not remain complacent in their situation; they incessantly learn from and engage with their environment in order to provide possibilities for future generations.

While the latter critics have done an exemplary job defining the critical dystopia and explicating various texts in this relatively new subgenre, one aspect of dystopian studies that has received little attention is a close study of the ideological implications surrounding characters' own writings within these novels. A close reading of characters' writings in the critical dystopia reveals a multifarious process that culminates in a discourse commenting on the ideological conflicts caused by the societal construct of the dystopian landscape. And while an in-depth analysis of rhetorical and discourse theory goes beyond the scope of this essay, it is important to acknowledge the apparent connections these theories have with the specific role of written discourse in the critical dystopia, for the creation of texts in this genre, I will argue, differs from all other genres specifically because of the conflict between two societal constructs: the pre-dystopian society and the post-calamity social construct. This social binary is significant for two reasons: its ability to create fragmentation and nostalgia within the psyche, and its ability to alter one's rhetorical ability to discuss societal change. Because characters commonly create texts in the dystopian genre with a focus on the present moment, it is important to read such texts as a discourse commenting on that historical moment, and since the majority of dystopias are not set more than a century apart from social catastrophe, the characters within these social constructs have not forgotten the morals, ethics, and social codes of the society before calamity. Thus, they initially remain faithful to the proscriptive norms of the pre-dystopia while in the dystopian construct. The introduction of a completely discordant social and ideological construct creates such a psychological conflict that this is the place where I find the genre capable of producing its most powerful discourse about individuals' capabilities to acclimate to new surroundings and to formulate new belief systems. A close study of the characters in the dystopian construct goes beyond the ostensible physical challenges of surviving in a resource-vacant and violence-prone landscape to one that is as much physical as it is psychological.

The main characters in critical dystopias are those who have avoided the many deleterious elements of the dystopian landscape. A reading of one of these texts will usually produce a list of a great number of fatal obstacles: weather, nuclear explosions/radiation, malnutrition, pollution, physical violence, disease, social unrest, fatigue, imprisonment, and physical illness. Once a character learns to take the necessary precautions to acclimate to the physicality of the dystopia, he or she then is faced with the psychological facets of the social construct, which, I will later argue, is one that is primarily ideological and understood through written discourse.

Because the pre-dystopian landscape no longer exists for these characters, for calamity has already occurred, irreparably changing it, they must adapt to the new social ideology before they can make any meaningful difference in the dystopia. There is no time machine in these worlds, there is no elixir, there is no deus ex machina, and there is no stoic hero who is capable of resetting the balance of society. If characters do not adapt to the new social construct, it will kill them.

One multifaceted process that provides the most direct insight into the process of ideological negotiation is that of discursive creation. Since dystopian and utopian authors have habitually utilized the epistolary, first person narrative in their novels, it becomes apparent that this technique is an important aspect of the genre. And while many dystopian texts are not written in direct epistolary form, the inclusion of journal entries, letters, and memoirs have produced nearly the same effect. Unlike the characters of dystopian novels, who remain firmly grounded in the world before calamity, a study of critical dystopian fiction reveals that characters in this subgenre often go through a process of self-transformation that enables them to adjust their values to meet the declining conditions of the dystopian landscape. This process, which is both physical and psychological, is commonly externalized through the use of written discourse, but as it is multifaceted, an examination of a critical dystopian novel is essential, for a close analysis of a character's individual transformation reveals the process's complexities. Such novels as Kim Stanley Robinson's *Pacific Edge* and Le Guin's many works are suitable for this kind of analysis, but Octavia Butler's emphasis on creating discourse in *Parable of the Sower* establishes it as a fitting text for a discussion of the ideological complexities inherent within discursive creation.

Unlike a "utopian impulse" or rebellious yearning, which any character can have, establishing a discourse to understand the dystopian construct is imperative for a novel to transform from the pessimism of the dystopia to the possibly inherent in the critical dystopia (Moylan 188–89). In these harsh dystopian societies, action and change cannot just happen, for their structure has become too defiled to allow a free movement of actions and ideas; thus the characters of critical dystopias go through a process that leads them to action. It is during this process that many characters use written discourse to voice externally their own ideological negotiations. Since the past is no longer accessible in the critical dystopia, characters must come to terms with their present reality—the horror of a dystopia—and discard nostalgia for the past and utopian promise. Along with discarding the past, characters also reject their preconceived notions of morality and the ideologies of a former society in order to understand the reality of the dystopian present. Oftentimes characters' rejection of finished texts and antiquated rituals from the past symbolizes social acclimation. Once characters have negotiated this psychological process, they are able to engage truthfully with the dystopian construct not only by voicing areas for possibility, but also by acting to foster a future with possibility.

Epistolary Form, Discursivity, and Ideological Negotiations

While reading a novel from the "topia" genres, it has become quite common for one to encounter novels written in epistolary form or peppered with the journal entries of a novel's protagonist. This epistolary structure becomes highly beneficial to the reader, for the entries often provide concrete dates and locations that assist with contextualization. Beyond such surface level features, the epistolary text also creates a window into a character's psyche, offering subjective narrative that often transforms into stream of consciousness dialogue. In dystopian novels and critical dystopias, the reader is often given a disturbingly truthful internal monologue that articulates the anxiety, paranoia, emotional instability, fear, hatred, and unabashed psychological violence that have instilled in the character's head. By providing this direct insight into a character's psyche and inherent suffering, the epistolary form has the unique ability to establish urgency in the text and create a direct emotional connection between the character and the reader.

In traditional dystopias, a character's writing is frequently a form of resistance against an authoritarian regime. Without any means to rebel collaboratively, characters who are under the rule of aggressive authoritarian regimes seek to disobey the ruling power during all possible instances, even if it is a solitary act of personal reflection. These rebellions, regardless of how small, often keep the spirit of the individual alive in a society that has ceased to have the pulse of revolt. Under the control of an omnipotent authority figure, one's own written text, even if not destined for any particular reader, becomes a politicized act discrediting an authority's attempt to force all citizens to conform to its ideology. Ultimately, the characters trapped within the dystopian landscape use language as a last means of rebellion and as a way to maintain a rational understanding of the transforming reality around them. It is this process of maintaining an individualized discourse that has the potential to establish power within the individual and the community. The writing process becomes more than affirming and articulating dissent; in many texts, it becomes a means to appropriate a discursive form that is able to conflict with the domineering discourse, which is functioning to affirm and reinforce an oppressive ideology.

As *1984* is a seminal publication in the dystopia genre, it is a fitting model for showing the differences in discursive creation among critical dystopias, traditional dystopias, and anti-utopias. In *1984*, Winston Smith is very much aware of the political ramifications of his own writings. Winston not only rebels against the Innerparty by keeping a journal, an act that symbolizes *personal* reflection, dissent, and intellect, but it is also the nature of his entries that commits the most heinous act possible against the Party, thought crime. Journaling becomes Winston's individualized discourse that reassures his own dissident place among the Party's arrested society. It is his way of creating a counter discourse that opposes the Party's overwhelming hold on language and ideology. The first time Winston writes in his journal, he instinctively and unconsciously writes "in large neat capitals" the powerful statement, "DOWN WITH BIG BROTHER" four consecutive times prior to awakening himself from a reflective trance (Orwell 104). Unbeknownst to Winston, his journaling has acted as a form of sublimation, providing an outlet for the repressed energies that have been subdued in the psyche. It is such psychological purging that authoritarian regimes fear, for the use of violence to suppress social rebellion only propagates the violence that will be used to overthrow the repressors.

Although Winston uses language to rebel internally against the ubiquitous rule of the Innerparty, his discursive act, which is similar to many other dystopian characters' writings, is practically insignificant in the larger society of Oceania; Winston is one man in a city full of thousands of Big Brother supporters. He writes truths that will go unread, unheard, and unchallenged. Winston's journaling becomes even more inconsequential once O'Brien, the voice of the Big Brother regime, informs him that the Innerparty has been meticulously monitoring every word he has written since the first day his "archaic instrument" tattooed the rusty pages of his outdated journal. The Party tells Winston that they have allowed him to continue his innocuous journaling for years, in order to learn from, and later use it, to do the opposite of its purpose: to formulate new means of further controlling forms of psychological rebellion. Readers cannot help but see the dark irony in this scene. As Winston once helped the Party destroy the language that would promote rebellion, the Party will now use Winston's own rebellious discourse to desist later forms of nonconformist writings.

Winston's initial consideration of creating a discourse that would communicate with future generations does give the work critical potential, for it would presumably offer clandestine information about the Innerparty's complex forms of societal manipulation; but Winston hastily dismisses his onset of a purposeful discourse. Unable to devise a means of connecting his solitary discourse with a mass audience, Winston realizes that his text is worthless since it cannot offer direction for future readers. Once Winston accepts this position, he is emasculated; he cannot produce and disseminate a counter discourse, and what he does produce is decontextualized and impotent. The omnipresent power of the Party immediately debilitates Winston's rebelliousness, and the narration of this scene provides Winston's internal dialogue to readers: "It was of its nature impossible. Either the future would resemble the present, in which case it would not listen to him, or it would be different from it, and his predicament would be meaningless" (95). The text does not empower Winston, nor does it elicit any public reaction. Rather, the Party's ideology prematurely defeats him before a plan for communication can even begin to develop. At this disconsolate point in the novel, it becomes apparent that Winston is no freer than the rest of Oceania's citizens; he too has internalized the panoptical power of Big Brother and immediately concludes that he will be caught before his writing can ever be read. This is exactly how the Party wants rebellious citizens to think; rebellion is crushed internally before it can be articulated externally. After Winston's realization, readers get a dismal picture of him "gazing stupidly" at his empty journal, having "forgotten what it was that he had originally intended to say" (95). The Party's power over the citizen immediately dismantles Winston's once rebellious and potentially meaningful act of creating a counter discourse. Aware of the complex power relations of the Innerparty, Winston loses his discursive ability, leaving him alone, defeated, and further from progressive action.

As critical dystopias have shifted away from the pessimism of the dystopian novel to texts defined by possibility, this subgenre has also begun to treat written texts differently from the classic dystopian models. In many critical dystopias, writing is not only a means for sublimation and rebellion, but also a way for characters to understand and alter the future of a declining dystopian society. Thus, writing is not merely a personal act; it carries a communal goal within its prose that is intended for a diverse audience of readers. With an audience in mind, it then becomes a discourse that attempts to rationalize, define boundaries, make meaning, and communicate with a designated readership. Furthermore, an individual's act of formulating a text in the midst of complete social breakdown clearly symbolizes the power and effectiveness of language.

What characters of the critical dystopia must do before they can progress in the landscape of the dystopia is reconsider the very concept of knowledge and discursive function. What was once considered applicable knowledge in one social construct is no longer meaningful in the dystopian construct. In effect, the violence and affliction of the dystopian landscape alters the historical period, thereby opening a space for a new discourse and, ultimately, a new ideological system. This idea of discourse changing over time is one of Foucault's foundational premises. In *Discipline and Punish* Foucault writes, "Discourse is a group of statements which provide a language for talking about ... a particular topic at a particular historical moment" (189). Foucault believes that the subtle variations of a discourse over time define the knowledge and "truths" of an active historical period. According to Foucault, the truth of a concept varies as competing ideas and counter discourses surface to disempower dominating discourses (188–89). Consequently, a new discourse produces new forms for understanding the world since discourse defines and limits how one is able to discuss a particular topic. This discursive revision is what takes place in the critical dystopia as characters strive to create new forms of meaning in a social construct that has lost any sense of purpose.

It has become a rhetorical standard to view writing as a multifaceted process that is as much audience conscious as author conscious. However, an analysis of a writer's process of understanding the subjectivities of discourse is often removed from the genre of fiction. In fiction the text's characters act as the subjects relaying discourse to the reader, which causes the reader to become so invested in the characters and plotlines that an analysis of discursive subjectivities is often overlooked. While this kind of rhetorical analysis does go beyond the confines of a novel's covers, an analysis of discourse holds power, for it forces one to go beyond surface level analyses in order to understand the ideological implications of the text. A reading of discursive practice forces the reader to put pressure on the discourse, asking questions of its origins, ideological framework, and sociopolitical position. In essence, discursive analysis asks the reader to go outside the text in order to further extract meaning from it.

In addition to the commonalities among discursive analysis with composition theory, psychoanalysis, and new historicism, Mikhail Mikhailovich Bakhtin's contribution to the field of literary studies and in-depth discussions of discourse and heteroglossia cannot be removed from this discussion. His demanding 1935 essay "Discourse in the Novel" is quite fitting here, for Bakhtin's commentary about discursive acts is one that views discourse as an underrepresented part of the novel that is highly conditioned by ideology. Similar to Foucault, Bakhtin also understands the relevance and effect of a language's historicized moment:

> At any given moment of its historical existence, language is heteroglot from top to bottom: it represents the co-existence of socio-ideological contradictions between the present and the past, between differing epochs of the past, between different schools, circles and so forth, all given a bodily form. These "languages" of heteroglossia intersect each other in a variety of ways, forming new socially typifying "languages'" [291].

Bakhtin's assertion that conflicting voices are always apparent within the novel's lingual structure is one of the theoretical components of discursivity that is apparent in the critical dystopia, for it is within the new social construct of the critical dystopia that readers will find characters struggling to find a means to understand and discuss a new historical moment that deviates sharply from their past. And while Bakhtin's focus is on the discursivity of the novel itself, his insights about language, ideology, and heteroglossia are applicable to an explication of characters' actions and discourse in the critical dystopia.

Discourses of the Future

In order for characters to create useful texts in the dystopian construct, it is imperative that they understand both their past and present discursive communities. Baccolini articulated this sentiment during her own discussion of memory and history: "History, its knowledge, and memory are ... dangerous elements that can give the dystopian citizen a potential instrument of resistance" (115). Ultimately, an effective text is a synthesis of past and present knowledge, contextualized in a way that is tailored to a designated audience; thus, it is heteroglot, as conflicting voices, readers, and languages are synthesized to articulate its message to readers. Traditionally, the characters of classic dystopias refrain from engaging in the present and rely on discourses from the past for guidance. These characters are dependent on what has been documented before catastrophe had irrevocably altered their society. According to Baccolini, these classic dystopian heroes offer no hope for communal resistance because they have not come to terms with their precarious position in the dystopian landscape, ultimately losing an ability to "gain any control over history and the past" and to create new texts of power (115). Because of this historical regression, old texts dominate the classical dystopias, typically reasserting outmoded ideologies in new social contexts and creating a palpable nostalgia that is often fatal. And while these old texts were once applicable for readers of their historical moment, they do not have the capacity to adapt to the present. They cannot promote change or progressive modes of thought because they cannot conceptualize the aberrance of the dystopian landscape.

In *1984,* Winston's decision to abandon his own writing for Goldstein's outmoded text is a primary example of reliance on outdated texts for guidance in the horror of the dystopia. While Winston knows he has a responsibility to pass his knowledge of the Innerparty on to future readers, he immediately supersedes his place of authority with Goldstein, and Goldstein's archaic text becomes the dominating mode of thought. Instead of taking action and accepting a personal responsibility to formulate a contemporary discourse to understand the society of Oceania, Winston looks to Goldstein's dormant text for answers. He ignorantly considers his own work "a truth that nobody would ever hear," and places all his faith in Goldstein's work, thereby exposing himself to the Party (283). Once Winston hears about Goldstein's furtively circulating text, its prose, much like the prose of the Bible—even being alluded to as "The Book"—becomes his sole embodiment of hope.

Rather than being subjects of the historical nostalgia of the dystopian genre, the characters in critical dystopias find new ways of producing progressive modes of thought that engage with their present society. While this discursive act is not usually completed immediately after calamity strikes these characters' societies, it is the ideological negotiation leading to their realization that past systems of belief are no longer applicable that is of primary importance and will be explicated in Butler's *Parable of the Sower.*

Octavia Butler's Parable of the Sower: "The Only Lasting Truth Is Change"

From the start, Butler's novel exposes the reader to the foundational concept of Lauren Oliminas's evolving text, *Earthseed: The Books of the Living*: "All that you touch/You Change./All that you Change/Changes you./The only lasting truth/Is Change./God/Is Change" (3). In *Parable*'s 2024 California, malleability, adaptability, and change have become the core concepts for survival in a society that has practically lost any regard for laws, community, responsibility, and altruism. In this dystopian setting, the lack of basic human resources, coupled with frequent droughts, has driven citizens to rob and, oftentimes, kill in order to survive. A global recession that never stabilized has left the few communities still functioning in the novel as enclaves, guarded by massive walls and barbed wire and on the brink of collapse. Gangs, thieves, drug addicts, arsonists, killers, and homeless families roam the streets of various towns and cities in the novel, and the police units, who are scarcely seen throughout the novel, take gang bribes or use their position of power as leverage to rape and kill on impulse. One also finds the corpses of men, women, and children scattered in the public streets, oftentimes charred and noticeably eaten by those without food. Lauren's dated journal entries, the context for the novel, articulate the chaos of her debased society. On the rare chance when she can come out from behind the gated walls of her isolated community, she describes the horrific scene she encounters. One of Lauren's first journal entries reads: "I saw at least three people who weren't going to wake up again, ever. One of them was headless.... After that, I tried not to look around at all" (Butler 9). Travelers on these city streets also find the once enviable homes of southern California burned, vandalized, and inhabited by the poor who ubiquitously line the streets and sidewalks. Ultimately, the social landscape of this dystopian society has actually altered the fundamental laws of how a society can function.

While *Parable* certainly creates the traditional setting that can be expected in modern dystopian novels, the novel's *critical* component derives from the ethical and ideological negotiations of its characters as they struggle to survive in and change their society. The novel goes beyond producing a metaphorical warning for social consciousness; it moves into the realm of action through its emphasis on education collaboration, and language. The novel's main character, Lauren Olamina, actually creates a discourse for understanding the dystopian construct. Because of the discourse's emphasis on malleability and the acceptance of diverse semantic codes, it is a discourse that fosters multiculturalism, diversity, and language's incessant transformation. Thus, it is an open discourse, acknowledging what Bakhtin terms heteroglossia. Lauren does not create a discourse that is static and unwilling to internalize external influences; rather, she accepts its malleability and encourages others to assist in developing its message.

Unlike many novels in the "topia" genre, Butler understands that once a society has declined past a certain point of debasement, there is no returning to antiquated notions of the past. The citizens of dystopian societies reach a point where they no longer have the physical resources or psychological strength to revert to a former existence. Because of this irrevocable change, utopian authors often remove their fictional societies from the historical moment of the present in order to establish feasibility with readers. This removal, I would argue, is pure fantasy. Unless the slate can be wiped clean, a utopian resurgence cannot occur, for once the majority of society's inhabitants devalue the fundamental concepts of empathy, benevolence, compassion, and unity, there is no possible way a society can find the means to replace the dominant ideologies that debilitated it—the historical moment has passed.

Butler uses the brutality of *Parable*'s historical moment to eradicate the possibility of a utopian resurgence within the novel's fragmented society. Tucked away from the main roads running through Robledo, sits Lauren's family's once idyllic community now on the verge of collapse. Guarded from the tumultuous public, families in this community continue to live with the belief that society will rectify itself before its cul-de-sac walls are breached by what Lauren's dad refers to as the "maggots" of society (7). Mr. Olamina's disillusioned idea that society will evolve back to a state of prosperity and safety reflects this community's regressive and antiquated beliefs. In order to convey the community's dangerous complacency, Butler intelligently uses the symbolism of the cul-de-sac to convey that no future progress can occur within this group. The community's placement in a cul-de-sac not only symbolizes an illusory removal from the dangerous reality of society, but also a stagnant way of living that does not adjust to the new ideology of contemporary society. Unwilling to engage with the declining reality of Robledo, this community remains faithful to the Christian ideology of one God as savior and fails to account for the changing conditions of the contemporary world. Lauren's father's antiquated system of beliefs maintains the social codes of a past historical moment. Altruism, community, family, and empathy are attributes of the pre-dystopian discourse that no longer communicate with the new discourses of the dystopian construct. In order to survive, Lauren, who symbolizes a new generation, is forced to leave her father and remove herself from the outmoded ideologies of a past historical moment.

While the older generations refuse to acknowledge the inevitable destruction of their community, Lauren's progressive thinking and preparedness save her from death when the outside breaches the cul-de-sac's gates. Lauren has not only accepted that her community's austere values are outdated, but has already begun to educate herself and others for survival in the present dystopian landscape. Lauren does not limit herself to one particular set of beliefs or religious discourse, as her father and community does, but she seeks the voices from multiple discourses. In drastic opposition to the inflexibility of her community's religious doctrine, Lauren begins engaging in a polyphonic education open to more than one source of truth. Lauren's new ideological belief that God and the world are rooted in change and malleability saves her from the fate of her brother Keith, her father, and the majority of other community members inside the cul-de-sac's walls. Critic Jerry Philips has also noticed Lauren's transgression and finds that her belief in change and adaptability is a rejection of fatalism, monotheism, and traditional religious texts (307). The discourse of *Earthseed* reflects a new belief system that opposes the fatalism of Christianity and rigid structures of finished texts. One section of *Earthseed* states, "We do not worship God./We perceive and attend God./[...] We adapt and endure,/For we are Earthseed,/And God is Change" (17). The text reflects Lauren's refusal to put her future in the hands of a superior power outside her own control, and because of her empowered position, she begins to recreate her own identity to one that can adapt to and survive in the historical moment of the dystopian social construct.

Lauren's recreation exemplifies the ideological negotiation characters must undergo to ensure survival in the dystopia. Lauren knows she must discard many of the ethical codes of the past in order to engage purposefully with the realities of the present historical moment. Prior to her community's destruction, Lauren spends ample time educating herself in all subject areas that would assist her survival among the thieves, rapists, and killers of the outside world. She realizes that the monological education she received from her father's community is not applicable in the new social construct and begins studying self-defense, botany, chemistry, philosophy, and first aid in order to prepare herself physically and mentally for survival in the dystopia. Instead of embracing the attitude of her father, which is to "hold out. Survive," Lauren understands that her future depends on embracing a new discourse that prepares her for the challenges of the present historical moment (70). It is during Lauren's conversation with Joanne that we begin to understand Lauren's dedication to preparing herself for the future. When Joanne asks Lauren about her interest in the severity of the outside world, "Why do you want to talk about this stuff," Lauren responds emphatically: "We can get ready. That's what we've got to do now. Get ready for what's going to happen, get ready to survive it, get ready to make a life afterward" (52). As painful as it is for Lauren, she is able to reject the outmoded ideologies of her community for the new discourses of the dystopia. She has come to terms with the reality of the present and places herself in a position where she can adapt to the challenges of a new social structure.

While traditional dystopian heroes attempt to rectify a once purer society from the past in order to overcome an authoritarian power, *Parable* is unique in that no dominant power like Big Brother exists to be defeated; practically all members of society have been forced to disregard any sense of collective unity and to capitalize on one another's weaknesses. There is no underlying ideological purity with the power to regulate society back to normalcy. Any internalized notions of communal responsibility have been replaced with a desperate urge to survive in any way possible. Unique to the modern dystopian structure, *Parable*'s society has no collective suffering, only a collective violence that has displaced the traditional ethical responsibilities of its former existence. The discourse of *Earthseed* embraces this reality, providing guidance and a system of beliefs complementing the social construct of the dystopia.

Lauren's rejection of her community's antiquated societal beliefs symbolizes a departure from the past and traditional Christian beliefs, and begins her process of creating a new discourse for understanding the world. In *Earthseed*, a metaphysical God no longer dictates one's own survival in society, but it is one's own ability to shape and to adapt to the world that will dictate his or her own destiny. *Earthseed* becomes an embodiment of Lauren's ideological negotiation, for it articulates a new discursive structure that allows an understanding of a new social construct. Reflecting a departure from traditional monotheistic religion, the text states, "*Earthseed* deals with ongoing reality, not with supernatural authority figures. Worship is no good without actions. With action, it's only useful if it steadies you, focuses your efforts, eases your mind" (202). Unlike monotheism, *Earthseed*'s principles put the individual in a place of power, for his or her own dedication to malleability and preparedness will lead to survival. "Show me a more pervasive power than change," Lauren says confidently to Travis as they discuss the implications of internalizing *Earthseed* discourse. Lauren realizes the virtues that were once equated with piety and honor now cause suffering and death, which is the end result of the cul-de-sac community. Ultimately, the dangerous conditions of the novel's fragmented society create a new medium for understanding its present ideological structure. *Earthseed* becomes the discourse that provides an alternative way to understand and to live in the dystopian construct.

The creation of a new text during a time of complete social breakdown has ideological value that goes beyond only replacing antiquated modes of religious discourse. A close examination of Lauren's *Earthseed* text portrays a clear connection with discourse theory. An incorporation of Foucauldian discourse theory alongside the creation of *Earthseed* is particularly applicable, for Foucault understands discourse as being something created from the particular cultural conditions of a particular moment and capable of being replaced as history progresses (89). Thus, the social breakdown in the world of *Parable* offers a new cultural condition extricated from its past ideological structure and vulnerable to new discursive formations. While it is difficult for many citizens in *Parable* to reject the ideological teachings of religious fatalism, Lauren engages with the conditions of her society enough to realize that a rejection of the rigid discourses of the past is necessary. Through a critical engagement with her society, Lauren obtains what Foucault terms a "subject position" of discursive power. She understands that the frameworks of thinking that once governed society before calamity are inadequate and this knowledge empowers her. Because power is not only directly linked to knowledge, which can be both oppressive and liberating according to Foucault, it also has the capabilities of producing new forms of discourse that, at times, act as counter discourses (189). Ultimately, Lauren's engagement with the chaotic world of Robledo not only empowers her understanding of humanity, but also creates urgency for a new discursive community.

New discursive formations are possible because there are always multiple discourses for discussing an event and understanding a historical context. And since one of the main objectives of a discourse is to produce new forms of knowledge that are historically conscious, different ways of defining a particular event become possible. Sarah Mills's discussion of Foucault and language also emphasizes discourse's contextualized position as a priority. She writes, "We categorize and interpret experience and events according to the structures available to us and in the process of interpreting, we lend these structures solidity" (56). Because *Earthseed* is a new discursive form, it must interact with the chaos of the dystopian structure and attempt to provide a means of understanding it. Centered on the concept of change, *Earthseed* teaches its readers that they can take control of their own existence by synthesizing their past beliefs with the realities of the contemporary world. Such ideological negotiations create a subject position that is malleable and engaged with the formation of the present. Chapter 21's passage clearly articulates *Earthseed*'s emphasis on self-empowerment: "The Self must create/Its own reasons for being./To shape God,/Shape Self." (237). *Earthseed* no longer places God at the center of its discourse, but places the individual's ability to adapt to his or her world as the ultimate power. In essence, *Earthseed*'s own discursive function incessantly revises itself, for it is an open discourse that allows individual experience to dictate its shape.

Although *Earthseed* principles do place immense emphasis on the individual's power to shape his or her own destiny, it does not deny a connection to others. While Lauren's emphasis on the individual as God and God as change conveys the necessity of focusing on ongoing reality rather than a religious afterlife, it also acknowledges that all individuals understand and shape God in different ways. Critic Jim Miller also sees *Earthseed*'s principles supporting concepts of diversity: "God is Change … suggests that the point of *Earthseed* is not to reify some cannon of ideas or create a rigid set of rituals, but rather to maintain a radical openness toward others and the world" (356). Furthermore, *Earthseed*'s intentions are not to create a new religion for worship, which would then produce an unchanging text like Christian doctrine, but to provide a discourse embracing a multiplicity of voices that is ready for the revisions that will provide a better chance for survival in a dystopian landscape.

Lauren's *Earthseed* text in *Parable* is immensely more powerful than what the characters of traditional dystopias have composed because it *does* articulate answers to the most difficult questions and *does* provide a discourse for understanding the present. It is an authentic discourse that not only synthesizes the past and present, but also attempts to provide possibilities for future generations to learn from and expand upon. Its discourse is not rigidly defined for one particular readership, but it is polyphonic and malleable, which makes it capable of reaching a universal audience. Lauren refuses to confine her thinking only to the ideologies of the past, which ostensibly keep failing everyone around her, and uses the present rhetorical situation to develop an open discourse that suits the instability of the future. Lauren informs those around her that *Earthseed* is a text that "deals with ongoing reality" (202) "exists to be shaped" (70) by its many different readers, and does not attempt to redefine the ideologies of the past.

As the critical dystopia continues to develop as a genre and move away from the pessimism of the dystopia, readers may begin to see texts emerge that deal implicitly with the economic pressures our county has faced in the last ten years, for it is clear that Butler's *Parable* is very much responding to the social conditions of her historical moment. Many of today's writers have already begun explicating the effects of global capitalism since the 1980s, but the twenty-first century is offering a whole new set of environmental, sociological, educational, and economic conflicts that begs for the promise of possibility that is ingrained within the critical dystopia.

Works Cited

Baccolini, Rafaella. "'A useful knowledge of the present is rooted in the past': Memory and Historical Reconciliation in Ursula K. Le Guin's *The Telling*." *Dark Horizons: Science Fiction and the Dystopian Imagination*. Ed. Tom Moylan. New York: Routledge, 2003. 113-134. Print.

_____. "Gender and Genre in the Feminist Critical Dystopias of Katherine Burdekin, Margaret Atwwod, and Octavia Butler." *Futures Females, the Next Generation: New Voices and Velocities in the Feminist Science Fiction*. Ed. Marleen Barr. Boston: Rowman & Littlefield, 2000. 13-24. Print.

Bakhtin, Mikhail. *Dialogic Imagination*. Ed. Holquist, Michael. Austin: University of Texas Press, 1981. Print.

Butler, Octavia. *Parable of the Sower*. New York: Four Walls Eight Windows, 1993. Print.

Foucault, Michel. *Discipline and Punish: The Birth of the Prison*. New York: Pantheon, 1977. Print.

Miller, Jim. "Post-Apocalyptic Hoping: Octavia Butler's Dystopian/Utopian Vision." *Science Fiction Studies* 25:1 (1998): 336-360. Print.

Mills, Sarah. *Michel Foucault.* New York: Routledge, 2003. Print.
Moylan, Tom. *Scraps of the Untainted Sky.* Boulder, CO: Westview Press, 2000. Print.
Orwell, George. *1984.* Orlando: Harcourt, 2003. Print.
Philips, Jerry. "The Intuition of the Future: Utopia and Catastrophe in Octavia Butler's *Parable of the Sower.*" 35:2/3 (2002): 299–311. Print.
Robinson, Stanley Kim. *The Novels of Philip K. Dick.* New York: Umi Research Press, 1989. Print.
Sargent, Lyman Tower. "U.S. Eutopias in the 1980s and 1990s." Lecture at the Comparative Thematic Network Project (COTEPRA) conference, Centro Interdipartimentale di Ricerca Sull' utopia, University of Bologna, Rimini, Italy, 9 July 2000.
Walsh, Chad. *From Utopia to Nightmare.* New York: Harper & Row, 1962. Print.

About the Contributors

Susan M. Bernardo teaches science fiction, literary theory and British literature at Wagner College, where she is a professor of English. She co-authored (with Graham Murphy) *Ursula K. Le Guin: A Critical Companion* (2006) and contributed a chapter to *Environmentalism in the Realm of Science Fiction and Fantasy Literature*. She also co-edited *Gender Reconstructions: Pornography and Perversions in Literature and Culture*. Her articles on Tim Burton's *Batman Returns* and *Sleepy Hollow* appeared in *Film/Literature Quarterly*. She has presented papers on science fiction, Victorian literature and film.

Shayani Bhattacharya is a PhD student in English at SUNY Buffalo. She is interested in postmodern fiction and culture, experimental fiction and popular culture. She focuses on the effect of paranoia on American popular culture and in postmodern American science fiction and fantasy literature. Her paper "Why I Am What I Am: Issues of Cultural Identity in Orhan Pamuk's *Istanbul* and *My Name is Red*" was selected at the International Symposium at the University of Edinburgh to be published as part of its annual web publication.

Keith Elphick is an instructor of English at San Juan College in New Mexico. He has taught courses in various areas of literary study and composition. He received both his bachelor's and master's degrees from Salisbury University. His master's thesis examined the rhetorical practices and ideological implications in contemporary dystopian literature. He has presented on displacement in contemporary American literature, exilic literature, the works of Brett Easton Ellis, and the racial components of Langston Hughes's poetry.

Matthew Hadley is a lecturer in the Department of Cultural Studies and Comparative Literature at the University of Minnesota. His research deals with the practices of biotechnology in Anglo-American literature from historical moments of drastic technological change that correspond to the emergence of various forms of capital. He is working on an article that reveals deep affinities between Mary Shelley's *Frankenstein* and Virginia Woolf's *A Room of One's Own*. He teaches courses in media studies, sexuality studies, and literary criticism.

Margaret S. Kennedy is a doctoral candidate at Stony Brook University; she holds an MA from Binghamton University and teaches in the English Department at Suffolk County Community College. Her interests include the long 18th century, Victorian literature and ecocriticism. Her dissertation discusses environmental advocacy in the Victorian novel. She has published articles in *The Wildean* and *Anglistik* and contributed a chapter to *Wilde's Wiles* (2012). She is the editorial assistant for the journal *Victorian Literature and Culture*.

Lauren J. Lacey is an associate professor in the English Department at Edgewood College in Madison, Wisconsin, where she teaches courses in postmodernism, postcolonial fiction, feminist theory, environmental literature, and science fiction. She is the author of *The Past That Might Have Been, the Future That May Come: Women Writing Fantastic Fiction, 1960s to the Present* (McFarland, 2014). Other publications include articles in *Critique: Studies in Contemporary Fiction*, *Doris Lessing Studies*, and *The Intersection of Fantasy and Native America*, ed. Amy H. Sturgis and David D. Oberhelman.

Adam Lawrence is an assistant professor of English at Concordia University, where he teaches writing and science fiction. He has published articles on gender and myth in contemporary Irish fiction, and the human-"alien" encounter in twentieth-century science fiction. A forthcoming article examines the theme of hospitality in Ray Bradbury's *Martian Chronicles*. He is working on a project that examines the "changeling" legend in British and American science fiction.

Jonathan P. Lewis is an assistant professor of English at Troy University's Covington/East Atlanta campus where he teaches composition, world literature, and modern and contemporary literature. He has a PhD from the University of California at Riverside and edited the first book of scholarly essays on Neal Stephenson, *Tomorrow Through the Past* (Cambridge Scholars Publishing, 2006). He has also published and presented on such authors as Thomas Pynchon, James Joyce, David Foster Wallace, and Sylvia Plath, among others.

Melanie A. Marotta is a lecturer in the Department of English and Language Arts at Morgan State University, where she received a PhD in English. She published an article in *Theory in Action* and a chapter in *Creoles, Diasporas, Cosmopolitanisms*. She is awaiting the publication of her chapter on the works of Nathaniel West and Sam Shepard and is working on an article about male first-wave cyberpunk writers. Her interests include U.S. literature (19th to 21st centuries), Renaissance, ecocriticism, feminism, and science fiction.

Justin T. Noetzel is an instructor and PhD student in the English Department at Saint Louis University. His research interests include manuscripts, monster studies, ecocriticism, and landscape theory. He has presented on topics including Anglo-Saxon saints' lives, Viking-age Iceland, Middle English prophecy, Irish travel writing and fairy tales, and British fantasy. He has published in *Mythlore*, the *Ashgate Encyclopedia of Literary and Cinematic Monsters*, and *Newfound: An Inquiry of Place*. His forthcoming work includes a previously unpublished Middle English political poem, with commentary, and he is working on a cultural history of the English fens.

Index

After London, Wild England 101
Ahlbäck, Pia Maria 13
Althusser, Louis 50, 51
Anand, Mulk Raj 149
Anathem 5, 46–52, 54–60
Anti-Oedipus: Capitalism and Schizophrenia 73, 74
Arachne 40–41

Baccolini, Rafaella: "Gender and Genre" 173–174, 181
Bachelard, Gaston: *The Poetics of Space* 122, 124, 128, 132, 134
Bakhtin, Mikhail Mikhailovich: "Discourse in the Novel" 181, 184
Baldick, Chris 83
Ballard, Lester: *Child of God* 129
Baratta, Chris: *Environmentalism in the Realm of Science Fiction and Fantasy Literature* 2, 114
The Baroque Cycle 46, 49
Baudrillard, Jean: *Simulations* 159
Baxter, Samuel R.: *The Long Earth* 10, 23–26; *see also* utopia
Berry, Wendell 103
Blanchot, Maurice: *The Space of Literature* 92, 93–94
Blood Meridian 129
Booker, M. Keith 76–77
Boos, Florence 103, 104
Brave New World 172, 173
Brewton, Vince 129
Broun, Paul 52–53
Buell, Lawrence: *The Future of Environmental Criticism* 1, 2–3, 10–11, 165–166
Butler, Octavia E.: *Parable of the Sower* 7, 176, 183–189; *see also* dystopias; epistolary text

Cabe, Richard 155
The Calcutta Chromosome: A Novel of Fevers, Delirium and Discovery 6, 137–152
Cant, John 125, 126, 134, 135
Čapek, Karel: *War with the Newts* 5, 64–80; *see also* gender
"The Cask of Amontillado" 128
Chambers, Claire 147, 150
Cixous, Hélène: "The Laugh of the Medusa" 138, 140
Clark, Timothy: *The Cambridge Introduction to Literature and the Environment* 1
Coburn, Tom 47–48
colonialism: in *The Long Earth* 26; in *The Word for World Is Forest* 18, 25
Cryptonomicon 49
Csicsery-Ronay, Istvan, Jr. 29–30, 32, 34–35, 36, 39, 40
cyberpunk 29–30, 32, 35–36, 37–38, 39, 43, 44

Dalrymple, William 149
darwinism 65, 73, 78–79
Davis, J.C.: *Utopia and the Ideal City* 29
De Bruyn, Ben 124–125, 135
Delany, Samuel R.: *Stars in My Pocket Like Grains of Sand* 4, 10, 13–14, 17, 19–23
Deleuze, Gilles 2, 5, 78–79; *Anti-Oedipus: Capitalism and Schizophrenia* 73, 74; *A Thousand Plateaus* 48–49, 50, 52, 55, 57, 58, 65–66, 71, 74, 76, 80; *What Is Philosophy?* 90, 92–93, 97, 98
Delveaux, Martin 106
deterritorialization 52, 54, 64–65, 71, 75–76, 80; *see also* reterritorialization
The Diamond Age 46, 52
Dick, Philip K.: *Do Androids Dream of Electric Sheep?* 6, 154–168; "Man, Android and Machine" 156, 166
Dickens, Charles: *Our Mutual Friend* 108

Do Androids Dream of Electric Sheep? 6, 154–168
Donaldson, Laura 109
Downton, Paul F. 106
dystopias: critical dystopian fiction 171, 173–177, 179–180, 181–182, 189; in George Orwell's *1984* 172, 173, 174, 182; in Octavia Butler's *Parable of the Sower* 183–184, 185, 186, 188–189

Easterbrook, Neil 22
ecocriticism 1–2, 11
ecoscience fiction 11
epistolary text 177–178; in George Orwell's *1984* 178–179; in Octavia Butler's *Parable of the Sower* 183
Ertung, Ceylan 42–43

feminism: in *He, She, It* 37–38; in *Trouble and Her Friends* 43
Foucault, Michel 4, 11–12, 13, 181, 187, 188; *Discipline and Punish* 180
Frank, James: *The Development of the Laboratory: Essays on the Place of Experiment in Industrial Civilization* 86
Frankenstein: James Whale's 1931 film adaption 83–84; Mary Shelley's 5, 83–85, 87–88, 90–92, 95–99; *see also* laboratories
The Future of Environmental Criticism 1

gender: in *Stars in My Pocket Like Grains of Sand* 20–21; in *Trouble and Her Friends* 43; in *War of the Newts* 72–73; in *The Word for World Is Forest* 17
Ghosh, Amitav: *The Calcutta Chromosome: A Novel of Fevers, Delirium and Discovery* 6, 137–152
Gibson, William 43
Gilbert, Nathanael 113–114
Gomel, Elana 79
Gordon, Joan 11
The Greatest Hoax: How the Global Warming Conspiracy Threatens Your Future 53
Guatarri, Félix 2, 5, 78–79; *Anti-Oedipus: Capitalism and Schizophrenia* 73, 74; *A Thousand Plateaus* 48–49, 50, 52, 55, 57, 58, 65–66, 71, 74, 76, 80; *What Is Philosophy?* 90, 92–93, 97, 98

Hage, Erik 122–123
Hayles, N. Katherine 164
He, She, It 4, 28–36, 44; *see also* feminism
Heise, Ursula: "Lost Dogs, Last Birds, and Listed Species" 155–156; *Sense of Place and Sense of Planet* 3

heterotopias 4, 11–14, 16–26
Hetherington, Kevin 12
Hibbs, Thomas S. 125, 133
homosexuality: in *Trouble and Her Friends* 38, 39, 41; in *The Word for World Is Forest* 19
Horowitz, David 53
Hovanec, Carol P. 14–15
Huffman, Bennett 11
Hutcheon, Linda 150–151
Huxley, Aldus 47; *Brave New World* 172, 173

Inhofe, James: *The Greatest Hoax: How the Global Warming Conspiracy Threatens Your Future* 53

Jameson, Frederic 94
Jefferies, Richard: *After London, Wild England* 101
Jung, Carl 155, 156

laboratories: in Amitav Ghosh's *The Calcutta Chromosome* 141, 145; history 85–88; of literature 93–94, 96, 99; in Mary Shelley's *Frankenstein* 84–85, 87, 91–92, 97–98
Latour, Bruno: *Science in Action* 85, 88–90, 94–95, 98–99
Lavigne, Carlen 35–36, 42
Lawrence, D.H. 92
Leary, Timothy 38–39
Leblanc, Laurie 43
Le Guin, Ursula K. 176; *The Telling* 4; *The Word for World Is Forest* 4, 10, 14–19, 21, 24; *see also* colonialism; gender; homosexuality
Leopold, Also 103–104, 107
Levitas, Ruth 29, 40, 41
Lincoln, Kenneth 126
The Long Earth 10, 23–26; *see also* utopias
The Lord of the Rings 137
Love, Glenn 2

Macherey, Pierre 92
The Magic Flute 161
Marx, Karl: *Capital* 155
Massumi, Brian: *User's Guide to Capitalism and Schizophrenia* 55
McCarthy, Cormac: *Blood Meridian* 129; *The Road* 6, 120–136
McCarthy, Patrick 161
Mehan, Uppinder: "Postcolonial Science, Cyberpunk and *The Calcutta Chromosome*" 141
Miller, Walter A.: *A Canticle for Leibowitz* 46

Mills, Sarah: *Michel Foucault* 188
Milton John: *Paradise Lost* 96, 97, 98
Molloy, Claire: "Dreaming of Electric Sleep and Negotiating Animality" 160
Mongol empire 48–49
Morris, William: *News from Nowhere* 5–6, 101–115
Morton, Timothy 2
Moylan, Tom: *Scraps of the Untainted Sky* 173, 176
Mozart, Wolfgang Amadeus: *The Magic Flute* 161

Nelson, Diane M.: "A Social Science Fiction of Fevers, Delirium and Discovery" 141
News from Nowhere 5–6, 101–115; *see also* utopias
1984 7, 172–173, 174, 178–180, 182; *see also* dystopias; epistolary text

Orwell, George 47; *1984* 7, 172–173, 174, 178–180, 182; *see also* dystopias; epistolary text
Otto, Eric: *Green Speculations* 2

Parable of the Sower 7, 176, 183–189; *see also* dystopias; epistolary text
Paradise Lost 96, 97, 98
Pasteur, Louis 94–95, 98
Piercy, Marge: *He, She, It* 4, 28–36, 44; *see also* feminism
Poe, Edgar Allan: "The Cask of Amontillado" 128
The Poetics of Space 122, 124, 128, 132, 134
Pordzik, Ralph 12
Pratchett, Terry: *The Long Earth* 10, 23–26; *see also* utopia

Rancière, Jacques: *The Flesh of Words* 97
reterritorialization 5, 59, 65–66, 68, 71–72, 75–76; *see also* deterritorialization
The Road 6, 120–136
Robinson, Kim Stanley 172; *Pacific Edge* 176

Santorum, Rick 53
Sargent, Lyman Tower 174
Scholem, Gershom 93
Schumacher, E.F. 106
Science in Action 85, 88–89
Scott, Melissa: *Arachne* 40–42; *Trouble and Her Friends* 4–5, 28–29, 38–44
Shelley, Mary *see* Frankenstein
Shelley, Percy 98
Sims, Christopher 168
Singh, Khushwant 149

Snow Crash 49
Soper, Kate 103–104
"The Soul of Man Under Socialism" 110
The Space of Literature 92–93
Spencer, Herbert 69
Spivak, Gayatri Chakravorty: "Can the Subaltern Speak?" 138, 143–144, 147
Stars in My Pocket Like Grains of Sand 4, 10, 13–14, 17, 19–23; *see also* gender
Stephenson, Neal: *Anathem* 5, 46–52, 54–60; *The Baroque Cycle* 46, 49; *Cryptonomicon* 49; *Diamond Age* 49, 52; *Snow Crash* 49
Sterling, Bruce 31, 37

The Telling 4
terraphilia 155, 156, 168
Thomson, Sir William (Lord Kelvin) 86
A Thousand Plateaus 48–49, 50, 52, 55, 57, 58, 65–66, 71, 74, 76, 80
Thrall James H.: "Postcolonial Science Fiction?" 144–145
Tolkien, J.R.R.: *The Lord of the Rings* 137
Topinka, Robert J. 13
Trigg, Dylan 124
Trouble and Her Friends 4–5, 28–29, 38–44
Tuan, Yi-Fu: *Space and Place: The Perspective of Experience* 124, 126, 135
Tweit, Susan J. 155

User's Guide to Capitalism and Schizophrenia 55
utopias: in *The Long Earth* 25; in *News from Nowhere* 101–103, 105–106, 111, 114–115

Vint, Sherryl: "Speciesism and Species Being in *Do Androids Dream of Electric Sheep?*" 159–160, 163
von Liebig, Justus 86

Walsh, Chad 172
War with the Newts 5, 64–80; *see also* gender
Warde, Anthony 133, 134
WarGames (Movie) 38
Wells, H.G. 91, 101
Whale, James *see* Frankenstein
Wilde, Oscar: "The Soul of Man Under Socialism" 110
Woolf, Virginia: *A Room of One's Own* 92
The Word for World Is Forest 4, 10, 14–19, 21, 24; *see also* colonialism; gender; homosexuality

Zamyatin, Yevgeny: *We* 172, 173